CONNALLY

The Adventures of Big Bad John

CONNALLY

The Adventures of
Big Bad John

by Charles Ashman

WILLIAM MORROW & COMPANY, INC., NEW YORK

1974

BOOK DESIGN BY HELEN ROBERTS

PRINTED IN THE UNITED STATES OF AMERICA.

1 2 3 4 5   78 77 76 75 74

Library of Congress Cataloging in Publication Data

Ashman, Charles R.
  Connally: the adventures of Big Bad John.

  1. Connally, John Bowden, 1917–   I. Title.
E840.5.C66A93   973.924'092'4[B]   73–20248
ISBN 0–688–00222–6

As in all things, this book is possible because of a patient and remarkable woman, Pamela, and our equally remarkable daughter, Shireen. It is also dedicated to my mother and father—who were always there.

Foreword BY MELVIN BELLI

John Connally makes little attempt to disguise his greed. Certainly no one can doubt the intensity of his ambition to reach the White House one way or another, but it takes no more than one way—a close examination of Connally's own words and deeds—to convince the reader that Big Bad John should be excluded from consideration for further high office in our Government.

Charles Ashman has exceptionally keen political instincts and possesses the unique ability to dissect effectively his subject with that subject's own words as his tools. Ashman's study of our Secretary of State in *Kissinger: The Adventures of Super-Kraut* gave us a glimpse of Kissinger the private man as well as the public figure. Next Ashman invaded the inner sanctum of judicial life by assembling a sparkling rogues' gallery of seventy-four classic cases of "judicial pollution" in *The Finest Judges Money Can Buy*. But in telling the saga of John Connally, Ashman has done more than solidify his position as the nation's most successful pop biographer. While adhering to the need for entertaining style, this book documents a compelling argument against the Connally brand of arrogance in American politics.

The Watergate era and error will be with us for quite a while, but there is always the hope that the Seventies' exposure of high-level malfeasance and abuse of public confidence may dissolve our traditional national apathy. If that is so, then a Connally presidential candidacy can no longer be treated seriously.

It is terribly important that we learn the facts about those who govern us and so critically affect our lives. It is equally important that a book in this field be accurate, honest and well written. This book is all three.

In a democracy a book can affect history.

This one can and should cost John Connally the presidency of the United States!

Acknowledgments

I gratefully acknowledge the cooperation of those who manage the research facilities of *The New York Times,* the Library of Congress, and the libraries of UCLA, the University of Texas and Washington University in St. Louis. The *Texas Observer* is unquestionably the foremost reservoir of Connallyphenalia.

The candid comments of Congressman Henry B. Gonzalez of Texas, Congressman Paul McCloskey of California, former U.S. Senator Ralph Yarborough, former Congressman and presidential candidate John Schmitz, Kenneth O'Donnell and Jimmy Hoffa are appreciated.

Further, the cooperation of Bob Guccione and the *Penthouse/Viva* family was essential to this and related projects.

Finally, to Susan, Sandra, Rose, Michael and Lloyd, whose investigative and research talents were indispensable, thank you.

My editor's pen was a guiding light—since John Willey is one of the outstanding editors in the country.

Contents

	Foreword by Melvin Belli	vii
	Acknowledgments	ix
[1]	Prologue	1
[2]	The Bullet-Made Man	15
[3]	Little John	49
[4]	On the New Frontier	73
[5]	The Manicured Man in the Statehouse	101
[6]	Nixon's Economic Guru	175
[7]	Democrats for Nixon	257
[8]	Epilogue: 1976	287
	Index	297

CONNALLY
The Adventures of Big Bad John

John Connally, June 20, 1973
On this day Connally broke more than a month of silence about his status as unpaid adviser to President Nixon to tell a White House news conference that he was "catching up on his reading" and was not unhappy in his role. *Credit: United Press International Photo.*

(1)
Prologue

There are a handful of Americans who overinfluence our lives. They manipulate our economy, motivate our politics, regulate our culture and, more recently, denigrate our rights of privacy and individuality. Some achieve this awesome ability incidental to their responsibilities as high-ranking elected officials. This breed includes most Presidents, a few Senators, a rare Congressman and even an occasional Governor. Coincidental with the emergence of our American Government as a technocratic demo-glomerate, appointed officials are now clothed with a degree of authority and audacity that surpasses that of those who chose them. Once in a while they are caught and their power is shut off.

The back-room bosses, who previously were content to appear publicly only at an annual Labor Day picnic or an inaugural ceremony, have also become more sophisticated and audacious. A few of their number must be included on any prime list of American power brokers.

Then there is John Bowden Connally, Jr., who has

1

never needed any book of precedents to guide his progress. He has advanced as a power merchant without peer by smothering the competition and integrating three roles. First, and most effectively, he is a political and financial behind-the-scenes strategist. Second, he became the immaculate candidate. Finally, he has become a professional presidential appointee.

The chain-smoking but teetotaling Texan enjoyed notable political success long before he became Richard Nixon's financial guru and a presidential contender. As a campaign aide and confidant, Connally was regularly at Lyndon B. Johnson's side as LBJ New-Dealed his way from the House of Representatives to the United States Senate and, finally, to the White House.

Then there was Connally's ironic association with John F. Kennedy, Johnson's principal Democratic rival. At the Democratic National Convention in 1960, Connally was director of the "Citizens for Johnson" movement. When it appeared doomed, Big John and his followers hatched a vicious anti-Kennedy smear campaign: LBJ's faithful charged that Kennedy was dying of Addison's disease. Connally desperately tried to convince convention delegates that Kennedy could not realistically function as a candidate or as a President. Although some party regulars dismissed the attack as routine intraparty maneuvers, members of Kennedy's personal and official family did not forget. Even after Connally became a member of the Kennedy Cabinet, he was never very close to the White House team.

In that 1960 campaign labor leader Jimmy Hoffa was determined to defeat John Kennedy. The would-be President's brother had already been a thorn in the Teamster's side. Forgive and forget is not Hoffa's motto. When LBJ challenged Kennedy for the Democratic nomination, Hoffa was quick to offer support. Hoffa met secretly with John Connally to promise that support for

Lyndon Johnson if he was nominated. When LBJ failed
to make it, Hoffa renewed an earlier pledge to Richard
Nixon. But, once again, Connally was the man in the
middle.

The peacemakers in the Democratic party tried to
portray Connally's appointment as Secretary of the Navy
as a magnanimous gesture by President Kennedy. They
were determined to heal the party's wounds left over from
the election. But according to another account, Connally
was a compromise designee selected by Kennedy only
after Secretary of Defense Robert McNamara had rejected the President's earlier suggestions for the subsidiary post.

Connally had Vice President Johnson's patronage
approval as well as McNamara's backing, and the Senate
Armed Services Committee approved his nomination
unanimously. But watchdog Senator William Proxmire,
the Wisconsin liberal Democrat, opposed him vigorously
in Senate debate. He believed that Connally's intimate
association with the oil industry represented a conflict of
interest since the Navy Department was that industry's
biggest customer.

Although Connally was confirmed as Secretary of
the Navy by Senate vote, the resultant publicity focused
attention on Big John's wheeling and dealing and financial machinations in Texas. The extent of his influence
in the industry and banking worlds first became known
when an alert press expanded upon Senator Proxmire's
inquiries.

In 1952 John Connally became attorney for the
firm of Richardson and Bass, independent oil operators,
in Fort Worth. Eventually he became chief administrator
and lobbyist for Sid W. Richardson's numerous interests,
principally in the oil and gas industry. He acquired directorships in Richardson's Texas companies and later,
through Richardson's holdings, in the Atlas Corporation

and the New York Central Railroad. Along the way he became secretary of the Sid W. Richardson Foundation.

On September 29, 1959, the fabulously wealthy Richardson died, and Connally discovered when the will was read that he was co-executor of the oilman's estate, estimated to be worth hundreds of millions. Big John, one of seven children of a dirt-poor farmer, butcher, and part-time bus driver, would never be poor again.

During his earlier Richardson days, there had been whispers in Texas that Connally was defecting to the Republican party. Richardson had guaranteed General Dwight D. Eisenhower a bankroll befitting a presidential campaign if Ike would seek the Republican nomination. There are still many in Texas who swear that Connally engineered the successful "Democrats for Eisenhower" campaign which helped Ike win in Texas twice. Connally has consistently denied this. Yet, one Richardson aide verified to me that his late boss had called Connally's advice "essential" to the Eisenhower victories.

Notwithstanding the suggestive revelations concerning his oil ties, personal finances or even the 1960 anti-Kennedy campaign, Connally made it into high government circles. Big John served a brief and uneventful stint as Secretary of the Navy.

President Kennedy and Vice President Johnson were both vitally concerned about keeping the lid on the Texas Democratic party. It was a wildcat state, and the GOP had made dangerous inroads which could affect the next presidential election. They decided that Connally should be sent home to become Governor and hold onto the Texas delegates counteracting the Republicans. The executive team had not realized that Big John was primarily known as a manipulator in Texas and was not yet popular in the precincts; and it proved to be an embarrassingly close race for the stylish but still folksy Connally, who ran for Governor waving the Administration's blanket endorsement.

After a blistering primary campaign which ruptured the Democratic party, John Connally narrowly beat his Republican opponent, Jack Cox. Ironically, Big John's principal weapon was a barrage of verbal attacks charging that Cox had once been a Democrat and had switched to Republicanism.

The next time Connally did not want it to be close. The Governor planned to ask President Kennedy to come to Texas to dramatize to voters the truth of Connally's campaign claims that, if he were elected, the pork barrel contracts would continue to reach the state, along with new post offices, military bases and federal jobs. Patronage traditionally flourishes in Texas. It was Connally's insistence upon a Kennedy visit that brought the President to Texas and changed the history of this nation.

The United States was to enter an era of violence and instability. For Connally it would be one of those bizarre events when horror would breed a beneficiary— like the loss of a father providing an unexpected legacy.

With the assassination Connally became a wounded hero. He was easily reelected in 1964. The Governor continued to defend the constant theme of the Warren Report despite nagging inconsistencies and the arguments of those determined to prove a conspiracy.

John Connally served three terms as Governor of Texas despite a campaign promise to abolish a third term.

In 1968 Connally stood at the Democratic National Convention where Lyndon Johnson might have stood had he attended and forced a pro-Vietnam war plank into the platform that Hubert Humphrey was destined to fall from.

During that presidential campaign, Connally was courted by the Nixonites, who sensed his awareness of the futility of the Humphrey nomination. Connally sat it out. In the closing days of the campaign, the pundits finally began to predict that the Democrats had a chance. Big John, in bandwagon garb, slipped into high gear and helped Humphrey carry his Texas by 38,000 votes.

The Democrats began to lick their wounds and Connally left the Governor's Mansion. He joined a prestigious law firm in Houston which became Vinson, Elkins, Searls and Connally. He would continue his chores as a multi-corporation director and powerhouse par excellence in the oil industry and the world of dollars.

From the time Connally left the governorship until he assumed his duties as a Democratic Secretary of the Treasury in President Nixon's Cabinet, Big John concentrated on expanding his own treasures. Connally had been a property buff since he was a boy. Perhaps it was the insecurity of being the son of a tenant farmer in Wilson County, southeast of San Antonio. Or perhaps George Christian, a former Connally aide, is right when he says, "John just likes houses."

Since his governorship, Connally's homes have multiplied. There is the elegant suburban residence in Houston. There is, also, a gentleman's "ranch house" on the family homestead near San Antonio.

Connally has always been fascinated by foreign relations and international trade. What better way to understand the economy (or lack of it) of the independent Caribbean island of Jamaica than to have a home there. Connally's Oriental-style mansion overlooking the ocean near Montego Bay cost over $250,000. It is within two miles of one of Jamaica's most depressing slums.

Prior to and since his government service as head of the Treasury Department, Big John has collected diversified company directorships as other men collect neckties. These have produced a minor fortune but, more important to the Connally scheme, a network of influential contacts—the kind that elect presidents.

Among Big John's new companies is the huge American General Insurance Company based in Houston. There is also the First City National Bank of Houston, which boasts assets of over two billion dollars. The bank was started by J. A. Elkins, who was also the founder of Connally's law firm.

Connally is now an important man at Texas Instruments, Inc. The Dallas-based electronics company is listed on the New York Stock Exchange and does over half-a-billion dollars' business annually. As a director, Connally has applied his political savvy to guide this conglomerate to lucrative government contracts.

Big John's interests have included an oil pipeline company, large real estate holdings, a drugstore chain, broadcasting firms, more than one oilfield equipment company, a local telephone system and even restaurant franchises. As I said earlier, John Connally will never be poor again.

After his Treasury job and a newly acclaimed political intimacy with President Richard Nixon, John became unquestionably the man to see in Texas.

An impressive caravan of elegant chariots arrives daily at Connally's Houston manor when Big John is in town. He is not the kind of Texan to come to you, and he is most at ease when he is holding court. His law and business associates double as public relations men ready to defend a Connally business deal or attest to his hard work or political popularity as needed.

Connally is unencumbered by modesty or shyness. And so the super-rich and the power seekers come to pay homage, remind him of their support and hunt for a hint of inside information. Mostly they are looking for a word about a corporate or government policy change to which

Connally may be privy—the kind which produces fortunes.

Meanwhile, lower-income Americans are definitely divided in their feelings toward John Connally. Almost all are either for him completely or absolutely against him. There is very little middle ground. Many admire his stylish oratory but abhor his arrogance. Too many share the view of the outspoken Liz Carpenter, Lady Bird Johnson's former press secretary. When Connally switched loyalties to head up "Democrats for Nixon," she poignantly charged that Big John was a "political transvestite who, at the battle of the Alamo, would have organized Texans for Santa Ana."

As Richard Nixon and his plotters began charting their 1972 reelection strategy, Texas loomed high in national strategic importance. The country's economy would be the key domestic issue and the Republicans were in trouble in at least ten large states.

This was before the White House realized that they would have only minimal opposition from George McGovern. The Democratic nominee would be too busy defending his dumping of vice-presidential candidate Tom Eagleton to give Nixon much trouble. But, back in 1970, President Nixon was worried.

Richard Nixon always enjoyed a political coup. The first announcement of Connally's selection as Secretary of the Treasury came in a telephone call from the White House to the LBJ ranch. The President called former President Johnson and told him an "old friend of yours is joining the White House team." An unusually timid Connally was handed the phone by a gloating Richard Nixon. For thirty years Big John and LBJ had talked about everything. When the former President realized the appointment had been maneuvered without his being consulted, he was furious. The call ended much of the Johnson-Connally love affair.

On paper Connally would pass as somewhat qualified for the top Treasury job. He was a director of some banks, a lawyer and a self-made millionaire. Yet, to the conservative Republican economic regulars who are concerned with every fractional change in a price index, Big John was an unqualified upstart. Nevertheless, the Nixonologists were pleased that the President had added the promised extra dimension to the Cabinet in the form of an acceptable Democrat. Speculation as to why Connally received the job ranged from the President's need to carry Texas in 1972 to the possibility of a Nixon-Connally ticket.

The "dump Agnew" rumor mill worked overtime. There was so very much to be said about the political repercussions of Secretary John B. Connally's new job that little attention would be paid to what he actually did in office. When the Texan stepped down from the Cabinet post, an observer for *The Times* of London summed it all up—"Connally is just another Phase Nixon is going through."

After serving for eighteen months as the token Democrat in the Nixon Cabinet, Connally resigned with a declaration of independence and a promise of complete support for the President's economic policies. He also revealed he would personally vote for President Nixon in the 1972 election, despite the fact that the Democratic nominee had not yet been selected.

Connally often finds himself in the storm center of conflicting loyalties. He came home to Texas after brief service in the Kennedy Administration to serve three terms as Governor and then ignored several of Kennedy's pet programs. Next he alienated many of those Texas Democrats who had made the governorship possible when he agreed to serve in Nixon's Administration.

Connally' s ferocious pursuit of power and his constant trafficking in financial and political influence has nurtured his critics' claim that Big John is an obvious opportunist. For a while there was speculation that Connally would switch parties in time to seek the vice-presidential nomination from the Republicans in 1972. But Spiro Agnew and the party regulars had other ideas.

When Connally came forward as leader of the "Democrats for Nixon," it was, again, an obvious ruse since the GOP funded the group. But Big John, as always, would do his job well. It was thought that he might end up as Secretary of Defense or even Secretary of State.

Elated by the overwhelming Nixon victory, Connally focused on the State Department as his next home. When a folksy former Governor wants to be President, he needs the experience of involvement in foreign affairs as part of his image as an attractive candidate. Henry Kissinger and company feared that if Connally were Secretary of State his blatant ambition would threaten the delicate balance of international relations which had opened the door to China and cooled down the Russians, and was leading to the end of the war. If Big John were in charge of foreign relations, every word he uttered would be measured by American consensus and his personal future plans. The mechanical objectivity Kissinger had established in international negotiations would be lost. Kissinger applied his Svengalian influence on the President, and Connally was eased out of consideration for the coveted senior Cabinet position. When it became imperative that a Watergate President reestablish a modicum of national respect for his Administration, Super-Kraut took the State job himself.

Connally celebrated May Day 1973, and surprised no one, by formally joining the Republican party. The former Texas Governor had denounced Senator George McGovern when the South Dakotan was the Democratic standard-bearer. Connally had claimed that the Democratic candidate had "jeopardized the Vietnam peace negotiations in Paris, advocated the glorification of draft dodgers and proposed irresponsible government programs." Since he had campaigned for Nixon's reelection and disassociated himself from the Democratic platform, his official conversion was incidental to the philosophical changeover the year before.

The expected conversion was a planned step in the Connally campaign to seek the 1976 presidential nomination. It became apparent some time ago that the Democrats would never make another Johnson type their heir apparent and so the basically conservative Connally had nowhere else to go. His link with President Nixon had eliminated any chance of further Democratic leadership. At the time, of course, the former Cabinet member was asked whether he would rejoin the Nixon Administration. Connally assured the public that he was his own man and not interested in coming back to Washington in any capacity. Obviously, the label of opportunist would be hurled more readily if it appeared that Connally had merely taken a sabbatical to bolster the party as a prelude to returning in another Cabinet position. Significantly, Connally praised the Republican party in general and Richard Nixon in particular for a "tremendous job well done" in foreign policy and bringing new "hopes of peace."

And then all hell broke loose. "At that point in time" and "White House plumbers" became household words as millions of Americans became mesmerized by a clever Southern Senator and his vigilante committee investigating Watergate and pouring salt on the President's wounds. White House aides were being fired right and left and old regulars called in to help out.

John Connally came forward—this time as an unpaid White House consultant on anything and everything. Big John would show the nation just what kind of Republican he was and would help his old friend President Nixon out of a spot. However, when he got to the White House there was such tumult that Nixon was not listening. There was really very little time to worry about the business of a possible successor. The President of the United States was preoccupied with his own survival. And so, as noisily as he had arrived, Connally left. He had done all he could do as an adviser and he still stood firmly behind the President. Big John was going home to ranch, lawyer a little and take a trip around the world.

But, twelve hours after his resignation, instead of showing up in Houston, Connally appeared in Florida to meet with a group of millionaires to discuss the 1976 presidential race.

Connally has avoided reference to the Teapot Dome of the Seventies except to echo President Nixon's plea for a return to more routine matters. Before the Circuit Court of Appeals upheld Judge Sirica's ruling that Nixon turn over the controversial White House tapes, Connally repeatedly and enthusiastically endorsed the President's reluctance to diminish the Executive branch's authority notwithstanding legislative or judicial dictates. On September 20, 1973, Connally told a *Newsweek* reporter that "The President must always have the final word in inter-branch disputes." The former Texas governor did not bother to offer any statutory precedent for his position. In place of reasons, he proffers his loyalty to the President and his apparently sincere belief that we have once again established a philosopher-kinglike government with high officials engulfed in a coat of armor protecting them from other men's laws.

John Connally walks and talks and looks and seems like a President; indeed, he may look and sound too much like a recent President even to get elected.

But the silver-haired Texan is a natural. He thrives

on the pursuit of power and usually achieves it. He has relished his roles as counselor and companion to Presidents, conspirator with the boys in the back room and darling of the moguls in the board room.

His will be a familiar face on the 1974 congressional campaign trail, helping to reelect Republicans whom he will need two years from now.

If just the right combination of contingencies fell into place, Big John might have sat in the chair in the Oval Office he has visited so often. Yes, there is only a handful of those who have great power in our nation. John Bowden Connally, Jr., is one of that handful. This is his story.

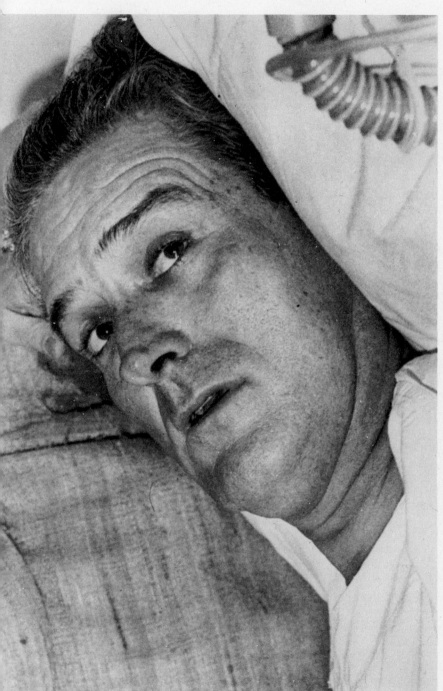

Texas Governor Connally rests in Parkland Hospital, Dallas, after being injured by a sniper's bullet during the Kennedy assassination. After recovery he enjoyed greater political potency

(2)
The Bullet-Made Man

The good Lord chose to leave me here, so I feel that
instead of being elected, maybe I'm one of God's elect.

JOHN BOWDEN CONNALLY, JR.

Texas politics is a tribute to paradox, and the cruelist irony of them all came that day in Dallas when an assassin struck.

Whatever powers there are that decide these things decided that the destiny of John Fitzgerald Kennedy and John Bowden Connally, Jr., should be sealed in that common shattering tragedy. But their destinies were to be radically different. When the President was killed, the Governor was reborn. The same bullet that passed through Kennedy made Connally a minor martyr, a role he was to exploit to such an extent that four years after the assassination the Baltimore *Sun* and other newspapers suggested with editorial sarcasm that "the black arm sling that Governor Connally is so fond of wearing is getting frayed."

The unprecedented expansion of John Connally's personal political power appears directly attributable to his association in the public mind with every American's emotional experience occasioned by the killing of a popular new, young President. The ex-Governor's image was that of the faithful wounded companion of our nation's martyred chief executive. Together with a seemingly endless supply of cash and a Grecian god-like demeanor, this has made him one of the most powerful public figures in current American history.

Assassination day also claimed as a victim the embryonic Republican party in Texas. The wounded included the liberal Democratic arm. For as his wounds healed, Governor Connally and his personal conservative team sought and secured unrivaled power. The state's political options were stifled by a unique mixture of Connally patronage, kindness, cleverness and cruelty.

The opposition became critically fragmented and eventually proved ineffectual.

Now in a wider spectrum, the nation began polarizing on Connally as a potential President of the United States. Is he a dangerous exploiter or a 1976 Republican savior? Whichever characteristic suits, there are included realities which demand explanation.

Before Connally's political rebirth, the secure Texas Democratic establishment dominated by the conservative Johnson-Connally faction was beginning to falter. Their politics had always been run under the convenient "Democratic" label, but they felt it would be much safer to continue operating Texas as a one-party state. The dynamic duo had taken over the party in 1956 when they ousted Governor Allan Shivers by more than a three-to-one majority in what *The New York Times* called "the dirtiest campaign of the year."

A slow evolutionary change had begun in LBJ-land. The conservative regime of Governor Shivers became the target of the national Democratic party because Shivers had not only supported Eisenhower against Adlai Stevenson but had run for Governor of Texas as both a Republican and a Democrat.

"There was a real chasm between the state and national factions of the Democrats," a Connally aide explained. Shivers did nothing to discourage the nationalites, and they flourished. And many independent conservatives joined the Republican party. Shivers left the governorship in 1957 with a fractured Democratic party and the beginnings of a two-party system in Texas. The next governor, Price Daniel, did little to help the problem. He was an average politician, and although a conservative, he was not successful in designing tactics to defeat his opponents in the party. He gave up a U.S. Senate seat and beat liberal Ralph Yarborough for the governorship. But then Yarborough won a vacant Senate position in a special election.

In 1961 John Tower, a conservative Republican relatively new to politics, won election to the Senate as a Republican. It was the first time that party had sent anyone from the Lone Star State to the Senate in eighty-four years. If the GOP continued to gain, it would mean that even more conservative voters would drift away from the Democrats, thus leaving the liberals—of whom Texas has a greater number than any other Southern state—in a position to seize control of the Democratic party. The comfortable status quo would then be disturbed and could mean danger for select power in Texas. Labor reforms, corporate tax changes and oil restrictions were frightening possibilities if your name was Connally.

Ironically, the candidacy of John Kennedy for the presidency was the key boost to surging Republicanism in Texas. The radical Right, which still flourishes in Texas with Klan meetings and isolationism, attacked the Kennedy campaign as it would later attack the Kennedy Administration. On the other hand, Texas liberals had found a home.

The ambiguous misfit was Lyndon B. Johnson. He was distrusted and disliked by most of the liberals for some sound reasons and some unsound ones. And he was thought of as a sellout by his fellow-conservatives for accepting the vice-presidential spot.

After the election the pressure was put on Connally to return home. His brief stint as Secretary of the Navy was innocuous. There had been far more excitement over accusations of his conflicts of interest by those opposing the Connally nomination than over his actual service.

Any identification with Kennedy was a peculiar hue in the Connally spectrum because through all the previous days of his lengthy political life, Connally had been identified with JFK's leading Democratic rival, Lyndon Johnson.

No matter which of his own several interests he pursued, Connally never really left Johnson. He worked as a campaign manager every time that Johnson had one, and he nominated him for President at the Democratic National Convention three times—including 1964. They were so close that when a friend once suggested that Connally had withheld information from LBJ at President Kennedy's request, Johnson exploded to the friend, "But you tell your own wife!"

President Kennedy was terribly upset by the election of John Tower in 1961 to fill out Lyndon Johnson's unexpired term, and, to reverse the Republican trend, John Connally, the most powerful behind-the-scenes manipulator in Texas politics, was sent home to take over. Nobody had done more than Connally to keep Texas' rickety Republican movement in a condition of near chaotic collapse. His reasons were strictly practical and much admired by the hierarchy of the Texas cashocracy. Connally knew his way around, and he knew what he had to do in 1962. "I came home to run for Governor," he said at the time, "because when John Tower was elected to the Senate I felt Texas was going to hell in a handbasket."

Connally had come back as a dragon-slayer; he would slay the GOP for President Kennedy and the opposition for Vice President Johnson. But something was wrong with his terrible swift sword. After a brutal primary contest with a liberal Democrat, Don Yarborough, he was forced into a runoff and won by only 26,000 votes out of more than a million cast. Then the Republicans had the gall to put up a real live candidate in the general election and nearly found enough votes to defeat John Connally.

In that primary election, Connally's young opponent, Don Yarborough (no relation to Senator Ralph Yarborough), had promised to repeal the sales tax, improve state services and increase the days each month that Texas oil wells could operate. His supporters were pushing for the development of an honest two-party system. Many liberal Democrats and labor leaders conceded privately that they weren't sure what they'd get if New Frontiersman Yarborough were elected—but they were adamant about not giving an inch to Connally. And that's why Connally only squeaked through.

Connally, a back-room political entrepreneur, was relatively unknown to the electorate. The early polls showed that virtually no voters knew his name, much less his qualifications. But with barrels of oil money his public relations brigade blanketed the state with expensive billboards and stylish radio and television spot announcements. Connally had put together a coalition reaching from the Dallas *News* on the Right to some Negro and civil rights groups on the Left, and used it, as one critic said, "to play the same damned no-party, no-issue politics Lyndon has always played."

In some areas he spent vast sums of money for what both opponents alleged was vote buying. On the Chicano west side of San Antonio, for example, Connally forces hired three dozen leafleteers for each precinct. (In the past, candidates had hired only one or two for each precinct.) Lalo Solis, an old-timer in San Antonio's precinct politics, said, "I've never seen so much money spent in a campaign. On election day you could hardly go into the voting places, the sidewalks were so crowded with campaign workers." A "worker" and his family were paid $10 a day plus $1 for lunch.

And the Connally tactics were often vicious. First, he charged primary opponent Yarborough with being a tool of a "diabolical plan" of the "left-wing radical Americans for Democratic Action" and "Eastern labor organizers" to capture Texas for "outsiders." He later denounced Cox, his Republican opponent, as "a renegade turncoat opportunist" because the man had once been a Democrat.

The gubernatorial contest had attracted national attention. Both candidates were basically conservatives. There was little discernible difference in their platforms or personal views, but Jack M. Cox made a major issue of Vice President Johnson's alleged control of Texas politics.

The prestige of the Kennedy Administration would have suffered heavily from a Connally defeat and any lingering ambitions of LBJ to be President in 1968 would almost certainly have been extinguished if he had lost his Texas political base.

But the liberal faction viewed John Connally with tepid feelings and would have preferred Donald Yarborough as the Democratic candidate. Liberals then regarded Connally as a stand-patter who would try to hold the conservative Democrats while doing nothing to calm the discontent on the party's left. Connally had criticized such New Frontier proposals as medical care for the aged under social security and federal aid to schools.

But the money really made the difference. And so

John Bowden Connally, Jr., became the thirty-first Governor of Texas.

At the same time Connally's future boss and political ally, Richard M. Nixon, was in California running a bitter race for Governor. Pat Brown had put Nixon on the defense about a loan by Howard Hughes to Donald Nixon, the former Vice President's brother. And it worked. A decade later more Hughes' money, this time funneled through Bebe Rebozo, would again jackpot Nixon.

While Connally was celebrating his election as a Democratic Governor, the future President, who was to woo him to Republicanism, was telling the press:

"As I leave the press, all I can say is this: For sixteen years, ever since the Hiss case, you've had a lot of—a lot of fun—that you've had an opportunity to attack me and I think I've given as good as I've taken.

"I made a talk on television, a talk in which I made a flub—one of the few that I make, not because I'm so good on television but because I've done it a long time. I made a flub in which I said I was running for governor of the United States. The Los Angeles *Times* dutifully reported that.

"Some newspapers don't fall in the category to which I have spoken, but I can only say that the great metropolitan newspapers, they have a right to take every position they want on the editorial page, but on the news page they also have a right to have reporters cover men who have strong feelings whether they're for or against a candidate. But the responsibility also is to put a few [reporters] on, on the candidate they happen to be against, whether they're against him on the editorial page or just philosophically deep down, a fellow who at least will report what the man says. . . .

"You won't have Nixon to kick around any more, because, gentlemen, this is my last press conference."

Nonetheless Jack Cox had waged an impressive campaign against Connally. He scored in attacks on Lyndon Johnson and his alleged control of the Texas political scene. At Tyler, Texas, days before the election, he told an audience that he was within a "heartbeat" of victory, and that the people would reject John Connally, the "hand-picked candidate" of Lyndon Johnson. Cox told another enthusiastic GOP rally that "six flags have flown over Texas, . . . but we are determined that the seventh flag, the flag of L.B.J., will not fly over the capitol at Austin."

An encouraged new Republican organization swept across Texas, enabling the party to enter the November elections in its most favorable position as a Texas political organization since the Reconstruction Era. As a result, the 1962 election saw the largest Republican vote ever in a state gubernatorial race.

Cox carried fifty-five counties, including Harris and Dallas, which reflected the urban appeal of new Republicanism, and polled a total vote of 715,025, while John Connally, the heavy favorite, polled a vote of 847,036. (Previous Republican candidates had been lucky if they got 75,000 votes in all.) In the race for lieutenant governor, O. W. "Bill" Hayes carried only sixteen counties and got a vote of 612,568, or 214,468 votes fewer than Cox.

But the congressional races gave Texas Republicans even more cause to cheer than did the gubernatorial contest. Bruce Alger easily won reelection in Dallas over his Democratic opponent, Bill Jones. A Republican, Ed Foreman of Odessa, was elected to Congress from the giant sixteenth district of West Texas. Foreman won

over four-term Congressman J. T. Rutherford by a vote
of 44,095 to 37,821. In a close race in the third district
in East Texas between veteran Congressman Lindley
Beckworth and Bill Steger, who had been the Republican gubernatorial nominee in 1960, Steger came within
2,112 votes of winning, out of 51,718 cast.

The gigantic vote polled by Jack Cox against Connally proved that Texas Democrats could no longer take
state elections for granted.

Governor Connally claimed the strong GOP vote
was evidence that the party had a better precinct organization than the Democrats. Connally said "the Republicans worked hard, while the Democrats did not get
busy until the final weeks" before the election.

The Democrats also had trouble keeping party
discipline. "There were defections among Democratic
precinct chairmen either positive or negative, or for different reasons. Some just did nothing, while others refused
to help the Democratic ticket. Some did this because
they were conservatives and favored Cox. Others did so
because they were liberals and favored Cox as a means
of breaking the moderate-conservative control of the
[Democratic] party machinery in Texas," the Democratic
campaign chairman in a major county observed.

It was precisely that split that would nurture the
controversy and dissension in Democratic ranks in
Texas, requiring a personal visit by President Kennedy
if Connally were to ever get reelected.

Things did not go well for the new Governor; the
start of his term was far from promising. He appeared
crude and insecure in his dealings with the Legislature,
and his prejudices were much too obvious. Within a year
after taking office he had alienated the minorities that
had supported him because of President Kennedy by
vetoing federal antipoverty programs, denouncing the

Medicare program and opposing the public accommodations sections of the Kennedy Administration's civil rights bill.

In reflecting on Connally's years as Governor, former Senator Ralph Yarborough told me: "He was the worst, most reactionary and vicious governor in Texas history. . . . He was just nasty and vindictive. . . . He wouldn't cooperate with our congressional delegation or leaders back home. It was pathetic."

Senator Yarborough had been close to President Kennedy politically and personally, and he more than any other Texas leader opposed Connally's involvement with the Administration. Connally ignored criticism from Capitol Hill and in the press about his iron-handed rule but found an opportunity to insult Yarborough publicly when the President made his fateful trip to Texas.

Connally tried to hold the party together by telling blacks that he was against the poll tax. Connally's enemies accused him of wanting to substitute literacy tests, but the Governor claimed that was a lie. He told labor groups: "It's no use kidding ourselves, we have differences. I know a lot of you did not support me, but the great strength of the Democratic party is that we are big enough to have our own views and yet follow the majority opinion."

Political trouble was increasing in the state's Democratic party despite Connally's having won. Liberals complained that the Governor, with Vice President Johnson's blessing, had frequently ignored or sabotaged their proposals. Senator Yarborough had been a longtime irritant to LBJ but a regular backer of liberal legislation. He was expected to seek renomination in 1964, and Don Yarborough was planning to oppose Connally again for the gubernatorial nomination.

On November 21, 1963 (the day before the assassination of President Kennedy), the Houston *Chronicle*'s poll—reputed to be one of the most accurate in Texas—showed that Connally would have at best a fifty-fifty chance of being reelected the next year. The Governor's loss of support was so dramatic that the Dallas *News,* the outspoken voice of Texas conservatism, wrote ominously about the possibility that if Connally lost control of the state delegation to the 1964 Democratic National Convention, Lyndon Johnson might not be put back on the Kennedy ticket. To say the least, on the eve of tragedy things already looked bleak for Big John.

The bitter factional dispute in Texas had become a national problem for President Kennedy. The White House was concerned with the voting habits of the big Texas delegation in the House of Representatives. Only eight of the twenty-one Texas Congressmen voted with Kennedy as often as the average Democrat. In at least three Democratic congressional primaries, Johnson-Connally men had worked for the conservative candidates and against those who would have voted for the President's programs. The situation might also jeopardize Kennedy's 1964 reelection prospects in Texas. The state's twenty-five electoral votes were a vital bloc, whether Lyndon Johnson was on the ticket or not. Kennedy and LBJ had secured Texas in 1960, but now Democratic factionalism and the rise of a tough Republican party made the forecast for '64 appear at best cloudy. And if Barry Goldwater should be the GOP nominee, Texas could be written off as safe for the Republicans. President Kennedy began selling a compromise plan under which all Texas Democrats would join in supporting Governor Connally and Senator Yarborough for reelection in 1964. The Johnson-Connally wing was reportedly willing to go along, but neither of the Yarboroughs appeared interested.

Since the President had supporters on both sides

of the controversy, it was suggested that Kennedy make a political fence-mending visit to Texas in order to bring the compromise plan to fruition. Kennedy had visited the state only briefly since the 1960 presidential campaign and had made no formal visit to Texas or any other state in over two years. The trip was under consideration by Vice President Johnson and Governor Connally for nearly a year before it took place. Finally, it was decided that President Kennedy should definitely go in the fall of 1963 rather than in 1964 when, according to Connally, his appearance might have had "more political overtones."

The basic decision for the tragic visit was made at a meeting of the President, Vice President Johnson and Connally on June 5, 1963, at the Cortez Hotel in El Paso. Kennedy had spoken earlier that day at the Air Force Academy near Colorado Springs and had stopped in El Paso to conduct an inspection of military facilities and to discuss the proposed visit with the Vice President and the Governor. The three agreed that Kennedy would come to Texas in late November 1963. The original plan called for Kennedy to spend only one day in the state, making whirlwind visits to Dallas, Fort Worth, San Antonio and Houston. But, in September, the White House decided to extend the trip from the afternoon of November 21 through the evening of Friday, November 22. On October 4 Governor Connally traveled to Washington to discuss the details of the visit and to ask President Kennedy what he would like to do. The President agreed that the details of events in Texas should be left largely up to the Governor.

The first information that Lee Harvey Oswald received regarding Kennedy's trip to Texas was the three-column front page headline in the Dallas *Morning News* of October 5 that announced: "Connally Tells J.F.K. Texas for Democrats." The story said that the Governor, in the course of a recent visit to Washington, "had been asked to make recommendations on plans for the President's Nov. 21-22 visit to Texas and that he expected to present something to the White House in about a week." " 'Many places in the state want him to come,' " Connally said. Among them, he added, were Corpus Christi and San Angelo, plus the four big Texas cities: Dallas, Houston, Fort Worth and San Antonio.

Although the public purpose of President Kennedy's fateful trip to Texas was to attend the dedication of a new aerospace center in San Antonio, the visit was actually designed to mend the serious wounds that had developed within the Texas Democratic party. Kennedy hoped that his presence in Texas would bring together the liberal and conservative wings of the party into a working unit, so that the traditional Democratic control of Texas politics could be preserved and the state counted on to support Kennedy's reelection effort.

It was ultimately agreed that the presidential party would stop in five cities—San Antonio, Houston, Fort Worth, Dallas and Austin. The Dallas leg of the journey was originally to be an evening affair. But Governor Connally decided that the evening event should be in the capital city of Austin and that "we should hit Dallas around noontime." A political fund-raising dinner was scheduled for the night of November 22, after which the President was going with the Johnsons to their ranch on the Pedernales.

Letters from Governor Connally and packages of tickets for the $100-a-plate dinner started arriving at the offices of the Texas congressional delegation the first week of November. Connally was asking each Democrat in Congress to sell 200 tickets. Senator Ralph Yarborough was sent 250.

Connally's public insult to Yarborough—not inviting him to the formal reception for the President—only further complicated the Kennedy trip. When he was asked on board the presidential plane headed toward Texas about his feelings concerning not being invited, Senator Yarborough responded: "I desire that my friends take no offense at this. I want everyone to join hands in harmony for the greatest welcome to the President and Mrs. Kennedy. Besides, Governor Connally is so terribly uneducated governmentally, what else could you expect?" But Senator Yarborough's plea had little impact on other liberal Democrats in Texas, who protested against the $100-a-plate presidential dinner on the grounds that many of their lower-income supporters, including blacks and Mexican-Americans, would not be able to attend. They also feared that the money collected would be used to finance Connally's 1964 primary campaign against Democrat Don Yarborough. Liberals were demanding assurances from President Kennedy that the proceeds would be evenly distributed amongst conservatives and liberals. Amidst all this in-fighting and public bickering, Kennedy wasn't sure whether he had created or solved more problems. The prospect for unity in the Texas Democratic party that Kennedy was seeking was very dim.

Moreover, the Republicans had recently captured eight out of nine Dallas county seats. Dallas County constituted the single most important county in the state because of its high population. Republican Jim Dobbs had even forced a runoff election for the tenth congressional district seat, once held by Lyndon Johnson. Dobbs had taken advantage of the Democratic split between J. J. Pickle, a Connally Democrat and onetime aide to Lyndon Johnson, and Jack Ritter, a liberal. Although Pickle won, he made many enemies among the liberal Democrats. Pickle's race for Congress was sensed to be a test case to see if liberal and conservative Democrats would be able to cooperate in backing a single

candidate. Kennedy supported Pickle's campaign and
tried to use his influence to get the liberals to fall in line
behind his candidacy. If the Administration was able to
work out a compromise in that instance, there might be
hope for a similar compromise on some of the more important races.

Kennedy again found himself in the middle, supporting one of Johnson's and Connally's men in the interest of party unity, against the wishes of his most ardent
liberal supporters in Texas. If the compromise could not
be reached, the winners would be the Republicans, who
would profit from Democratic factionalism.

But Governor Connally did little to further the
spirit of compromise between the two factions. Although
his own political future depended upon the compromise
that the Administration was attempting to work out in
Texas, he was notably uncooperative with their efforts.
His refusal to invite Yarborough to the presidential reception was not an isolated example. The compromise
that Kennedy was trying to work out would allow for all
the Democrats to support the reelection of Connally for
Governor and total party backing for Senator Yarborough's reelection as well. John Connally had no intention
of becoming Governor at the expense of giving up Democratic control of Texas politics.

Unquestionably John Connally owed his political
life to Lyndon Johnson and Kennedy's recent support.
Yet a breach was obviously growing between Connally
and the Administration. In some respects the support of
the Kennedy Administration was a political liability to
Connally. When he had left his position as Kennedy's
Secretary of the Navy in 1961 to run for Governor, he
was thought of by some Texans as a political "appointee"
of the Administration. In Texas more than any other
state, many resented the interference of the national
party leadership in their local political affairs. It was

even rumored at that time that the Kennedy Administration had offered a federal post to the incumbent governor, Price Daniel, in consideration for not running for reelection. Perhaps this outside interference would not have been as much resented if the Kennedy Administration had not drifted so far toward liberal policies. Even Texas' native son, LBJ, seemed to have been "infected" by the liberal spirit of the Kennedy team. That fear and the established intimate relationship between Connally and Johnson did not improve Connally's standing with the dogmatic Right in the state.

Many conservative Democrats had bitter memories of the last time in which the Administration had intervened in Texas politics and thrown its support behind liberal Democrat Henry Gonzalez in a congressional race. His victory in 1961 marked the first election of a Mexican-American from Texas to the Congress. Behind Gonzalez' victory lay a significant threat to conservative controls of the Democratic party in Texas and a vast potential of liberal strength. And a great Kennedy ally came to Congress. The huge sleeping giant of Texas politics, the Mexican-American and Negro populations, which made up a potential of over one million votes, seemed to be stirred by Gonzalez' victory. The Administration's support for Henry Gonzalez and the manner in which they paraded him around the nation after he won, to drum up minority support for the Democratic party, politically repelled conservative Texas Democrats.

But that sleeping giant was a reality with which Connally was forced to deal. By November 1963 a very strong liberal coalition threatened to turn traditional Texas politics upside down. The new coalition, made up of Mexican-Americans, blacks, labor unions and independent liberals, was gaining great momentum through various subsidiary organizations. Texas, which has the largest Mexican-American population of all states, was being organized by the Political Organization of Spanish-speaking People (PASO) with considerable success. Their leader Albert Pena had successfully led the Crystal City movement in April 1963 in which, after a massive voter registration drive, Mexican-Americans were able to install their first slate of Chicanos as mayor and city councilmen. In addition to the emerging brown-power politics, the Kennedy Administration was busy registering and organizing liberal Democratic support in other minority groups.

All of these minority political organizations and the liberal coalition chose the repeal of the poll tax as a major objective. Although the poll tax charged was only $1.50 to $2.00 per person, it served as a major barrier to the low-income voters in registering. If the poll tax could be repealed, it could be the beginning of the emergence of liberal control of the Democratic party. Connally was well aware of the potential threat that elimination of the poll tax could mean to his faction. Although his close association with the Kennedy Administration and its civil rights legislation forced him to favor the repeal of the poll tax officially, he was notably inactive in organizing support for the repeal vote in early November 1963. Two months earlier he had lashed out at political organizers who supported the repeal. He deplored "efforts by self-seeking politicians to turn poll tax repeal into a sideshow for their own purposes. We have the would-be bosses like Albert Pena of San Antonio, whose favorite term is 'political action' by bloc vote as a means of solving all the ills of our times, whether in Crystal City or throughout Texas." Connally's opposition to the poll tax repeal infuriated the liberals, who based their support on the emergence of that minority voting power. Albert Pena responded to Connally's speech by saying: "Actually the Governor's speech was

a sadistic, cruel, under-the-table oblique way of telling
the people of Texas he favored retaining the poll tax. If
95 percent of voter participation in a campaign such as
Crystal City is repugnant to the Governor, then it's
doubtful he believes in majority rule."

The poll tax failed to be repealed in the election
held two weeks before the arrival of President Kennedy
in Texas. But it would only be a matter of time before
minority voters in the liberal coalition or new federal
civil rights legislation would repeal the archaic tax. Governor Connally had only postponed the disaster he feared.

When President Kennedy finally arrived in Texas,
the liberal Democrats were hardly in the mood for a
compromise which involved the reelection of John Connally, who had helped defeat their primary objective,
the repeal of the poll tax. Yet both Connally's personal
and the Texas Democratic party's future depended upon
reaching a workable compromise which would prevent
the further disintegration of Democratic strength and
proportionate upsurge of the Republicans.

Texas was viewed as a test case for the entire South
to see if Southern conservatism was still compatible with
Kennedy's liberal leadership of the Democratic party.
Thus, if Connally's reelection was unacceptable to the
liberals as a compromise, he might have to be sacrificed
in order to preserve party unity. By his stubborn resistance to liberal demands for repeal of the poll tax, Connally had destroyed any chance the liberals might
genuinely support him as a party compromise. His continued close relationship with the liberal Kennedy leadership of the national Democratic party and crossover of
conservatives to the Republican party further undercut
his chances of staying Governor. Connally's political
position was eroding from both sides and his viability as
a candidate was close to exhausted.

As if all these developments were not enough to

threaten Connally's political future, in October 1963 a federal court ruled that the congressional districts of Texas were unconstitutional. All subsequent elections would have to be held at large until the Texas Legislature was able to design an acceptable plan for reapportionment. Connally refused to call a special session of the Legislature because reapportionment would be most harmful to his conservative faction which had so carefully gerrymandered the state's congressional districts to its favor.

In short, in November 1963 John Connally was in such serious political trouble that only a personal presidential visit could bail him out. Whether or not the visit would solve or intensify Connally's problems was a moot question. But the actual events of Kennedy's final visit transformed Connally from a political pawn into a man of incomparable stature, one with the instant charismatic appeal of a Texas folklore hero.

In order to avoid any risk of a relatively small turnout in Dallas, it was decided to stage a downtown motorcade in conjunction with the noon lunch hour. The final decision as to the route of the motorcade was held up due to a controversy involving Governor Connally, local Democratic leaders and Ken O'Donnell's presidential liaison staff as to the best place for the President to give the speech. The choice was between the Trade Mart and the Women's Center. Connally insisted on the Trade Mart, and the others finally acquiesced to his views. That made it virtually certain that the caravan would proceed down the Elm Street approach to the Stemmons Freeway (since Elm was the main civic center entrance to the freeway) and past the Texas School Book Depository. It was Governor Connally's office that innocently issued the press release detailing the motorcade route that served as a blueprint for assassination.

Public interest and concern about the impending Kennedy visit spread throughout the state. Texas newspapers provided their readers with a steady stream of information and speculation. An editorial in the *Times-Herald* of September 17 called on the people of Dallas to be "congenial hosts" even though Dallas hadn't voted for Mr. Kennedy in 1960 and might not endorse him in '64. On October 3 the Dallas *Morning News* quoted Congressman Joe Pool's hope that the President would receive a "good welcome" and would not face demonstrations like those encountered by Lyndon Johnson during the 1960 campaign (Johnson was spat upon).

The situation became more delicate as a result of an incident involving Adlai Stevenson, United States Ambassador to the United Nations. On the evening of October 24, after a speaking engagement, former Governor Stevenson was jeered, jostled and spat on by hostile demonstrators outside the Dallas Memorial Auditorium Theater. Mayor Earle Cabell called on Dallas to redeem itself during President Kennedy's visit. He reassured the nation that Dallas had shed its reputation as the "Southwest hate capital of Dixie."

The volatile party split continued right on through the very week of the Kennedy visit. On November 20 *The New York Times* featured an article entitled "President's Trip Arouses Texans." The story noted that "squabbling Texas Democrats" were "making a political stew out of President Kennedy's upcoming swing through their state." White House Press Secretary Pierre Salinger was quoted as saying, "Every faction in Texas will be taken care of." Mr. Salinger labeled the President's trip, which was to start the following Thursday, as "nonpolitical" except for a loop into Austin for the fund-raising dinner to be hosted by Governor Connally. The President's scheduled appearances included a testimonial dinner for Representative Albert Thomas, a Houston Democrat. Salinger said it would be a "bipartisan event." And maybe somebody somewhere believed him.

Two members of the Texas Democratic Executive Committee, Maury Maverick and Sarah McClure, complained to Congressman Henry Gonzalez about Connally's high-cost dinner. Maverick said he was taking up a collection for his $100 ticket and that his wife would "have to eat chili con carne with some poor liberal friends in Austin." Mrs. McClure wrote to John Bailey, then Democratic National Chairman, saying she could not afford $100 and that many Democrats could not afford even a $5 dinner. "When brazen public recognition goes to the moneyed minorities who most suspect vote Republican anyway, with no offsetting recognition given to the faithful, hard-working majority, it rankles in the souls of the little man, causing bitter resentment," she wrote. The ticket dispute continued even after the assassination. On November 26 the Associated Press reported that no decision had been reached on disposition of the more than $300,000 that had been raised.

On November 21 there appeared on the streets of Dallas anonymous handbills fashioned after Wanted posters. Beneath two photographs of President John Kennedy, one full-face and one profile, appeared the caption, "Wanted for Treason," followed by a scurrilous bill of particulars. And on the morning of the President's arrival, there appeared in the Dallas *Morning News* a full-page, black-bordered advertisement headed "Welcome Mr. Kennedy to Dallas," sponsored by the American Fact-Finding Committee. The "welcome" consisted of a series of statements and questions critically embarrassing to the President and his Administration. At the time of the visit, the Dallas *News* reported that Governor Connally had gone to Washington days before to try to per-

suade the President not to come to Texas at all. The
Governor feared that the visit would only tend to exac-
erbate the party's wounds.

As Kennedy's plane was en route to San Antonio,
the battle wore on. It is a matter of protocol that the
President take members of his party from Congress with
him when he goes into their state. And so Kennedy invited Senator Yarborough and a number of Democrats
from the House of Representatives to join him on the
trip to Texas. When Connally did not invite Yarborough
to the predinner reception for Kennedy at the Governor's Mansion in Austin, he had used the excuse that
the party was limited to members of the Texas Legislature.

The presidential entourage landed in San Antonio
at one-thirty in the afternoon of Thursday, November
21, 1963, where it was met by Governor and Mrs. Connally. The Kennedy-Connally party then motorcaded to
the new Aerospace Medical Health Center at nearby
Brooks Air Force Base, where this new six-million-dollar
facility was dedicated. They next flew to Houston for a
dinner honoring influential Representative Albert
Thomas. Again, they followed the pattern and traveled
by motorcade from the airport to the dinner. After dinner
the presidential party flew to Fort Worth and spent the
night at the Texas Hotel. They had breakfast there the
next morning and left about ten o'clock for the flight
to Dallas.

Governor Connally rode in the same car with
President Kennedy in both the San Antonio and the
Houston motorcade. In both of those cities they were
welcomed by large, enthusiastic crowds lining both sides
of the streets. Anti-Kennedy sentiment seemed to lose
out to a patriotic welcome for the Chief Executive.

Senator Yarborough twice refused an invitation
from Vice President Johnson to ride with him and Lady

Bird. Instead, Yarborough chose to ride in another car farther back in the caravan. But in Dallas, when Johnson insisted, Yarborough finally accepted the Vice President's invitation.

When the President and his party arrived at the Dallas Airport about noon on the twenty-second, he was greeted by an enthusiastic crowd of several thousand people. The motorcade for the journey through the city immediately began to take shape. Secret Service Agent Roy Kellerman took his place in the front seat of the presidential limousine next to the driver, William Greer. On the jump seats in the middle were Governor John Connally and Mrs. Connally. The Kennedys occupied the elevated rear seat, with the President sitting directly behind the Governor.

As the motorcade proceeded through the more thinly populated areas of the city, the crowds were sparse and somewhat restrained in their reactions. But, as it approached downtown, the crowds were tremendous. "They were stacked from the curb and even outside the curb, back against the walls." It was estimated that over 250,000 people lined the streets along the downtown route. The cars slowed to approximately twelve miles per hour. The farther they went, the more enthusiastic the response. Just as the motorcade turned onto Houston Street off Main, down by the old courthouse, Mrs. Connally turned to Kennedy and, referring to the wildly enthusiastic crowds, remarked, "Mr. President, you can't say Dallas doesn't love you."

As the limousine turned onto Elm Street, its occupants could see that the crowd was beginning to thin along the banks just east of the freeway. They were right on schedule. It was twelve-thirty, and they would be at the Trade Mart in another five minutes. But, approximately 150 to 200 feet after the turn, a deadly sound pierced the air. President Kennedy slumped silently in his seat. In the space of a few seconds, a thousand things passed through Connally's mind, he reflected later as he testified before the Warren Commission.

He heard what he immediately took to be a rifle shot from behind and up to the right. Instinctively he turned (and, in so doing, undoubtedly saved his own life) to look back over his right shoulder in the direction of the sniper's nest in the Texas School Book Depository building about a hundred yards away. He saw nothing unusual. Almost at the same time he heard the shot, the thought of an assassination attempt crossed his mind. Failing to catch the President in the corner of his eye, he started to turn to look back over his left shoulder. But he never got that far in his turn. He felt a smashing blow to the right-center of his back and immediately thought he had been shot—and knew it when he looked down and saw that he was covered with blood. It passed through his mind "that there were either two or three people involved, or more, in this, or someone was shooting with an automatic rifle. . . ." Assuming he had been fatally hit, he cried out, "Oh, no, no, no. My God, they are going to kill us all."

The bullet had drilled down through his chest, fractured his right wrist, and lodged in his left thigh. Connally doubled up, turning to his right, and Mrs. Connally pulled him over to her lap. Several reports confirm that Mrs. Connally reacted calmly whereas Mrs. Kennedy and others seemed to panic. Another shot sounded. Connally later told the commission that on his trousers "there was a chunk of brain tissue as big as almost my thumb. . . ." As he lay there conscious with his head in Mrs. Connally's lap, his eyes wide open, she told him, "Be quiet, you are going to be all right. Be still, you are going to be all right."

After the third shot, Kellerman ordered the driver

to "get out of line," and radioed to the motorcycle police
escort leading the parade to "get us to a hospital quick."
As they pulled out of line, Connally lost consciousness
and didn't come to until they reached the hospital. The
limousine raced beneath the underpass, up a ramp onto
the Stemmons Freeway, off onto Industrial and down
Harry Hines Boulevard. When the car came to a screeching halt five minutes later at the emergency entrance to
Parkland Memorial Hospital, the Governor was jolted
back to consciousness. The only thought that occurred
to him was that he was "in the jump seat next to the
door, that everyone concerned was going to be concerned with the President; that I had to get out of the
way so they could get to the President." He suddenly
lurched out of Mrs. Connally's arms and tried to stand
upright to get himself out of the car. When he collapsed,
he was picked up, placed on a stretcher and wheeled
down the passageway into Emergency Room Two. On
the stretcher lay the bullet that had become dislodged
from his thigh. Next to it lay his wide-brimmed, Texas
ten-gallon hat. Beside it, as if in mute comradeship, was
the soft felt hat that President Kennedy often carried
but seldom wore.

Following a five-minute checkup, Governor Connally was removed to a surgical suite. Inside, he was
quiet and calm in his pain as surgeons prepared to operate. The Governor's assistant, William Stinson, asked,
"How did it happen?" "I don't know," Connally said.
"Where'd they get you?" "I think they shot me from the
back. They shot the President, too. Take care of Nellie
[Mrs. Connally]." For four hours the doctors worked,
cleaning the wounds, removing bone splinters from the
chest cavity, stitching a hole in one lung, and treating
the wounds in his thigh and wrist.

The nature of Connally's wounds and the position
of the presidential car at the time of the shots tend to

prove that the bullet was fired from above and behind. The bullet had traveled downward at a twenty-five-degree angle and entered the Governor's back just to the right of his shoulder blade and toward the middle of the crease formed by the armpit. It went clear through and out his chest just beneath the right nipple, fragmenting his fifth rib and puncturing his right lung.

Having turned to look over his right shoulder and then revolving to look over his left shoulder, he had moved his right wrist over his left leg. The bullet entered the inner side of that wrist about an inch above the bone and came out in the center of the wrist on the other side, about three-quarters of an inch from the base of the palm. One of those doctors who first treated the Governor confirmed to me that his "turn" saved his life. The bullet then struck Connally's thigh about six inches above the knee. This wound was open, raw and about an inch and a quarter long and a third of an inch wide. Connally was not really aware of these two wounds until he came to in the hospital on Saturday morning. He looked up, saw his right arm tied up, and asked the nurse, "What is wrong with my arm?"

His chest wound was both "shocking and painful" and "very dangerous," according to the Emergency Room staff, because it was a "sucking wound of the chest which impedes breathing." However, while en route to the hospital, Connally must have instinctively put his right arm across his body, thereby closing the "sucking area" to some extent. An occlusive dressing was placed over it as soon as he got in the Emergency Room to keep him from sucking air in and out of the right chest. When the doctors got inside and saw the extent of the injuries, and how soon afterward he had reached them, they had no doubt that he could recover.

Dr. Tom Shires was chief surgeon at the University of Texas–Southwestern Medical School. He verified that

Connally probably would have been killed if he had not turned. The shot would have gone through his heart.

Later the Warren Commission hearing dispelled any doubt as to whether Connally and Kennedy were shot by the same weapon. Despite many controversial theories, the one-weapon decision stands.

Witnesses at the scene of the shooting saw a rifle being fired from the sixth-floor window at the southeast corner of the Texas School Book Depository, and some witnesses saw a rifle in the window immediately after the shots were fired. The bullet that was found nearly whole on Governor Connally's stretcher at the hospital and the two bullet fragments found in the front seat of the presidential limousine were fired from the 6.5-milli-meter Mannlicher-Carcano rifle found on the sixth floor of the building. The three used cartridge cases found near the window also matched.

But there was continuing conflict in the testimony before the commission regarding which bullets hit the President and which hit the Governor.

The Governor said he believed he was hit by the second bullet and President Kennedy, the first and third. Connally based his conclusion on the fact that he remembered hearing the first shot before he felt any impact, and the bullet from a high-powered rifle travels faster than the speed of sound. He explained that he failed to hear the second shot because the bullet reached him before the sound, thereby momentarily throwing his body into a state of shock such that he was not conscious of hearing. Connally reasoned that he couldn't have been hit by the third shot, since he was then lying down.

But experts had demonstrated to the commission that Oswald's rifle could not physically be reloaded in less than 2.3 seconds, and it would have been impossible for two shots to have been fired in sufficient time for

Connally to have heard the first and have been hit by
the second. Also, if all three bullets had hit persons in
the car, the three would have either been found or
evidenced by some specific damage inside the car. One
bullet was found on Connally's stretcher and one fragmented when it struck the President's head. There was
no sign of any other bullet mark on the limousine, so
one of the shots must have missed the car completely.
And so the commission adopted what has since become
known as the "one-bullet theory," determining that the
first bullet to strike Kennedy hit him in the neck-shoulder
area and continued in a downward path, exited from his
neck below the Adam's apple and continued downward,
striking Governor Connally. Could the relationship between the two, the day and John Connally's future, be
more ironically linked than by one bullet? It killed and
gave birth.

At first there was speculation as to whether Connally, rather than Kennedy, was the intended victim of
the assassination. In the course of the Warren Commission's investigation, it was discovered that Lee Oswald
had written a letter to John Connally on January 30,
1962. While Oswald was still a member of the U.S.
Marine Corps Reserve, he went to live in Russia. At
the American Embassy in Moscow, he announced that
he meant to become a Soviet citizen and swore out an
affidavit that said: "I affirm that my allegiance is to the
Soviet Socialist Republic." The Marine Corps got news
of Oswald's action, convened a special board and gave
him an "undesirable" discharge. Enraged, he wrote a
letter to Connally as Secretary of the Navy, promising
to "employ all means to right this gross mistake or in-
justice to a bona fide U.S. citizen and ex-serviceman."
Connally sent Oswald's letter to his successor, Fred
Korth, and the matter went no further. Oswald evidently
hadn't realized that Connally had stepped down from his

post as Secretary of the Navy a few weeks before he received the letter.

The Warren Commission was also told that Oswald had visited Governor Connally's Austin office in 1963. According to the published Report, however, this information was never substantiated from state visitors' records. Connally himself denied having any knowledge of such a visit.

If Connally had been Oswald's target, shots would probably have been fired when the limousine was still on Houston Street, where the Governor would have been exposed to direct fire. It is also significant that, when Oswald was told after his arrest that Connally had been shot, his reaction was, as described by one policeman, that of "genuine concern and surprise."

In his testimony before the Warren Commission, the Governor said he felt that the bullets were not intended for him and that there had been no conspiracy of any kind. His theory of what happened was that ". . . you had an individual here with a completely warped, demented mind who, for whatever reason, wanted to do two things. First, to vent his anger, his hate, against many people and many things in a dramatic fashion that would carve for him, in however infamous a fashion, a niche in the history books of this country. And I think he deliberately set out to do just what he did, and that is the only thing that I can think of."

The infamous Garrison investigation in New Orleans and the score of exploitation books claiming conspiracy have titillated some but convinced few that Connally was wrong. There are nagging inconsistencies in the Warren Report. Now, in the era of Watergate when the real extent of government secrecy is being exposed, the Kennedy conspiracy rumors are being rekindled. The Warren Commission report must be examined again with the realization that high-ranking government officials can and will lie and then document their untruths.

On Saturday, November 23, the day after the assassination, Connally was reported to be in "good condition." Doctors announced that he would stay in the hospital another ten or eleven days. From his bed he proclaimed the day of Kennedy's funeral "an official day of mourning in Texas." The chief of the Texas Highway Patrol ordered twenty extra men into Dallas to guard the Governor. A temporary headquarters was set up in the hospital for Connally's staff. Only members of his family and some staff personnel were permitted in his room.

On Sunday Mrs. Connally told the press that her husband was "now apparently out of danger." He was able to walk from his bed to a chair, sit there for a few minutes, and walk back to the bed. He was well enough to shave himself. Each day he was up and about for a bit longer. By the end of his first week in the hospital, half of the stainless steel wires used to stitch together his torn thigh had been removed. Doctors predicted that he would recover with little more to show than "a collection of scars, possibly a stiff wrist—and a horrifying memory."

And the state's political wounds were healing as rapidly.

Although he still required round-the-clock nursing attention, and tubes still protruded from both his back and chest, Connally's doctors reluctantly permitted a press interview on November 28. One reporter noted that the United States had been given a President from Texas for the first time in history and asked Connally to comment on "the way that fate intervened to literally change the world at this moment." Governor Connally responded, saying: ". . . I thought how ironic in spite of the fact I managed his campaign unsuccessfully for

President that the man who defeated him named me
Secretary of the Navy, a highly treasured position as far
as I'm concerned, and then on the very day that the
President was assassinated and I was wounded as a re-
sult of that, Mr. Johnson became the President of the
United States—a rather strange set of circumstances."
He later said of Johnson that he knew of no man he
"would rather have dealing my hand than him."

Mr. Connally ate Thanksgiving dinner with Nellie,
his three children, and his brother in the hospital room.
He also managed to watch a portion of the Texas A
& M–Texas University football game on television after
eating.

On December 5, 1963, Connally's physicians looked
over final X rays and decided that he could go home. As
he entered the hospital cafeteria, just before leaving, he
was met by representatives of the press and an applauding
group of more than 150 nurses, doctors and technicians.
He spoke for ten minutes, praising the hospital staff and
answering a few questions.

During his successful gubernatorial reelection campaign the following fall, Connally was reported to be
uneasy in large crowds, often jumping nervously at
sudden noises. His right wrist still gave him trouble. He
was compelled to eat left-handed, had difficulty brushing
his teeth, and couldn't handle coins with his right hand.
At a press conference in late November 1964 he said:
"More than ever before, I have tried to keep uppermost
in my mind what things are of lasting value and to be
grateful for the time I have, to be more aware of the
things you really hold dear and to be constantly grateful
for the things you really know in your heart to be of
lasting value and strength."

Even as those wounds were healing, his political
fortunes soared. As early as November 27, 1963, *The
New York Times* reported that the "assassination appears

to have had an unprecedented unifying force on feuding Democratic factions in Texas." Senator Ralph Yarborough, leader of the faction that had opposed the Johnson-Connally wing, told the President, "I pledge to you my support in Texas and the nation."

After the shooting, Connally could do no wrong—or at least he wouldn't be called on it. He had come into office promising to cut state spending by 10 percent. But suddenly his budget doubled. He came into office promising to pass legislation limiting a governor to two two-year terms; but he never mentioned that again and was elected three times. He persuaded two of his three legislatures to raise taxes on consumers and lower taxes for industry despite campaign rhetoric to the contrary.

A strange, oppressive atmosphere began to build up in Texas. The Governor established a super-regency over the state university system which became nationally infamous for the manner in which it put down dissent among students and faculty. Texas Rangers, at Connally's request, broke up a strike by Mexican-American farmworkers who wanted to be paid more than forty to eighty cents per hour. He became increasingly careless about —or indifferent toward—the opinions of minority groups.

No matter. Connally was still the most popular Governor in recent Texas history and in total control. By the start of his last term, his appointees held a majority of the seats on every important regulatory commission and agency, including, of course, the Railroad Commission, which regulates oil production. In matters affecting all business and industry, the hard-line conservative Democratic clique reigned supreme.

John Connally had become Mr. Texas. His power and influence exceeded LBJ's at his peak. Now there was the future—bigger and better things. One anti-

Connally newspaperman in San Antonio called the Governor's slogan, "Today, Texas—tomorrow the world."

He had become a bullet-made man, or more accurately, a re-made man. But it had begun a long time ago when he was Young John.

In 1938 young John Connally became a volunteer campaign worker for a congressional candi-

[3]
Little John

There's a rather odd twist to the whole business, since the mass of American people travel the wide middle of the road, but when the American electorate creates a political hero, the preference is generally for one whose beginnings are at one extreme or the other of the socio-economic spectrum.

At the one end are the heirs of extreme wealth, the patricians whose service to government and nation may stem from an unselfish and philanthropic attitude —men like the Roosevelts, the Kennedys, the Rockefellers.

At the other end are those who billboard humble beginnings and exemplify the struggle up from poverty to success and social standing. Abraham Lincoln, of course, is the most hallowed of this group, but the Trumans and the Johnsons also fit the mold as men who followed the American way and the Protestant ethic of industry, frugality and sobriety to grow in their chosen professions.

John Connally fits it, too. Or at least he wants to.

The tall, handsome man who now wears $300 cus-
tom-tailored suits and sports expensive haircuts has come
a long way from Floresville, Texas, where he wore faded
Levis and threadbare shirts while he hung around his
father's butcher shop. One Dallas reporter has dubbed
him "the manicured man," attesting to his immaculate
grooming.

The Great War and the prospects for American
involvement in it were the major topics of discussion
around Floresville when John Bowden Connally, Jr., was
born on February 27, 1917, the oldest child of John
Bowden Connally and his wife, the former Lela Wright.
The first son, in the American and especially Texan tradition, was named for the father, a hardworking, in-
dustrious man in a tiny southern Texas town.

Even today, only a handful more than 3,000 people
live in Floresville, and in the second and third decades
of the twentieth century, it was a typical country small
town. Connally is its one and only favorite son. All the
residents knew one another, and there would be smiles
and waves to "Junior" and his friends as they scuffed
their bare feet along the sandy streets. Floresville is the
county seat of Wilson County, and on Saturdays the
farmers and ranchers of the area would drive their
bonnet-wearing wives in the dusty pickup trucks to town.
Small-town Saturday has always been an exciting day,
and southern Texas won't let go of its touch of the
frontier. The tall men with their heavy boots and wide
brimmed hats, a chaw of tobacco tucked into the cheek,
were an impressive sight to a small boy.

The countryside is nearly flat as Texas slopes south-
ward toward the Gulf of Mexico, and the blooming
mesquite brightens the spring. The San Antonio River
runs by, providing water for the cattle ranches, and a

spot for young John and his friends to swim on hot summer days.

Floresville is some thirty miles southeast of San Antonio, an easy ride on U.S. Highway 181 today, but a full day's journey when the Connally family visited the "big city" in the 1920's. The frequent trips to San Antonio, which may be Texas' most hallowed city, helped instill in the boy some of the conservatism and other traditional values which he still holds. The Alamo is in San Antonio, perpetuating loyalty to Texas and enmity to Mexico, and its status as a shrine to independence, loyalty, patriotism and the great traditions that made the nation survive is so secure that it even has been able to ignore the irreverent line that if the Alamo had had a back door there would be no state of Texas today.

When fall came, young John would don shoes and go to the public school, his clutch of books surrounded by a leather strap, his pockets filled with the usual collection of a small boy—an old marble, half a lucky piece, a few coins, maybe even an apple. The schools were all white, since segregation was the law of the land at the time and the ranchers of southern Texas were not about to change it. Private education and prep schools were unknown, except for the handful of Catholics who attended parochial schools in the face of sneers from their young Protestant compatriots. Mexicans and blacks, who made up the manual labor force in the area, struggled for what little education they received, usually giving it up early in the face of family pressures to get a job.

About this time Little John got his first taste of politics, when his father ran for County Clerk. The Governor-to-be and his sister Carmen were told to knock on doors and ask people to help Connally, Sr. in his campaign. At first John, Jr. was shy, but, according to his sister, he learned quickly to communicate.

The Depression brought hard times to the Connallys, just as it did to everyone else, and the nation was
deep in the throes of it when young John, his one dark
suit neatly pressed and a tie knotted tightly around his
neck, marched to the auditorium platform to receive his
high school diploma. The band played "Pomp and Circumstance," and the elder Connallys and their neighbors,
smiles deep in wrinkled, leathery faces, were extremely
proud of their sons and daughters. John was one of the
15 percent of his classmates going to college. He was
enrolled at the University of Texas.

Austin was about 120 miles away, in perhaps the
nicest part of the state, and a higher education was still
available there at minimal cost. The Austin area, thick
with woodlands and surrounded by lakes, is in sharp
contrast with much of the remainder of Texas, and the
city houses the state capitol as well as the keystone of the
state university system. The campus was smaller then,
but the tall tower dominated it as it does now. It had yet
to become known as a sniper's hiding place, and it served
as the university's administration center. For football
victories and commencement week, it is bathed in an
orange light which adds an eerie glow to the night sky.
For students with dreams, like John Connally, the top of
the tower was a place to read in, to enjoy a late-afternoon
breeze or just to dream about his future while staring off
at the city and the faraway hills.

Hair was shorter and shoes were usually worn on
college campuses in the 1930's, and though there was
less feeling of political activism, there were plenty of
things for the students to do. Campus life appealed to
the young man from Floresville, and he entered into all
activities with the same sort of zeal and energy that he
later displayed as a professional politician. In particular
he liked debating, dramatics and individual speech-
making. He won his first competition with a recitation

of Patrick Henry's "Give me liberty, or give me death" speech. While an undergraduate, he visited area civic clubs and high schools as a public speaker on what was happening in college. The most memorable aspect of his standard speech, according to those who remember, was that it was always so long.

There is a strong link between the courtroom and the political arena and the dramatic stage, and Connally embraced drama as one of his major extracurricular interests. The Curtain Club, the University of Texas dramatic organization, produced in the 1930's broadcaster Walter Cronkite and actor Eli Wallach. Connally earned the lead in a major university theatrical production and went from goat to hero during opening night. He blew his entrance lines and departed the stage in despair and confusion, but returned to dominate the evening and receive an impressive ovation during the curtain calls. Even then Big John was indeed a leading man.

After rehearsals or after classes John and his friends drank beer at Schultz's, and talked and walked along Guadalupe Street, known to generations of Texas students as "the Drag."

In the fullness of time, he won the Inter-Society Oratorical Contest, was elected president of both Alpha Psi Omega, the dramatic fraternity, and the Athenaeum Literary Society. He was chairman of the Student Assembly and later president of the Student Association. Hours of work on stages and practice for his oratorical competitions added polish to Connally. Some of the south Texas accent was softened. His delivery improved and he became a poised speaker, at ease before any type of audience. Oratory polished his pacing, theater taught him the dramatic effect of timing and phraseology and colorful language rolled off his tongue.

But student activities, even when they lead to campus honors, aren't always enough for some young men, and John Connally, showing then the immense energy and stamina that would help him over the next 35 years, was such a young man. The fascination of politics already had a hold on him, and in 1938 he became a volunteer campaign worker for a young congressional candidate named Lyndon Baines Johnson. The campaign worker was barely old enough to vote, and the candidate was nine years older. Johnson had won a special election in 1937 to fill a House vacancy, and he was running in the general election of 1938. It was the two men's first association, and the beginning of the formation of a political team that would leave a solid mark on the nation for more than a generation.

In the 1930's a Texas law student could, by examination, be admitted to practice and begin lawyering before graduation. And so the handsome barrister characteristically began his legal career as well as his campaign responsibilities for LBJ in 1938, three years before even receiving his law degree. He eventually received his benedictory baccalaureate in advocacy in June 1941.

But campus life wasn't all work for the young John. One of the major social events of the school year is the selection of the Texas Sweetheart, crowned each spring during Roundup, a longtime tradition. The 1938 Texas Sweetheart was a lovely young co-ed named Idanell Brill, and her beauty caught the eye of the tall young man from Floresville. They were married two years later, while Connally was working toward his law degree and the nation was moving toward World War II.

In 1940 Lyndon Johnson again ran for reelection to Congress without real opposition, and with the help of Connally as campaign manager was again victorious. The unopposed status gave the duo time to take an active part in the tense maneuvering over selection of the Texas delegation to the 1940 Democratic National Convention.

The state's leaders were divided on the question of a third term for President Roosevelt. The prime issue was whether or not the Texas delegation would go to Chicago instructed to support the "Stop Roosevelt" movement. Pro-FDR elements argued that renomination and reelection of Roosevelt was necessary in view of the war in Europe. The opposition revered the two-term tradition and would not support a presidential third term for any reason. Johnson and Connally helped forge the compromise on which the Texas State Convention finally agreed: The delegation went to Chicago pledged to support John Nance Garner (the favorite son) for President but instructed not to take part in any "Stop Roosevelt" bloc that might form. The Johnson-Connally move was right and their power base was beginning to grow. FDR was grateful.

With the death on April 9, 1941, of United States Senator Morris Sheppard of Texas, Lyndon Johnson immediately seized the opportunity to fulfill his political ambition. He knew that if he waited for Sheppard's seat to come up for grabs in 1942, it would be virtually impossible to dislodge whoever was the short-term incumbent.

On April 19 Governor W. Lee (Pappy) O'Daniel, himself expected to be a candidate for the Senate seat, set June 28, 1941, as the date of the special election to fill the vacancy. That set off a flurry of hopeful candidates filing for the race. The final printed ballot would contain the names of twenty-nine candidates, including twenty-five Democrats, two Republicans, one Independent and one Communist.

Johnson was in Austin to speak before a joint session of the Texas Legislature. Under the guise of a commemorative address in honor of Sam Houston, he delivered a rousing speech in honor of Lyndon Johnson. At its conclusion he received a standing ovation. He then held a meeting with the Governor and cautiously sounded out O'Daniel's intentions regarding the up-and-coming race. Pappy finally agreed that he would not run for the Senate. Johnson was elated.

The next day he flew directly to Washington, burst into the White House Oval Office half an hour before FDR's scheduled news conference and told Roosevelt about his successful speech. He reported that Governor O'Daniel was out of the race. Roosevelt glanced at a statement Johnson showed him announcing his candidacy and suggested that Johnson read it to newsmen from the White House steps. A little help from the top never hurts.

A few minutes later Lyndon Johnson appeared outside the West Wing of the White House and, emphasizing that he had just come from the President's office, made his announcement. News stories in Texas the next day said that Johnson's candidacy had the "blessing" of the President of the United States.

The LBJ campaign, under the able leadership of managers John Connally, Alvin Wirtz and Raymond Buck, got off to a slow start, with Johnson ranked as the weakest of the four big candidates despite his public clutching of Roosevelt's coattails. By accepting the Administration's blessing, he found himself trapped within the confines of New Deal policies. His speeches took on a somber, preachy tone. O'Daniel had changed his mind and was running hard. LBJ couldn't seem to match the brassy, homespun style of Pappy O'Daniel, who campaigned from a flatbed truck with a country band whooping it up behind him. A state poll published on May 4 made Johnson's cause appear hopeless. O'Daniel, who hadn't even announced his candidacy until May 10, led the field with 32.8 percent of the voters while Johnson trailed with only 9.3 percent.

Heavy spring rains and cold weather hampered all the candidates as the campaign continued. Connally and Wirtz advised Johnson that the only way he could compete with O'Daniel was to put on a bigger carnival than the old hillbilly Governor. They planned a heavy saturation program but told LBJ not to launch it until the rains stopped.

The uneasy Johnson, however, refused to delay, and in a beating rainstorm he took off by plane for talks with local political leaders around the state. A month of lunches and dinners in soggy clothes brought on a serious throat infection that put him in the hospital for ten days.

When he was able to leave the hospital, LBJ was sure that his illness had doomed his campaign. But he was surprised to learn that the next state poll showed that his popularity had increased from 9.3 to 17.6 percent. Connally and Wirtz had been ready for the crisis. They took over Johnson's speaking engagements, and through influential friends kept his name in the limelight. In addition, they cleverly spread the false rumor that President Roosevelt would soon come to Texas to speak in Johnson's behalf. Uncertain how to handle that possibility, the Texas Legislature even approved a resolution inviting the President to inspect busy Texas defense plants when he came.

The cluttered race began thinning out as the weather cleared. By June 6 several candidates had dropped out, although their names remained on the ballot.

Because Johnson had started out low in the polls, his campaign team decided that more funds were essential. Although federal law limited Senate campaign expenditures to $25,000, they knew that there were ways to circumvent those rules. Total compliance would only mean defeat. There were charges later that the Johnson campaign chest grew to over $500,000. The candidate's official report claimed receipts of only $9,645 and expenditures of $11,880. But Watergate and public indignation over campaign spending were thirty years away.

Johnson had a personal airplane, hundreds of paid campaign workers, extensive newspaper advertisements, expensive radio spots, cash prizes for those who attended his rallies, and highway billboards throughout the entire state showing him and Roosevelt shaking hands.

A large part of these campaign funds were collected from Brown and Root, the construction company being promoted by Alvin Wirtz's law firm. They had fast become multimillionaires with Wirtz representing them and Johnson helping them get business from the Government.

The Bureau of Internal Revenue later uncovered some of the loopholes that the company used to get around campaign financing laws. One of the widely employed subterfuges was to issue large bonuses to employees, who in turn gave their "bonuses" to local Johnson campaign managers. Another scheme was to pay high "fees" to lawyers connected with the campaign, who then passed the money along. Since all of these transactions were in cash, they were impossible to trace. When Internal Revenue obtained sworn statements and was on the verge of proceeding with a criminal prosecution against Brown and Root, Wirtz and Johnson visited President Roosevelt and the anticipated action was canceled. Some years later when there was talk of reopening the case, all of the records involved were removed from a fireproof building in Austin and placed in a flimsy Quonset hut. They were reduced to ashes when the hut mysteriously caught fire and burned to the ground.

Connally had active Johnson organizations in every

Texas community. Along the Rio Grande they competed
with O'Daniel forces to buy off local political dictators
to bring in the vote for their man through their established Texas-style ballot-box-stuffing techniques. Connally also milked Johnson's newspaper friendships.

The Connally-Wirtz strategy was to have LBJ begin
the campaign as a statesman and then outdo Pappy as
an entertainer. As the campaign progressed, they soft-
peddled issues and staged what turned out to be a spec-
tacle that one observer called "the biggest musical
comedy floor show in the history of politics." A Johnson
rally included a swing band screeching out jazz, a black-
face act, dancing girls, an overweight singer of patriotic
songs, comedy routines, a long patriotic pageant, a lot-
tery—and, finally, a speech by the candidate.

As the campaign moved toward the homestretch a
new gimmick was Johnson's reading of telegrams sent to
him by President Roosevelt. On the days when there was
no FDR telegram, there were wires from other prominent
Washington officials.

But all of the chicanery, money, pressure and show-
manship were to no avail. Pappy O'Daniel was not con-
fined by the ideological strictures of the New Deal. And
Johnson could not hope to match Pappy's natural touch,
which brought him almost instant close rapport with
crowds. Roosevelt's bouquet became a campaign funeral
wreath.

Governor O'Daniel traveled the countryside with
his nine-piece hillbilly band, a sound truck, "Mickey-
Wickey, Patty Boy, Molly, and Texas Rose." Pappy
appeared without formality and without introduction
from local politicos. He gave homey rambles about his
platform, wrapped himself in the Ten Commandments
and the Golden Rule, and let everyone know that he was
the only candidate with such lofty purposes. Following

his homey bits he would rip into the Texas Legislature and lobbyists. He was guaranteed prolonged cheers when he told how he was fighting for the people against "influence-peddling politicians" who were occupying "mahogany-lined offices" at taxpayer expense.

Five hours after the polls closed, Johnson was leading by 3,000 votes. The next morning the Houston *Post* announced that he was ahead by 5,000. On June 30, two days after the election, the headline in the Dallas *News* read: "Only Miracle Can Keep FDR's Anointed LBJ Out." But the following day's paper revealed a Johnson lead cut to 700 votes. By the end of that day, the lead had dwindled to 77 as corrected totals began coming in from rural counties in east and south Texas. On July 2, 1941, O'Daniel was declared the winner by a margin of only 1,311 votes out of 600,000 cast.

Many of LBJ's friends expected him to contest the election since there appeared to be ample evidence of tampering with the returns. But Wirtz and Connally advised against the challenge. They couldn't afford to have the fund-raising particulars exposed. And some of their other campaign techniques could not stand close scrutiny.

On July 3 the Texas Senate voted to permit its investigating committee to look into the peculiar election. And E. B. Germany, chairman of the State Democratic Executive Committee, wired the United States Committee on Elections urging similar action. But in both instances when requests were made to examine the financing of Johnson's campaign, the proposed inquiries were quickly quashed. In the next U.S. Senate race Connally decided to pay more direct attention to the ballot boxes.

The 1941 defeat, together with Roosevelt's declining support in the South, signaled the disillusionment of Connally and Johnson with the New Deal. They began touting support by the more conservative elements represented by oil, gas and broadcasting interests.

Like almost every other university graduate of the class of '41, John Connally received his diploma and his welcome from Uncle Sam at almost the same time. Connally was standing very tall at commencement, his lovely bride at his side, and soon he would shift from the robes of graduation to the natty whites of the U.S. Navy, his LL.B. tucked in his pocket.

Bright young men moved fast in the service in those days, and no one has ever accused John Connally of not being bright. He received a commission as an ensign on June 11, 1941, and already displaying both education and practical experience, he was assigned to the Office of the Chief of Naval Operations.

Once again, things broke well for the young man from Floresville. He was stationed in Washington, D.C., and it was—like the meeting with Lyndon Johnson in 1938—a perfect match of a man and a situation.

Whether in wartime or peacetime, there is a very special aura about Washington. It is the seat of the Government, of course, but it also has a worldliness, a sophistication, an air of action and power and decision that can have an extremely potent effect upon a young and ambitious man. It had all this effect—and then some—on twenty-four-year-old John Connally. It was the beginning of a romance that still flames high in the Connally ken. He has been in and out of public life on many occasions, retiring to Texas and private life and business numerous times. But the siren song of Washington asserts a constant pull on him.

Washington was an even more attractive spot in the days of World War II. Because of the war, there was even more influence, even more power, and the young Texan survived the first shock of the city to post solid personal and professional advances.

Connally's legal background helped in his first naval assignment, as a legal assistant to James V. Forrestal, then Under Secretary of the Navy. A year later, he was wearing his officer's whites in Africa, assigned to Algiers as part of the planning staff for the invasion of Africa under General Dwight D. Eisenhower.

The tall, tanned, handsome Texan looked trim and dapper in his uniform and cut an impressive figure in Algiers. He is still trim and dapper, and he has the habit of leaning on associates whose dress is not up to the standards that Big John desires.

Action always appealed to Connally, and after his tour of duty in Africa he was transferred to the South Pacific, where he served with distinction. He was a fighter-plane director aboard the aircraft carrier U.S.S. *Essex* and won a Bronze Star for bravery. Later, he was shifted to another carrier, the U.S.S. *Bennington,* and was awarded a Legion of Merit for his service. In all, Connally was involved in campaigns in the Gilbert, Marshall, Mariana, Ryukyu and Philippine islands, and battle stars sprouted across the ribbons that adorned his chest.

Connally rose steadily, if undramatically, in the official grades and was discharged from active duty in January 1946 with the rank of lieutenant commander to go with a chestful of ribbons and a cap spangled with gold braid.

Like many other young Americans, John Connally returned from World War II with a large chunk missing out of his life. He had been gone from Texas for four and a half years; he had seen his wife and his young children on but a handful of occasions. He was twenty-nine years old, an attorney with limited legal experience, and it was time to set out on a career.

With his boundless energy, and a group of powerful

friends, Connally went off in two basic directions. One was political, the other was in search of personal wealth. The friends were an Austin-based fraternity of politicians and businessmen and included names like Johnson, Ed Clark, Walter Jenkins, J. C. Kellam, Jake Pickle and Bob Phinney. The group had contacts, courage and the common aim of wealth and power. They were experienced in political dealing and knew the benefits of government help in cost-plus contracts and various favorable allowances.

Three weeks after he was mustered out of the Navy, Connally took his discharge pay and, with ten other men, applied for a license to operate a new radio station in Austin. In honor of their recent military service, they applied for the call letters KVET. The signers of the application to the Federal Communications Commission included Connally and his brother Merrill, college friends Kellam and Willard Deason, plus Jenkins, Pickle, Phinney and W. E. Syers. The business address was given as 1901 Dillman Street, in Austin, a location later described by *The Wall Street Journal* as "the crowded house at 1901 Dillman Street."

The house was owned by Lyndon Johnson, who was still serving in Congress. Johnson helped push the application through, even though he and Lady Bird owned KTBC, another station in Austin. More peculiarly, when Johnson requested a license renewal for his own station, he listed Connally, Deason, Syers, Kellam and Pickle among his employees, which meant that they were working for two competing stations.

The help of Johnson was evidently sought when KVET told the FCC it wanted to broadcast at 1300 kilocycles. An existing station in San Antonio was already broadcasting at that wave length, but a short time later the FCC announced that the San Antonio station had "voluntarily" moved to another wave length. Con-

nally served as general manager and president of KVET
for three years.

Connally's Navy whites had been carefully placed
in storage, and he was back in conservative suits that
would display his "good ol' boy" image, vital in the
Texas countryside. The Legion of Merit ribbon might
be discreetly placed in his lapel, with congratulations to
be accepted modestly as just part of the job. The Italian
suit designers would have to wait another generation or
so, until Connally was an established part of the international political scene.

The young man needed more than a handful of
money-making schemes, a radio station and an interest in
politics to keep his life full, and by 1948 Connally was
ready to make a major political move. He and some rich
and powerful supporters, especially his friend Alvin Wirtz,
wanted to control the Senate seat that was to be filled
in November. The logical candidate, one of the "family,"
was Lyndon Johnson, a three-term Congressman, but the
early front-runner was former Governor Coke Stevenson, who wanted to move from the state to the national
level.

In the one-party system that Texas long has boasted,
victory in the Democratic primary was tantamount to
election, and primaries were far larger campaigns than
the general election. Still, Lyndon Johnson was stubborn
and told Wirtz, Connally and his other cronies that he
did not want to run for the Senate but would campaign
for reelection to his House seat. The primary was set for
July 24 and the filing deadline was June 11.

On May 11 some members of the KVET-KTBC
crowd met in the crowded house on Dillman Street to
try to convince Johnson that he should run. The future
President remained adamant, however, and eventually,
according to Stuart Long, an Austin reporter who was
present, Johnson "said no and went to bed. We sat and

talked, eight of us, all convinced that former Governor
Coke Stevenson could be, and should be, defeated. Finally we agreed that John Connally should run. He was
big and handsome, with three brothers who were even
bigger and more handsome, and their father looked like
Old Man Texas himself."

The next morning the group told Johnson of its
decision and asked him to support his protégé. It was
the perfect tactic for what they really wanted. Johnson,
in a towering rage, stormed from the room shouting that
he would hold a news conference later in the day and
that he would have something to say.

What he said, of course, was that he would run for
the U.S. Senate. Connally became his campaign manager.

Connally and Johnson crisscrossed Texas through
the blazing July heat, ripping at Stevenson in every tiny
town, but when primary votes were counted, Stevenson
had 477,077 votes and Johnson 405,617. Other candidates were far to the rear, but a runoff was necessitated,
with Johnson and Stevenson head-to-head. With the runoff scheduled for August 28, only a month remained for
Connally to overcome a 70,000-vote deficit for his man.

The runoff primary may be one of the most fasci-
nating stories in American political and election history.
At midnight on Saturday, August 28, returns showed
Stevenson leading by 1,894 votes. At three-thirty the
next afternoon his lead was down to 315 votes, and by
midnight on Sunday Johnson moved into a lead of 693
votes out of a total of 980,877. On Monday it was Stevenson's turn to lead again, this time by 119 votes. On
Thursday, September 2, the Texas Election Bureau announced that the count was complete and Stevenson had
won by a margin of 362 votes, though the bureau reminded everyone that the count was unofficial and that
the State Democratic Executive Committee would meet
on September 13 for an official canvass. The bureau then

changed its count the next day, with Stevenson the winner now by 114, still unofficial and still awaiting September 13.

John Connally moved into action and promptly left Austin for points unknown. Two days later he surfaced in Alice, Texas, the county seat of Jim Wells County, hard by the Gulf of Mexico. From Alice on September 4, a full week after the election, came a report that Precinct 13 had revised its vote. The original totals were 765 for Johnson and 60 for Stevenson. Suddenly, another 203 votes were found and the new figures showed 967 for Johnson and 61 for Stevenson. Lyndon Johnson now led by 87 votes.

Jim Wells County and its neighbor to the west, Duval County, are almost barren, with mesquite growing thickly on the cracked clay. In 1948 it was a poverty area, but by 1965, when Connally was Governor, irrigation had helped. Most of the help had been to the owners, not the workers, and Connally ignored the workers when they tried to organize and fight for a minimum wage. Old debts have a way of coming to light.

The battle lines were drawn over the election, and Wirtz hired the Washington firm of (Thurman) Arnold, (Abe) Fortas and (Paul) Porter in case the legal phase really got hot. In the meantime they would fight within the Texas Democratic party. Stevenson's men charged into Alice, demanding to see the lists. The first few pages were signed in black ink with many different handwritings. Oddly, the final 203 names were signed in blue ink, all in the same handwriting. Stevenson's men were not allowed to copy names from the list, but they managed to memorize a few before the list was replaced in a bank vault. Three of the names were found in a local cemetery, and another two belonged to persons who denied they had voted at all.

Still, when the Democratic Executive Committee

met on September 13, the additional votes were allowed
and Johnson was the primary winner. The general election was a cinch.

John Connally had done his job.

As a reward, the man from Floresville was hired as
the new Senator's administrative assistant, and the Johnson-Connally team went to Washington in January 1949.

Once again, Connally found the Washington atmosphere as heady as wine, and now he was no longer
a very junior naval officer but administrative assistant to
a United States Senator. Favors were in demand, and
influence was strong.

Within a few months of their arrival in Washington
it became quite apparent that Johnson and Connally were
natural political partners. Like Johnson, Connally was
brash, talkative, homey and a little crafty—and he could
be ruthless if necessary. People noticed that John began
to parrot Lyndon's facial expressions, his slouch and his
dramatic gestures. After a while, they even began to
sound alike.

For the first time LBJ found that he had a loyal employee who was not afraid to criticize him when he
thought he deserved it. This criticism ranged from the
way he handled political issues to the way he shook
hands.

"John Connally taught me how to shake hands,"
Johnson once admitted. And he explained the technique
he had learned from Connally: "When you extend a
handshake to a fellow, you can tell from his pulse and
evaluate him by the way his hand feels. If it's warm and
if it has a firm grip, then you know he is affectionate and
that he is direct. And if he looks you in the eye, you
usually know he is dependable." Connally told him he
was a finger grabber and that he would make a better
impression if he took full grasp of the other person's hand

and pressed it hard. Johnson remembered the physical contact in his next election campaign, and put on a good show "pressing the flesh."

They had much more in common. They were both farm and ranch bred, with similar childhood experiences. Some years after their association began, when each was establishing his own financial empire, they swapped information on their ranches. Johnson had listened to Connally boast about his own ranch's coastal Bermuda grass pastures and had Connally supervise the planting of a similar pasture at the LBJ Ranch.

Johnson respected John Connally's independence and was always careful to praise him in public. Connally was not always as discreet. On one occasion he gave this description of LBJ: "In some ways he is unlettered . . . not the most well-read. . . . At times he can be almost brusque and rude, but he is always determined, always firm, working for perfection." LBJ did not appreciate the "compliment."

Johnson adopted John Connally as his first political protégé and heir apparent. He even sought John's advice in highly personal matters.

During Lyndon's early days in the House of Representatives, he and Lady Bird had kept moving back and forth from a rented place in Washington, D.C., when Congress was in session to another rented place in Austin that they used as headquarters for Texas fence mending. In five years of marriage they had lived in ten apartments. Mrs. Johnson was growing weary of repeatedly packing and unpacking, arranging and rearranging. But Lyndon said that it wouldn't look good back home if word got out among the voters that he owned property in Washington. Lady Bird was not convinced and finally began house hunting. She found three she could live with and narrowed these down to one just off Connecticut Avenue.

Johnson and Connally were discussing political business one day in LBJ's living room when Lady Bird burst into the room and enthusiastically related how she had just found the most' wonderful house to buy. After she had described every detail of the colonial brick structure's eight rooms, Lyndon merely grunted and went on with his political monologue.

Greatly irritated, she blurted, "I want that house! Every woman wants a home of her own, and all I have to look forward to is the next election!" and stormed out of the room. Johnson looked at Connally and, scratching his head in puzzlement, said, "John, what do you think I ought to do about that house?" "I would buy it," Connally wisely counseled. They did. And Lady Bird and John have been close ever since.

There is a restlessness that is inherent in John Connally's nature. He likes to get things started, but then he seems to lose interest. The pattern has been true throughout his political life. He takes a job, he works at it for a while, then it seems to lose its challenge and he is off to other things. As he himself has said, "I've been called an opportunist, and I do move from place to place and from thing to thing and I enjoy it."

True to form, Connally remained on the Johnson staff only six months, and then he returned to Austin and became a member of his friend Alvin Wirtz's law firm. This time, money was on his mind, even more than power, and he and his cronies moved ahead, consolidating holdings in oil, carbon black, real estate and cattle which provided a solid and continuous source of income. The group liked to play as hard as it worked, with horse racing and quail shooting among their major interests. The men owned large and well-kept ranch homes whose gardens and patios made excellent party sites as Mexican waiters dispensed drinks and hors d'oeuvres. Their women were elegantly gowned and beautifully made up.

The Connally family grew rich and powerful in the 1950's, when Big John privately supported Dwight Eisenhower rather than Adlai Stevenson for President though he maintained his Democratic party ties. John and Idanell had four children, Kathleen, John B. III, Sharon and Mark, and the family group was handsome and politically ideal as it appeared at social events and major Texas functions.

Like any father, Connally felt extremely close to his eldest daughter, and there was shock and dismay when Kathleen hurriedly married in 1959, at the age of only sixteen. There was the usual spate of behind-the-hand whispers, and then, suddenly, there was violent death. Kathleen was killed by a shotgun blast in her home. At the inquest, her young husband testified that he had returned home to find her holding the shotgun and threatening suicide. He claimed he had struggled with her for the weapon, and in the scuffle, the gun went off and she was killed. The jury returned a verdict of accidental death, and no one around Connally was permitted to speak further of the episode.

The year 1959 had another major impact on John Connally, and this one was financial. Connally had been attorney for Sid Richardson, one of the old-style Texas oil tycoons whose financial empire was estimated to be worth anywhere from $200 million to $1 billion. Connally and Richardson first began working together in 1952. Big John had left the Austin law firm of Powell, Wirtz and Rauhut after the death of Wirtz and moved to Fort Worth, where the Richardson empire was based. The financier and the attorney worked well together. Under Richardson's aegis, Connally gained management experience in a wide variety of enterprises and also received valuable tips on the purchase of real estate. When Richardson died in 1959, Connally learned that he was to be a co-executor of the estate; the executor's fees would be sufficient to keep him in steaks and fine suits for a long time.

Texans' guesses about the value of Richardson's assets may have some basis in fact, but the executors of the estate were satisfied with the final valuation by the Federal Bureau of Internal Revenue at somewhat more than $105 million. How much Connally received as co-executor's fee—and how he received it—became recurrent issues in his political career. Not until his confirmation as Secretary of the Treasury in 1971 depended on it did he make that information public.

The big money men—Richardson, John Mecom, Robert Anderson—were valuable aides to Connally in his acquisition of his two key goals, power and money. Reportedly, Connally engineered the deal whereby Anderson received a $1-million payment to accept the second spot on the 1956 Republican ticket. The politicians decided to keep Richard Nixon, and Anderson kept the million.

His movements back and forth across party lines continued as, in the same year, Connally and Johnson locked up total control of the Democratic party in Texas after ousting Governor Shivers in 1956. Four years later, Connally made the nominating speech and was the campaign manager as Johnson bid for the Democratic presidential nomination.

June 7, 1960. The Secretary of the Navy designate arrives at Norfolk Naval Base for a day's

(4)

On the New Frontier

It seems to me that we should not approve the nomination of a man who looks forward to a principal income in the future . . . a very, very large income . . . from an estate which is overwhelmingly an oil estate.

SENATOR WILLIAM PROXMIRE

My boy John—as Lyndon fondly called him—had this time backed a loser. His political idol and fellow Texan, Lyndon B. Johnson, had been soundly defeated in his bid for the Democratic nomination for President earlier that year at the party's 1960 National Convention. But not for lack of all sorts of efforts by John Connally.

As manager of Johnson's 1960 drive for the presidential nomination, Big John watched glumly as John Kennedy piled up primary victories. With each triumph, he added to his total of delegate strength for the upcoming National Convention in Los Angeles. LBJ's chances were slipping quickly and neither candidate nor campaign manager liked to lose.

With time running out and Kennedy apparently on the verge of an insurmountable delegate lead, Lyndon Johnson's supporters grew increasingly nervous. An air of anxiety and near panic began settling over the Johnson headquarters. Big John made his move.

On July 4 the LBJ team grabbed the offensive,

holding a desperation news conference at which questions were raised about Kennedy's health. India Edwards, the controversial National Democratic Women's chairman during the Truman days and later an ardent Johnson supporter, charged that Kennedy had Addison's disease. "Doctors have told me he would not be alive if it were not for cortisone," she declared. Under questioning, she said her information on Senator Kennedy's alleged ailment had come from several doctors. She said that to her knowledge none of the doctors she had spoken to had examined or treated Kennedy personally. Connally stood at her side and confirmed her statements.

Immediately, the Kennedy camp counterattacked. It issued a firm denial, complete with a letter dated less than a month earlier from two highly respected physicians who reported that they had been Kennedy's doctors for more than the last five years.

"Your health is excellent," the two physicians said in their report to Kennedy. "Your vitality, endurance and resistance to infection are above average. Your ability to handle an exhausting work load is unquestionably superior."

The physicians said that they could state with conviction that they found the Senator "fully capable of meeting any obligation of the presidency without the need for special medical treatment, unusual rest periods or other limitations."

The Connally-Edwards smear effort did not work. It was obviously doomed to failure. Neither delegates nor voters, regardless of political leanings, were ready to believe that the tirelessly campaigning Kennedy was about to die from adrenal deficiency. They knew that for months Kennedy had been keeping a grueling schedule.

Johnson claimed he had no prior knowledge of the smear. Robert Kennedy claimed Johnson's denial came

only after the smear had apparently failed. The day
after that press conference, Johnson repudiated Mrs.
Edwards' accusation. Asked about her allegation, Johnson said all the Democratic candidates were in good
health.

But on another point Johnson was less kindly to
the Kennedy family. From the time delegates had begun
arriving in Los Angeles for the convention, John Connally and other Johnson aides had been engaged in a
campaign of innuendo against Joseph P. Kennedy, the
Senator's father. The Johnson campaigners charged that
the elder Kennedy, who was United States Ambassador
to Great Britain at the outbreak of World War II, had
been pro-Nazi and had harbored anti-Semitic sentiments.
There were Jewish delegates and financiers to be considered. Observers said that Johnson himself took no part
in the smear campaign, although he was unable to resist
taking at least one shot at Joe Kennedy. At a meeting
with the Washington state caucus, Johnson shrilled, "I
wasn't any Chamberlain-umbrella policy man. I never
thought Hitler was right."

The health smear was touched off in part by the
Kennedy camp itself. Jack Kennedy began the intramural
scrap by declaring that the presidency demands "the
strength and health and vigor of . . . young men."
Connally and other Johnson supporters understandably
might have concluded that Kennedy was trying to remind
voters and delegates that Johnson had suffered a heart
attack in 1955. Big John promptly retorted that he
would be happy to submit Johnson's medical record and
have it compared with that of Senator Kennedy or any
other candidate.

For his part, Lyndon Johnson was fond of pulling
out of his pocket a card-sized, plastic-encased copy of
his last electrocardiogram, which his doctors interpreted
as normal. The impression was that of a street hustler

trying to establish her continued virginity. But it was a needless gesture by a man who drove himself at a brutal pace. Like Kennedy, Johnson's vitality was his best evidence.

But if the Johnson camp lowered itself to the level of smear-campaigning at times, the Kennedy forces showed themselves capable of similar excesses. Such appeared to be the case when they flailed at Hubert H. Humphrey in the West Virginia Democratic primary for his World War II draft deferment. Morality is in the eye of the moralist.

In that primary Hubert Humphrey had been expected to win. But he lost to a lavishly financed Kennedy campaign and retired from the 1960 presidential race. For Senator John Kennedy the victory all but assured his nomination and played a key role in closing the door on any chance that Johnson would carry the Democratic banner in the November election against Nixon.

Four years later Johnson was again on the trail trying to round up delegates, even though not yet a declared candidate, and obviously enjoying the chase. While in Pittsburgh one night, he invited the traveling press to his hotel suite and regaled reporters with a lengthy monologue. Suddenly, without notice, Johnson reached for the telephone and dialed long distance. It was after midnight.

"I'm going to call John Connally," Johnson explained. "If I was ever in trouble I'd want John Connally by my side."

Although Connally was a decade younger and undeniably more handsome than Johnson, the two men resembled each other on the speaker's stand, at least in mannerisms. Connally had carefully copied Johnson's style, although the pupil came through as more sophisticated and polished than his teacher. Speaking at a political rally, Connally's big chin would be thrust out as though daring an opponent to risk a punch. Big John would allow his fists to come crashing down on the podium before him and contort his face into quick smiles as he made a point. He was like a younger Johnson in action.

Even though Connally had angered most of the Kennedy camp by his smear efforts at the 1960 nomination convention, Kennedy could not ignore his contribution in helping the Kennedy-Johnson ticket carry Texas by about 50,000 votes.

When Kennedy chose Connally to be Secretary of the Navy, it was widely assumed that it was Johnson's doing. There are differing views, however. Kennedy had originally wanted to name Franklin D. Roosevelt, Jr., of New York to the Navy post. The son of the late President, he had been a Manhattan Congressman and a strong pre-convention supporter of Kennedy. His father had once been Assistant Secretary of the Navy, and so had his great-uncle Theodore; Kennedy was said to like the idea of continuing the family tradition. But the new Secretary of Defense, Robert McNamara, would not have FDR Jr., according to historian Arthur Schlesinger, Jr.; McNamara's staff, searching for administrative talent, came up with the name of John Connally.

Connally himself said he understood that the late Sam Rayburn, powerful Speaker of the House, had proposed him for the post. Another account has Rayburn suggesting Connally's name to Kennedy at a meeting at which Johnson endorsed the idea. The President-elect admired Rayburn's political savvy and listened to him often.

Whatever the circumstances, a desire by Kennedy to please Johnson in all likelihood was a factor.

Evelyn Lincoln, secretary to President Kennedy, in an Associated Press interview said that Johnson had asked that all job appointments for Texans be cleared by him.

"Every time I turned around," she recalled, "a new Texan was being considered for an appointment. One of the first was John B. Connally, Vice President Johnson's 'right arm' throughout his campaign for the presidency. He was proposed for the office of Secretary of the Navy and he accepted long before President Kennedy was inaugurated. Repeatedly, it seemed to me," she continued, "that Mr. Johnson was more interested in personal patronage power and his own image-making, than in the success of Kennedy's legislative battles."

In any political party, a man with Connally's proved charisma and access to hefty chunks of campaign contributions would be a welcome addition. As an attorney and trustee for oil tycoon Sid Richardson, he had learned how to prevail on the Texas oil rich to part with goodly amounts for political purposes.

One longtime newsman in Austin coined the phrase "airstrip set" to describe the Texas wealthy after he heard one oilman invite Connally to drop by for a Johnson fund-raising party in 1960 at the oilman's ranch. Connally responded, "Sure . . . if you've got an airstrip long enough to handle a DC–3." Not surprisingly, the oilman had such a landing strip.

Comedians often have enjoyed joking about affluent Texans and their sometime compulsion to flaunt their wealth or, at a minimum, their disinclination to hide their material success from the world. Consider one fund-raising rally for Johnson held in 1960 at the ranch of Pat Rutherford, an oil multimillionaire. Nearly a thousand wealthy guests from every section of the state turned up for the rally at the ranch near Austin. They arrived in chauffeured limousines or in private planes that landed on the ranch runway. But at least one partygoer felt compelled to revise his entrance plans. Rutherford recalled the incident: "I have a rich friend in Fort Worth. He flew in a single-engine, came down low over the runway and saw sixty-two twin-engine planes. Hell, he went over to Austin and came back by cab."

Kennedy obviously had his reasons for appointing to an important sub-cabinet post a man who had easy access to Texas votes and Texas money. But perhaps a more pertinent question would be why John Bowden Connally, Jr., was willing to give up or temporarily shunt aside a lucrative law practice and association with Longhorn oil money interests.

No one has ever questioned Connally's ambition and his willingness to do what is needed to forge ahead.

When he agreed to accept the Pentagon post, it was not as if he were deserting Texas for an unfamiliar setting. He was no stranger to Washington, having gone there twice to work under Johnson. More significant, he had become a frequent visitor and temporary resident of Washington as part of his job as a lobbyist for Sid Richardson. John Connally, a man who quickly learned his way around the corridors of money and power, could not help feel the pull of Washington, where power and influence ultimately focused.

As Secretary of the Navy, Connally would be in overall charge of an operation that encompassed the world, extending from the bottoms of the oceans out into space and embracing such seemingly disparate activities as oil reserves in California and frozen blood banks in Bethesda, Maryland.

The pay, $22,000 a year, had to be one of the least attractive features of the Pentagon post he was about to assume. One good legal fee earned by the right phone call could amount to that much. But the scope of the job and the influence inherent in it were readily apparent. And there were some fringe benefits that must have appealed to a man who had been born into a poor family and raised frugally on a Texas farm. As Secretary of the Navy he would have the trappings and symbols of power. Ronnie Dugger, a longtime Connally watchdog-critic and editor of the crusading *Texas Observer*, author of a perceptive article about Connally,* quoted an unidentified Texas insider who had known him for a quarter of a century.

"This much about John Connally: He never likes to drive his own car," the insider told Dugger. "You can't make enough money to have an air-conditioned plane and a limousine waiting every minute, twice or ten times the secretarial help you need, speech writers and valets; all that goes with high public office. He *likes* that. He got out of the peanut patch and fell in love with easy livin' as quick as any man I ever knew. . . . He was as ambitious a man as I ever knew, to rise above his early family.

"I remember when he didn't smoke, he carried a cigarette lighter in his pocket, but he never jerked it out to light anybody's cigarette—except a very rich man! His number-one ambition in life was to be rich. He was just overly solicitous to rich people who didn't know anything about anything, but had a lot of money—he would court 'em, and he knew how to take political money off of them. I have always thought he was the all-time champion in getting 'em to just *give* big bundles of it to him."

The question was put simply and without hostility. The Senator asking it knew pretty much what the answer would be. So did John Connally as he was asked whether he felt he could serve as Secretary of the Navy without any possibility of conflict of interest.

* "John Connally: Nixon's New Quarterback," *The Atlantic,* July 1971, pp. 82–90.

Connally leaned forward and said vigorously, "Without any question of a doubt."

The issue had come up because of Big John's aforementioned association with the oil industry and the late Sid Richardson, the legendary entrepreneur of the Texas oilfields and real estate mart; the connection had helped him climb his way to real wealth. But it had also made him suspect as a tool of the moneyed oil interests, at least in the minds of some, including segments of the liberal press.

Richardson and his nephew partner, Perry Bass, had amassed a fortune in oil and gas, radio and television broadcasting interests, drugstores, ranching, carbon black and a smorgasbord of other corporate ventures. One Texas oilman said that Richardson hired Connally because he had been Johnson's "right-hand man in the Senate and Sid was vitally interested in that [oil] depletion allowance."

Connally, in an interview with reporter Louis Hoffenbert, recounted how he and Richardson got together: "I went to Fort Worth and visited Mr. Richardson in his rooms at the Fort Worth Club. We talked most of the night. He invited me to join his organization and he said: 'I can hire good lawyers and good engineers and good geologists, but it is hard to hire good common sense.' At the end of our talk he told me: 'I'll pay you enough so Nellie [Connally's wife Idanell] and the kids won't go hungry, and I'll put you in the way to make some money.' "

Connally's duties as attorney for the Richardson interests often took him to Washington to find out about proposals for legislation relating to the oil and gas industry. He was probably more than a spectator in 1955 when Lyndon Johnson, then Senate majority leader, introduced a bill that would get the gas industry out from under federal price controls.

Shortly before a Senate vote on the bill in 1956, however, a minor scandal erupted. Senator Francis Case, South Dakota Republican, told the press that a lobbyist had offered him $2,500 as a campaign contribution if he would support the bill. The Senate did pass the bill, but Case's story reached the White House, and at least partly because of what were described as "arrogant" lobbying activities, President Dwight Eisenhower vetoed the bill.

Dugger in his *Atlantic* article gave this account of Connally's purported activities at the time:

"A Johnson insider of that period says that Johnson 'kept after [Connally] to register as a lobbyist, but he said, "I'm up here in my own interest and I don't have to register." ' Through his connection with Richardson, Connally had obtained some small interest in natural gas."

The Dugger account continued: "According to a wealthy oil operative who was also lobbying in Washington for this gas bill, Connally was 'up there with a big suite at the Mayflower Hotel' from the first of January until the bill was passed and vetoed. 'There wasn't anybody more active,' this source says. He also remembers the flap over Connally's refusal to register as a lobbyist. 'I recall Price Daniel [then the junior U.S. senator from Texas] complaining very bitterly because he didn't register. There was even some talk that . . . he was going to be denounced on the floor if he didn't. I know Johnson thought he should register. His [Connally's] position was, Mr. Richardson was his employer, he was there by right of petition to the government—it was just part of his regular duties.' "

At Connally's invitation, according to Dugger, a group of fifteen or twenty of the industry people partied in Johnson's office. The article continues: "One of the

guests recalls that Connally appeared to be the host until
the Majority Leader came in. But according to the Johnson insider, the moment the scandal over the alleged
effort to bribe Senator Case broke, 'Connally got out of
the Mayflower and was out of town overnight.' "

The late Drew Pearson asserted that Connally had
worked together with a lobbyist who was caught up in
the scandal and that "Connally was one of the most
brazen lobbyists in Washington for the natural gas bill."

Richardson was a man who could be friendly with
the powers-that-be on both sides of the political fence.
He is generally credited with having induced President
Eisenhower to name Robert Anderson, a Texan, as
Secretary of the Navy in 1953. Anderson became Deputy
Secretary of Defense a year later and in 1955 returned
to private life.

Thereupon he reportedly made at least several hundred thousands of dollars in a complicated oil transaction
said to involve Richardson before rejoining government
service in 1957 as Secretary of the Treasury. In this post,
Anderson helped impose tighter federal restrictions on
oil imports, which tended to keep domestic oil prices
high.

And thus did oil tycoon Richardson demonstrate
anew his ability to prosper regardless of which party
occupied the White House.

On the same day that Drew Pearson in his column
was castigating John Connally for his alleged role in the
passage of the natural gas bill, the Senate Armed Services
Committee was holding its hearing on the Connally appointment as Secretary of the Navy.

It was January 18, 1961.

Pearson tore into Connally, describing him as the
lawyer and lobbyist for a group of oil-gas companies
which raised $1.5 million to lobby the natural gas bill
through Congress. "Connally was the mainspring of that

lobby . . . [and] masterminded the battle on Capitol Hill," the gutsy columnist wrote.

Later that same day Senator Richard B. Russell, the chairman of the Armed Services Committee, would take a far different tack. Rather than criticizing Connally for any of his past connections, the Georgia Democrat praised the Texan for his knowledge of the oil business.

Russell, after the questioning of Connally, read into the record the titles of laws dealing with conflict of interest. And then turning to Connally, he declared: "We are fortunate to have a man who knows something about the oil business. It will be a distinct advantage to the United States." Connally was not about to argue with this evaluation. Instead he offered the opinion that his "experience will stand me in good stead."

The committee hearing on Connally's qualifications and background was neither superficial nor particularly comprehensive. Some committee members, mindful of frequent references in newspaper reports to Connally's oil connections, attempted to question him carefully. The issue understandably was a sensitive one. Ever since the Teapot Dome Scandal in 1921 over Navy oil reserves in Wyoming and California, Congress has been hypersensitive to matters affecting the Navy's oil interests.

In his appearance before the committee, Connally described in detail his role—so he described it—as a "salaried employee" in administering the extensive oil properties and other Richardson holdings. Connally told the committee he was now one of three co-executors of the Richardson estate. But, he said, he would accept no fees from it during his government services.

Additionally, he said, the estate was not involved in business with the Government. Connally also emphasized that the Richardson oilfield holdings were *not* geographically near Navy oil reserves.

Someone then asked again whether he felt he could

take over as Navy Secretary without being involved in a conflict of interest. "Without a question of a doubt," he repeated firmly. Subsequently his nomination was unanimously approved by Russell's committee.

The formal nomination of Secretary of the Navy John Connally ran into an immediate obstacle in the Senate, however. Oregon Democrat Wayne Morse served notice that he would oppose it. (Ironically, Connally would follow Morse's style in party switching.) Senator William Proxmire, Democrat from Wisconsin, said there "appears to be a serious conflict of interests here." Even a Republican Senator, John Sherman Cooper of Kentucky, also made it clear that there were questions he wanted answered.

They attributed their concern to Connally's known close ties with the oil industry barons. The Navy was one of the biggest oil purchasers in the world and as Secretary Big John could handpick many of its suppliers.

During his confirmation hearing, Connally was identified as an officer or director of some twenty-seven major corporations. He told the cynical senators that he had been involved, as a salaried employee for baron Richardson, in oil and gas, radio and television, cattle ranching, drugstores, mining, housing, carbon black, gasoline refining, oilfield service, hydrocarbon storage and a hotel. He also acknowledged holding shares in a California management company and an Austin bank and told of receiving about $315 a month in royalties from a Texas oil well.

In opposing John Connally's confirmation, Senator Proxmire said the Texan's oil ties constituted a blatant conflict of interest. The Connally critic warned that Big John as Navy Secretary "will have great discretion over the [oil] reserve, including unchecked power to reduce their production and to lessen competition with the private oil industry." Continuing on the attack, Proxmire added that Connally also "would be in a crucial position to influence the Navy's research and development program for atomic fuel, the big competitor of oil."

But when the Senate debate was over about three hours later, the Wisconsin Democrat was the only Senator to vote against confirmation. In his futile attempt to block the appointment, Proxmire cited the fact that Connally would be continuing as an executor of the Richardson estate. "It seems to me that we should not approve the nomination of a man who looks forward to a principal income in the future . . . a very, very large income . . . from an estate which is overwhelmingly an oil estate. . . . This constitutes a conflict of interest if there can be such a thing," Proxmire declared.

Senator Kenneth Keating of New York, a liberal Republican, on this point noted that Connally had given assurances that he would not receive any income as Richardson's executor during his tenure as Secretary of the Navy. Keating added, however, that he was "a little puzzled as to why the estate would run on so long. . . . Normally the estates do not run so long."

Such powerful senators as the late Everett Dirksen, Illinois Republican, and Minnesota's Hubert H. Humphrey expressed confidence in Connally's independence and qualifications. Humphrey, who was serving as Democratic majority whip, played an important role in convincing liberal senators to drop their opposition to having Connally confirmed to the Navy post. The action reportedly angered many Democrats outside the Senate, particularly Humphrey's supporters in the Americans for Democratic Action. In 1968 Connally remembered and although he was slow in getting involved, he did help carry Texas for presidential candidate Humphrey.

In the Senate debate on the confirmation, Georgia's Richard Russell said that other nominees had not been required to vow that they would not return to lucrative law practice with major firms, so why should the Senate require that Connally not go back to the Richardson estate?

Proxmire had a ready answer. Connally, he fired back, had not severed his connections with the Richardson estate and that was the difference. The Wisconsin Democrat also said Connally was oil-identified because of his leadership in the General Gas Committee, which was formed by the oil industry during the 1956 effort to push the natural gas bill through Congress.

Alluding to the alleged bribe offer to Senator Case and to the other lobbying tactics that had prompted President Eisenhower to veto the bill, Proxmire was careful to say that he wanted it very clear "that there is no evidence that would involve the nominee in these practices. But the fact is that a very aggressive, militant, special-interest group did select the nominee as one of the members of the twenty-four-man steering committee," Proxmire said. The industry committee had 780 members.

Fellow Democratic Senator Mike Monroney of Montana then questioned whether Proxmire meant "that one is guilty by association? The Senator [Proxmire] and I abhor that principle." Senators from both parties testified to Connally's competence and character and Proxmire carefully avoided attacking the Texan's integrity. Kennedy's Administration was still in its honeymoon era and critics were gentle.

Instead, Proxmire focused on Connally's economic ties. He said the nominee had been an active and efficient administrator, but his experience was strictly in the oil industry. This evaluation was disputed by Senator Russell, who retorted that Connally, before he became associated with Richardson, had operated a radio station, practiced law and assisted Johnson in Congress.

On January 25, 1961, John Connally finally took the oath of office as Secretary of the Navy. His brush with Senate liberals like Proxmire had not amounted to much in the end, but the Sid Richardson estate and his connections with it were to haunt him a decade later when he sought confirmation for another high government position.

As he prepared to lift his right hand to be sworn in as Secretary of the Navy, Connally looked over and saw his two close friends and political mentors, Lyndon Johnson and Sam Rayburn, sharing his honor. And if his memory intruded, Connally could have reflected back to his boyhood when he helped his father and a Mexican man butcher livestock for other ranchers.

John's job had been to carry buckets of water to the two men so they could wash away the blood as they worked. Thinking back to those early days, Connally once reflected, "Mostly, our Christmas presents were things we needed, along with some fruit and candy." When they got a football or a used bike that had been repainted to look new, the Connally children shared it. And now he was being sworn in as a high-ranking member of the new President's Administration. He was entering the New Frontier, at the behest of President Kennedy.

As Navy Secretary and a politician, Connally was to win President Kennedy's respect. But on this day John Bowden Connally, Jr., was venturing into a strange landscape. It was not that Washington was new to him. What was new was that he was becoming a part of the New Frontier, with its Kennedy-style version of liberal idealism and social programs that would later come to fruition under President Johnson. Many of these programs would be opposed by the future Governor of Texas, John B. Connally, Jr.

Temperamentally, Connally was not at home at the New Frontier. On balance, he would seem to be a conservative by instinct but a moderate when circumstances demanded; and although it was true that his role as Navy

Secretary did not push him to the forefront of the Kennedy Administration and New Frontier, he still doubtless felt somewhat out of place. Perhaps if he had been President and Kennedy the Secretary of the Navy . . . In any case, Connally eagerly began tackling his new role.

As successor to outgoing Navy Secretary William B. Franke, John Connally was about to take over a fighting force divided into four fleets. The Sixth Fleet was in the Mediterranean, the First in the Atlantic, the Fourth on the West Coast and the Seventh in the Far East. Each reported to the Chief of Naval Operations and through him to the Secretary of the Navy.

The Navy was one of the world's biggest employers, with 628,400 persons in uniform and 650,000 civilian employees. They were stationed around the world on ships and at bases and as naval attachés at embassies— they were involved in the operation of 222 major bases in the United States and 53 bases overseas.

In effect, the Navy also was operating its own air force, with some 6,800 aircraft of all types. He would be taking over the helm of a Navy made up of 817 ships. A number of admirals were lined up and anxious to convince him that many of the ships were too small to meet Navy commitments and also were becoming rapidly obsolescent. Of the total number of ships, 383 were warships and the rest were support and supply craft.

For a man of Connally's sense of adventure, the post clearly offered a challenge. He confided in friends that the Navy had always been the "glamorous" branch of the military.

One of the new Secretary's first tasks would be to pass judgment on and defend or criticize a budget calling for the expenditure of $14 billion. In a period of a few weeks after assuming the post, he would be expected to master a budget that had been two years in preparation and that represented the accumulation of financial obligations he had assumed or been assigned over decades.

Before immersing himself in a sea of budget figures, however, Connally started on a tour of naval facilities, including installations in the Norfolk, Virginia, area. On that trip he arrived by plane from Washington, accompanied by Admiral Arleigh A. Burke, then Chief of Naval Operations and one of the three most influential military men in the country.

The visits were the first of many to naval facilities, as Connally assumed the inevitable burden of tradition. Like others before him and others still to come, Connally filled the ceremonial role demanded by all bureaucracies, including the military. There were courtesy calls, inspections of the nation's latest advances in naval arsenals. There were ships to be launched and countries to visit. In August that year he talked with West German armed forces chiefs when he paid a courtesy call at the Defense Ministry in Bonn. Next Big John flew to Madrid and Rome on his first European trip since his appointment by Kennedy. His stay was officially described as an orientation visit. Overall, the trip lasted more than two weeks and also took him to London and to the Mediterranean, where he visited the Sixth Fleet. The public information officers loved him—he really looked the part.

During Connally's year as Navy Secretary, the Sixth Fleet participated in a new kind of gunboat diplomacy that won the United States thousands of friends in the countries that fringe the Mediterranean Sea. The new diplomacy had begun the same way as the old: a warship sailing into a foreign harbor. But this time the only shots came from toy cap pistols handed to children by sailors aboard the aircraft carrier U.S.S. *Forrestal* while it was assigned to the Sixth Fleet. The 4,200-man crew of the *Forrestal* had "adopted" the Maria Immacula Orphanage in Naples. Three times its crew had laden the orphanage and children with gifts. Extra gifts were given to a hospital in Cannes for children with bone diseases, to school children in Leghorn, to poor Greek children in Rhodes and to a hospital for spastic children in Palermo. There were also presents for Turkish children in Cyprus and to a camp in Beirut for Arab refugees left homeless by deportation from Palestine. Nor was the *Forrestal*'s the only crew to help out needy children in countries visited by their ship. The men of the destroyer *Laffey* passed the hat among themselves and contributed $1,000 for the welfare of children housed in an institution near Gaeta harbor, Italy. The dilapidated building was home to thirty-one boys and one girl, ages two to eight years old. The children's parents were convicts and were being held in a state prison. Later, while the destroyer exercised at sea, four of its crew members were at the orphanage planning the renovation of the building. When the *Laffey* returned to Gaeta, twenty-five crew members worked fifteen hours a day for four days to make the building a decent place for children to live.

Connally was to discover that the ceremonial trappings of a Navy Secretary were not without their own hazards. One fall day he arrived back in Austin for an appearance at the University of Texas. When his plane landed at the Municipal Airport, the transplanted Texan was welcomed by the university's naval ROTC Honor Guard. Ceremony, of course, required that he review the Honor Guard. He did so and in the process suffered a cut near his left eye from a rifle in the hands of one of the more efficient guardsmen. The cut required several stitches. The accident occurred as Connally asked the midshipman his name. As Connally leaned forward, the alert young man thought Connally wanted to inspect his rifle, so he brought the rifle sharply up into the traditional port arms position. Connally and the rifle barrel met unexpectedly.

Within two months after taking over the top Navy post, Connally found the National Association for the Advancement of Colored People seething over special restrictions allegedly imposed on black sailors during a goodwill visit to South Africa by a United States Navy task force. Roy Wilkins, NAACP executive secretary, fired off a telegram to Connally lodging a "most vigorous protest" against the purported restrictions. The telegram charged that Navy policy during the visit "heaps humiliation upon Negro officers and enlisted men." Wilkins was referring to reports from Capetown, South Africa, that American sailors visiting there had been ordered to abide by that nation's apartheid racial policies, which compelled strict separation of whites and blacks. Promptly the Navy responded to the charges of bias. It declared that when a United States warship is in a foreign port, in South Africa or any place else, "all officers and men are granted liberty with no discrimination whatsoever in regard to race, color or creed." "Navy policy," the statement continued, "concerning the visits to ports of the Union of South Africa is the same as for visits to ports of all other countries with whom we have diplomatic relations."

I interviewed Roy Wilkins recently and asked him for his view of John Connally today. The seventy-two-year-old moderate black spokesman was blunt and brief. "I don't like him and I don't trust him"—this despite the fact that Wilkins was a great admirer of Lyndon B. Johnson.

In his first and only year as Navy Secretary, Big John fought hard for those Navy programs he considered worthy and quickly scrubbed those he considered impractical—as when he concluded that after the U.S.S. *Enterprise* there should be no more nuclear aircraft carriers. On September 9 Connally presided over commissioning ceremonies as the *Long Beach,* the nation's first nuclear-powered surface warship, joined the United States fleet. The ship, built at a cost in excess of $320 million, made its debut at the South Annex of the Boston Naval Shipyard. "Her range is practically unlimited and

she will travel the sea-lanes at an unprecedented pace,"
Connally said of the 721-foot guided-missile cruiser,
equipped with nuclear armament. Connally referred only
discreetly to the ship's armament and seagoing capabilities, details of which were largely secret.

Late in November Connally praised the nuclear-
powered carrier *Enterprise* as she joined the fleet in
ceremonies at Newport News, Virginia. He predicted
that the 85,350-ton ship would rule as "queen of the
sea" for a "long, long time." But Connally also took the
occasion to emphasize that "his" Navy had no immediate
plans to build any more nuclear-powered carriers because they had proved "considerably more expensive"
than conventionally powered ships. At the same time,
he extolled the capabilities of the nation's nuclear-powered submarines equipped with Polaris missiles.

Connally, as might be expected of a second echelon
official, attracted the occasional attention of the news-
print and broadcast media, but not with the same fre-
quency he was later to achieve in his political odyssey.
Still he was regarded by many Pentagon watchers as
perhaps the most effective service secretary in the Defense Department.

For lovers of blimps, the Navy's lighter-than-air
fleet, Connally would be remembered as the man in office
when the great blimp eclipse occurred. Less than three
months after he assumed the Secretary's post, it was dis-
closed that the Navy planned to deflate its blimps, except
for two that would be kept for research purposes. Budget
cutbacks were blamed for the decision to place the blimp
fleet in mothballs.

Connally fought hard to protect the Navy's role in
the nation's space program. In late March he testified
before a House committee that he had been assured by
Secretary of Defense Robert S. McNamara that the Navy
would not lose the space programs it was interested in.
He told the committee of his opposition to a contro-

versial Pentagon directive assigning most space research
to the Air Force. When the question of whether he had
"resisted" the directive arose in the committee questioning, Connally said he would not use that word. Then in
a slip of the tongue, he continued, "We resisted it. . . ."
This brought laughter. "Did I agree with the original
draft?" the Navy Secretary asked rhetorically. "The answer is no. Do I now agree with it? The answer is yes."

He told the committee that a great deal depended
on how the directive was administered, adding that his
concern was that it might cause the Navy to "lose its
scientists to other pursuits."

From time to time Connally showed he could be a
tough taskmaster. At one point he publicly denounced
Navy officers who expressed opinions on Navy policy
matters and then hid behind anonymity. "If you are not
willing to be quoted by name, you should not be speaking," he declared in a policy speech before a gathering
of a thousand naval officers. In the same address Connally took public issue with the finding of the Navy staff
that nuclear power would *not* reduce the number of
ships needed by the Navy. In budget hearings that year
he was regarded as an effective spokesman for Navy
interests. He could vary his pitch, from low key to hard
sell, depending on what approach seemed best and on
how important he believed a project to be. Nor was he
unmindful of which power corridors were open to him.
Connally repeatedly has shown himself a man not afraid
to speak his own mind. He also has shown that he can
remain silent and refrain from rocking the boat when
political prudence dictates.

In April 1961, well before Connally became Navy
Secretary, the Navy had made what seemed to be a
routine contract award to a firm by the name of Transport Co. of Texas. It involved civilian operation of a
hotel, terminal, refueling and maintenance services and

other "housekeeping" functions on Kwajalein atoll in the Marshall Islands, which was scheduled to become an important adjunct of the Navy-operated Pacific Missile Range. The Texas firm, apparently benefiting from political influence and lax contracting procedures, got the contract on a cost-plus, fixed-fee basis. The estimate of the cost was $5 million over a fifteen-month period, with the Texas firm expected to earn a $340,000 fee. Ultimately, according to Herbert Solow in an article published in *Fortune,* the original estimate was followed by a $13 million estimate when the contract was extended another fifteen months. The $18.5 million total, according to Solow, included a projected $1 million in fees for Transport Co. of Texas. Edgar M. Linkenhoger, a former produce trucker who had become president and chief stockholder in the firm, was known to be friendly with Lyndon Johnson. Oilman Sid Richardson had been the third largest stockholder in the Texas firm when it was incorporated in 1951, according to Solow. He said that there was no evidence to indicate that Johnson was anything other than an innocent bystander in the Kwajalein housekeeping contract awards. There was no evidence to suggest that Johnson or Connally had sought to influence the contract award or that they had any real prior knowledge. Connally, of course, was not yet in office. But subsequently he apparently did not go out of his way to preclude extending the contract or to replace it with a contract issued on the basis of more competitive bidding procedures.

Connally's tour of duty as Navy head kept him out of trouble and earned him some good reviews. *Time* magazine, looking back on his brief tenure, termed his record as Navy Secretary a "first-rate appointment." It cited his willingness to fight hard for programs he believed in, while discarding those he considered impractical. But others, while also impressed with Big John's style, were less enthusiastic. They noted that the brevity of his service precluded any sustained or comprehensive achievements. In truth, Connally probably had only begun to grasp the budgetary insights and tactical intricacies and needs of a modern Navy. Most Pentagon watchers credit him with being a quick learner, a man capable of swiftly grasping a complicated situation. But he was, in effect, a temporary caretaker. Admittedly competent, but only temporary. *The New York Times,* in an editorial published a week before his departure from the Pentagon post, reflected its ambivalence:

"Mr. Connally's intelligence, warm personality, leadership, common sense and political shrewdness have established him as the most effective service Secretary in the Defense Department. But he leaves, as so many have done before him, just when he was getting to know the Navy. His successor, Fred H. Korth, also a native of Fort Worth, takes over in January, just on the eve of another Congressional session. With all due deference to Mr. Korth, he cannot be expected to comment with anything like expertise on the budget or any other plans of the Navy he will head. It was no secret in the Pentagon that Mr. Connally was not in sympathy with some of the plans and methodology of the Department of Defense. This dissent had nothing to do with his departure, but it was clear to all who knew him that Mr. Connally would have difficulty reconciling his private convictions with some of the projects and developments in the Department. More important motivations for change were the Texas political pressures exerted on Mr. Connally, his own ambition for a political career and his loyalty to President Kennedy and Vice President Johnson, who would undoubtedly like to return Texas, 'threatened' with a two-party system, to an uncomplicated allegiance to the Democrats. One can understand these motivations. But the Berlin crisis is still unresolved and there are major organizational and other problems pending. Mr.

Connally's talents are needed now more than ever, and
the office of the Secretary of the Navy should not be a
political stepping stone. What is good for Texas is not
always synonymous with what is good for the nation."

Exactly two weeks before Christmas 1961 John
Connally made official what had long been known—he
was resigning as Secretary of the Navy to return to Texas
and seek election as Governor the next year. His decision
came as no surprise to reporters who had sparred with
him as early as July over the upcoming Texas gubernatorial race. That summer, with only six months under
his belt as Navy Secretary, Connally mused over the
prospects. "I will say this: I believe that the next Governor of Texas will be a fresh face in statewide politics,
a new name on a statewide ballot." He did not say so at
the time, but as it turned out the description fitted his
purposes nicely.

In late October, news reports that Connally was
thinking of abandoning the Pentagon for a shot at the
Texas chief executive's office began to appear in increasing numbers. It was just a matter of time before it would
be made official. On December 11 Big John announced
he was leaving his Washington post, effective December
20. At the same time, President Kennedy appointed
another Texan, fifty-two-year-old Fred Korth, to succeed
him. Korth was a longtime Johnson follower and during
World War II served as a lieutenant colonel in the Air
Transport Command. In the Truman Administration
Korth had served as the Army's deputy counselor and
later as Assistant Secretary of the Army. His connection
with Truman was seen by Texas sources as a factor in
Korth's appointment. President Kennedy previously had
made several appointments of Texas Democrats who
supported Republican Dwight D. Eisenhower for the
Presidency in 1952. Korth had not crossed party lines,
and his appointment appeared to be in part an effort to

offset some of the bitterness caused by Kennedy's having named Eisenhower Democrats to some federal posts.

Connally's letter of resignation was made public by the White House. In it Connally said he believed he could make his greatest contribution to the nation, as well as to the future of his home state, "by offering whatever energies, experience and abilities I have to the people of Texas."

Thus, at age forty-four, did Connally prepare to become a candidate for major elective office, rather than limit himself to helping others finance their races. His entry pleased some and incensed others. Among those angered by his move was Will Wilson, Democratic attorney general in Texas. Wilson professed to see the political handiwork of Lyndon Johnson behind the Connally maneuver. "John Connally's candidacy," Wilson declared, "is a move by Lyndon Johnson to oust Price Daniel [incumbent Democratic Governor], oust me, oust Senator Ralph Yarborough and gain complete control of the state government."

What prompted Connally to jump into the race for Governor? The one obvious answer is that he wanted to. True, he may have been pressured, but if so he did not protest too loudly. State Attorney General Wilson, himself a candidate for the nomination for Governor, doubtless was close to the mark when he pointed a suspecting finger at Johnson as the force responsible for Connally's entry into the race. Johnson, according to some accounts, tried to portray himself as having sought to dissuade his friend, ultimately acquiescing in Connally's decision. Not so, argue many longtime observers of Texas politics. In their view, Johnson was the ramrod, not the casual bystander. Perhaps the entry of Connally into the Governor's race was inevitable from the time in 1960 when Republican John Tower, then a relatively unknown political science professor, ran against Johnson for the

Senate. He polled a surprising 925,600 votes to 1,306,-
600 for Johnson. And when Johnson left the Senate to
become Vice President, Tower won a special election in
1961 for the seat Johnson had vacated. Reporter Robert
Sherrill in the Chicago *Tribune* said that Tower's triumph, together with a growing revolt by the state's liberal
faction, placed Johnson in danger of losing control of
his power base in Texas. The Democratic conservatives
had to come up with a strong gubernatorial candidate in
1962. "It was at this point, with conservatives seeming
to waver in their support of the time-honored one-party
arrangement, that Connally was hustled to the front of
the Texas political stage," Sherrill recalled. "He made no
secret of his objective. Reporters who traveled with him
in the 1962 campaign say he was furious with then Governor Price Daniel for 'letting the party get away from
him.' Connally had been drafted from the job of Secretary
of the Navy to come back to Texas and reunite the party
for the conservative Democrats, re-recruiting the defectors to the Republican party," Sherrill contended. "He
did that job with great, if sometimes heavyhanded skill."

Connally began the race as an underdog, but was
able to cash in on his political ties with Johnson and
Kennedy and his contacts with most of the richest and
influential men in the state. He ran the longest and most
expensive campaign ever mounted in Texas, winning the
Democratic nomination by a margin of about 26,000
votes. More than a million ballots had been cast. Next
came the general election and victory over his Republican opponent.

And so John Bowden Connally, Jr.—son of a
tenant farmer, lawyer, right arm to Lyndon Johnson,
lobbyist for the oil rich and former Navy Secretary—
took over as Governor of Texas. What next, Horatio?

Still wearing a cast and sling on the arm injured by President Kennedy's assassin, Governor Connally stands under the Lone Star State flag. Texas Pavilion, New York World's Fair, Feb. 26, 1964. *Credit: Wide World Photos.*

[5]

The Manicured Man in the Statehouse

John Connally's years as Governor of Texas could most flatteringly be described as adequate and unsurprising. As expected, Big John was, throughout, the professional politician balancing the demands of the few who financed his career against the needs of the multitude.

Texas made some economic progress during the Connally administrations. His staff claims it was because of Connally's decisive leadership and original legislation; his enemies claim it was despite the Connally program. Both factions agree that union leadership, Democratic liberals and minorities never reached a position of any real influence in the Texas Statehouse while Connally ruled.

While his legislative record might be considered routine, Connally's political achievements were exceptional. He almost singlehandedly preserved the one-party system in Texas despite the aggressive raids on the Democratic machine by a sophisticated and well-financed Republican organization.

Economically and politically, Connally must be classified as a true conservative, but his personal morality did not preclude advocating the sale of liquor even in those ultraprovincial Texas communities where the electorate had voted to stay dry. During his last few months as Governor, Big John added parimutuel betting and racetracks to his program for posterity.

No single legislative issue escaped "Connallization." He wound up and delivered an energetic speech on just about anything when given the chance. More recently, he has become an extremely effective orator, but unfortunately, while Governor, he was prone to glittering generalities and the flamboyant recitation of such mundane subtleties as, "Never before in the history of this nation, and of this entire world, has there been a greater need for people with trained minds and practical intelligence and deep awareness of human needs." He sounded as if he were reciting from a high school civics text.

Connally confided in friends and staff members that he was frustrated by the weak Texas Legislature and a congressional delegation that did not always understand the "Texas way," which, translated, meant that other elected officials had the gall to express their own views.

Connally pointed out in several speeches how difficult it was "to move a monolithic structure of government" when the Legislature met only once every two years. "Nobody works for the Governor," Connally complained. "They work for their boards. Administrators won't volunteer anything—I never knew anything except by hearsay. They volunteer nothing."

"We've tried to move in a lot of directions, and I think we have," the Governor bragged. In 1968 he claimed that 1,494 new industrial plants had moved into Texas and there had been 1,976 new plant expansions, creating 150,000 new jobs. But the unions disputed Big

John's statistics as distorted and incomplete. Labor leaders still list Texas as one of their disaster areas.

As Governor, Connally was a big promoter of Texas tourism. In his final year in office, the state attracted more than 20 million tourists who spent over $1 billion, and this pleased the voters because it did mean new jobs and better wages for many already working. Yet one former Connally assistant confirmed that Connally most enjoyed tourists in Texas because visitors were beginning to recognize Big John as a national figure. The governor of any state, whether it be Reagan of California or Rockefeller of New York, can face monumental political crises at home but still be a fascinating celebrity to those who visit from other states.

John Connally enjoys being a star. He dresses the role and times his entrances with the precise taste of a Roman centurion. As Governor, he was surrounded by symbols of authority. More often than not, two tough élite Texas Rangers were at his side, ready to keep away autograph seekers and other pests, even when they weren't there. All the Rangers assigned to him were required to be three inches shorter than the Governor. This provided the "John Wayne look," according to one of his former capitol assistants. Big John likes to be bigger than life, and comparison with shorter men never hurts.

Connally orchestrates his appearance by combining immaculate grooming with a leading man's wardrobe. When he resigned as Secretary of the Navy to stump Texas for the Statehouse, he arrived in Houston wearing a homburg, a pin-stripe suit and a black silk vest. The local committee chairman told the Houston *Post,* "We can't elect a man in a homburg hat Governor of Texas." But they did—for three terms—because Connally stashed his homburg. His wardrobe also included a wide variety of silk cowboy shirts, more than a dozen pairs of handmade boots and even a collection of sheriffs' badges from most of the counties in the Lone Star State. He may be the only Grand Marshal of a Texas rodeo ever to wear an authentic cowboy suit with a Christian Dior label.

I thought about the Connally style recently when we passed each other in a San Francisco television station. It was one of those morning talk shows in which the host shuffles politicians, authors and entertainers in and out of a taping room with amazing dexterity. I was leaving after having discussed my Kissinger biography and Big John was next at bat. His entourage consisted of eight members of the local Democrats for Nixon organization. The chauffeur who waited outside could obviously double as a bodyguard. Connally strutted in and never stopped dictating to a male secretary, who had to run to keep up.

Big John was even more the star while Governor. He would begin each day just a little better groomed than the best of his staff. He was so good at looking the part that often the lack of impact of his statements was overlooked.

The survival instinct, strong in every man, probably is strongest among politicians. Even as the elected official drafts his acceptance speech, his thoughts are concerned with the problem of his reelection. As 1967 opened, John Connally looked to his third inauguration as Governor of Texas with the question of a fourth two-year term high in his thinking. Secondary matters were impending legislative battles over salary increases for state employees, difficulties with the Federal Government and a publicity plum like the HemisFair, scheduled for San Antonio in 1968.

Other problems, like pressures from neglected minority groups and the overriding pall of the Vietnam war, would have to wait their turn.

There was considerable irony in the Governor's considering a fourth term. His first gubernatorial campaign, against Governor Price Daniel in 1962, had included loud criticism of the incumbent, who was seeking his own fourth term. Connally had been quoted often as saying that two terms were enough for anyone.

First things first, however, and 1967 had to be completed before 1968 even could begin. The Governor had an inauguration speech to deliver, a speech which pointed out that mediocrity and conformity threatened to engulf the "uncommon man," though there was little indication of what type of "uncommon man" the Governor wanted around.

Obviously not a man like State Senator Charles Herring, who introduced a bill for an emergency pay raise for state employees on January 23, six days after the Governor spoke. Herring's bill would allocate $5.2 million from unpledged general fund surpluses to help until a general wage increase bill could be passed later in the session. Texas employees, like those in many other states, were woefully underpaid. Some 30 percent reportedly left state jobs every year to take more lucrative employment with private industry or the Federal Government. The legislators were also looking forward to helping themselves at paycheck time. After all, they were state employees, too.

One state representative spoke for the bill as "a humanitarian issue," adding, "I talked with one man who has three children and makes only $212 a month. They pay more than that in China."

The bill passed the Senate easily, but humanitarian or not, it was tabled by the House on February 6. At the same time, the House quickly approved a $5.5 million emergency appropriation to complete the state's work on HemisFair '68.

Why was one bill so promptly passed, the other just

as promptly sidetracked? Governor Connally had initiated the bill for the fair appropriation. He had not
initiated the bill for "humanitarian" salary increases.

More than 100 legislators voted to table the Herring
Bill, and Representative Bill Bass described the action
as one that "sort of set the tone for the session. What
the members were saying was that everything should flow
from the Governor to the House." Senator William N.
Patman noted, "Connally is real sensitive and touchy.
He wants to be the one to initiate things." Herring might
have been an uncommon man, but he obviously was
engulfed by conformity.

When the Governor was the initiator, he obviously
preferred to be cast in the role of the uncommon man,
even if it meant taking on the forces of Washington that
were led by his longtime friend Lyndon B. Johnson.

The traditional rallying cry of the South, that
of "States' Rights," was a clarion once again in two
struggles with the forces of centralized government.

Both came early in 1967.

First, on the day after his inauguration, Connally
proposed to the Legislature that the state of Texas initiate
an amendment to the United States Constitution that
would rebate 5 percent of all federal income taxes to the
states. He urged that the federal revenues be shared with
the states for "spending without restriction," and then
pointed out, "Federal grants, if allowed to proceed as they
are, will so entwine themselves that a state's freedom of
movement will be significantly inhibited."

Texas had no state income tax, by the way, either
corporate or personal, a situation that probably reflected
far more brightly on the profit-and-loss statements of
the corporations than of individuals.

Second, Connally and Secretary of the Interior
Stuart Udall clashed on a question of offshore oil and

its control. Oil long has been a vital force in the economy—and the political power—of the state. Oil made millions for many, and some of the profit obviously was funneled from the flat fields of East and West Texas to the hill country around Austin, where the Governor and the Legislature hold forth.

When it came right down to it, "oil" was a far stronger rallying cry in Texas than "States' Rights," and everyone from Washington to Austin knew it.

Therefore, when Udall proposed that the Federal Government take over regulation of oil and gas production on the Continental Shelf of the Gulf of Mexico, Connally saw threats in two directions, one to the sacred status of the oil industry, another in further incursion into state jurisdiction by the folks from Washington.

Udall had invited Connally or his representatives to participate in discussion of the regulations, and the state did take part. The Governor, of course, was not convinced. On receiving the first reports of the meetings, he said he was not sure that "the approach taken by you [Udall] will accommodate the national purpose or [that it] is in the public interest." The Government, which had yielded regulation of offshore oil and gas production to the states in 1954, was interested in moving back in, in terms of conservation of resources and under the new political-social-economic banner of "ecology as well."

Connally also pointed out that "several meetings with federal officials had failed to resolve Texas objections," though he did not state any specific objections.

Even oil was not a rallying cry that could assure Connally unanimous support. Former State Senator Franklin Spears had criticized him, saying, "Connally has perpetuated the control by out-of-state oil companies and gas transmission companies in this state."

The backwash of the oil industry involves pollution,

whether in water from offshore well leakage or ship collision, or in the air from the noxious fumes of refineries.

The chief antipollution official in Houston leaped into the breach at one point with a bitter criticism of the Governor for having appointed one of the city's major polluters to the state Pollution Control Board. Connally had responded with an illustration of a $10,000 fine levied against an industrial polluter in the city, though he passed over the obvious, if irreverent, retort that it would take a polluter to know a polluter.

The Governor, however, had not been oblivious to the problems of pollution. He praised the state's Water Quality Board for making some headway, and convinced the Legislature that some money was needed for state-wide planning.

"It's a beginning," he pointed out later, "but to say we've solved the problem is ridiculous, because we haven't." Connally feels that the state's water problems can be solved by large-scale planning that would control an entire river basin, with necessary authority given to the state, but his practical nature is quick to realize that this could infringe on the already autonomous river authorities.

"Galveston Bay starts with Dallas–Fort Worth," he said. "It's gonna be tough, but it's gotta happen."

Connally's irritation with Washington and federal intervention was a theme which recurred often during the year. He spoke to the New York Chamber of Commerce on March 3 and deplored "an overcentralization of federal power." Later in the year, when a friendly reporter obviously asked the proper leading question, he said that, as Governor, "it is a difficult task at best to cope with the manifold problems of the office when the federal structure is designed, almost, to prohibit and prevent any intelligent direction of state affairs."

But before the Washington juggernaut rolled over the state completely, there still was the opportunity for some fun and a chance to reap both publicity value and the tourist dollar from the big exposition of the following year, HemisFair '68, a fair which would be held in San Antonio, site of the state's most sacred shrine, the Alamo. Besides benefiting the city with some massive urban renewal projects, it would, by its very name, "carry out the theme that the fair is to be the confluence of civilization in the Americas."

One of the high spots of the whole thing, said Connally, would be a permanent Institute of Texas Culture, which would be "a dramatic showcase, not only to Texans, but to all the world, of the host of diverse peoples from many lands whose blood and dreams built our state."

Last, but not least, was the economic value of HemisFair as a stimulus to the economy of the state. "We anticipate," said the Governor, "more than $12 million in direct state taxes will result, not to mention the long-range benefits to the region, particularly in the field of tourism."

It is important, for a governor who has national ambitions, that he be heard on national topics, and the question of dissent was an overriding topic of Connally's third term. There was some of it in Texas, but far more in other places, and it is easier to tell other people how to raise their children than it is to raise one's own. As Mark Twain once said, "To do good is noble. To tell others how to do good is nobler still—and less trouble."

Therefore, when Connally made a speech in Des Moines during the month of May, while President Johnson had been discussing freedom of speech and dissent in Washington, the Governor of Texas discussed it in Iowa, saying, "Let it be clear that we do not question the right to dissent, but we do question the right of any-

one to subvert our society under the guise of dissent."
The public conscience was strongly aroused over the
war in Southeast Asia, but Connally was quoted as saying, "The critics of our policy in Vietnam, those who
engage in disorderly demonstrations in the streets, should
somehow be convinced that their irresponsibility is a
disservice to their country."

Still, the legislative session went on, despite Connally's commentary on national and international issues
during his visits to other parts of the. country.

When the session ended on June 3, the Governor
could point out the success of some of his proposed
legislation, but not all of it. The major failure probably
was in terms of modernizing government in twenty-four
metropolitan areas of the state. Connally recommended
the measure strongly, but it was blocked by the chairman
of the Committee for Counties, Cities and Towns, who
had vowed to impede any sort of urban reform bill.

Other legislation for revision of the state constitution, annual sessions of the Legislature and full-time
status for the lieutenant governor and the speaker of the
House, all urged by Connally, did not make it. Neither
did the bill for legalized parimutuel betting, which he
actively pushed behind the scenes.

Connally also felt the sting of failure over one of
his pet bills, that authorizing liquor by the drink. The
Governor had lobbied so ardently for this particular piece
of legislation that the liberal *Texas Observer* chided him
during March, noting: "All liberals—wet and dry—
agree that an industrial safety law is needed in Texas,
that farm workers should be encouraged to organize,
that a minimum wage should be passed, etc., etc. But
what does Connally place at the top of his list? Liquor
by the drink! Children die of malnutrition on the banks
of the Rio Grande—and Governor Connally's prize

concern is liquor." The booze barons rival the oil bosses in political influence.

The Texas liquor laws probably had been an embarrassment to the Governor for some time, reflecting, as they did, a small-time attitude on the part of a state that desperately sought status and image. The state had achieved big-league rank in the world of professional sports, but sports writers from other cities continually ridiculed the state's archaic laws for the sale of liquor. This was the sort of national reputation that irked Connally far more than things like malnutrition along the Rio Grande.

Taxation and appropriations, always matters of conflict between a governor and his legislature, or between a governor and his campaign contributors, were exactly that again in 1967. Connally had decided on an annual tax increase of $140 million, scheduled to come from increased taxes on corporations and on natural gas, plus the application of the state sales tax to beer and liquor. There were immediate rumbles from many of the Governor's supporters, and he quickly backed off. He settled for a one-year tax increase while he girded his loins for discussion of taxation and spending with the Legislature in the next session.

The sticky subject of pay raises for state employees, which began with the introduction of the Herring Bill in January, finally was settled on May 27. Connally had recommended an appropriation of $26 million, while Herring had sought $30 million. The compromise, at $27 million, was enough to provide raises ranging from 14 to 40 percent for about 40,000 state workers, and a 60 percent increase for the Governor himself, from $25,000 to $40,000 a year. The legislation was obviously necessary, from the Governor on down, though Connally did not originally seem too interested in those farther down. He had proposed a pay increase of about 7.5 percent for the lowest state salary group, but the Legislature, feeling munificent, provided a raise of almost 22 percent, from $2,820 to $3,432 on the lowest level. The highest classification of state employees received a salary increase of almost 26 percent, from $12,830 to $16,140, and the mood of generosity swept heads of agencies, certain commissioners and elected officials along in its wake with salary increases from 15 to 25 percent.

It was a good session, at least financially, for the legislators.

On the positive side of the session, the Legislature did provide for salary raises for teachers averaging $560 per year; increased spending for public welfare and state colleges and universities; made plans for water development and the control of water pollution; and repealed all the state segregation laws of 1957 relating to public facilities.

A minimum wage of $1.60 an hour was set for all state employees, but the legislators ignored a plea from the Mexican-Americans of South Texas who had requested a minimum wage law of $1.25 an hour for themselves. Texas had no minimum wage law of its own, though lip service was paid to minority groups by the establishment of two study committees who were to deliver reports in 1969.

The problem of the Mexican-Americans in the Rio Grande Valley area was becoming a serious one, but it got sidetracked while Connally visited with President Johnson's representatives on their "peace mission to the governors," which arrived in Texas on June 6.

Connally discussed Texas and national political questions with Johnson's liaison man, Farris Bryant, former Governor of Florida, and predicted that Johnson would be able to carry the state again in 1968. Connally and Bryant also discussed the Governor's own future, with the fourth term mentioned again. Connally people believed that his name on the ballot would help the Democratic ticket throughout the state when election time rolled around.

But Connally also had to return to the subject of States' Rights and the difficulties that he felt existed between Washington and Texas. He described the relationship as "characterized by misunderstanding, disharmony and, in some cases, utter confusion."

The Governor proposed a simplification of the system of federal financial assistance and sought the opportunity for the state to participate in the drawing up of programs and their operation. He was critical of the administering of federal contributions to the total cost of state and local government, estimated to rise from $1 of $15 in 1945 to $1 of $3 in 1975, and he predicted a deterioration into "a veritable jungle of mismanagement, suspicion and recrimination."

The Mexican-American minority makes up about 16 percent of the Texas population. Many work on farms in the blistering hot summers of the Rio Grande Valley, others are employed in a variety of menial occupations. Without a state minimum wage law or a viable organization, they were both poor and powerless. Still, in a time of national turmoil, a dispute broke out in Edinburg, deep in the valley. On May 27 a union attempted to picket a trainload of cantaloupe and honeydew melons coming from neighboring Starr County. The famed Texas Rangers, the state's glamorous and movie-famous law enforcement agency, arrested twenty farm labor union members, sympathizers and bystanders and charged them with unlawful assembly. Bond quickly was provided, and the twenty proceeded to protest to both Connally and the White House.

The situation had been deteriorating all spring, and

the use of the Rangers was an exacerbating force. Questions arose as to their responsibilities in keeping order, and even more difficult questions about who had assigned the Rangers to the area and to whom they were to report. Four Rangers, including Captain A. Y. Allee, were named in a suit by the Texas Council of Churches as having infringed upon the civil rights of persons observing the situation in the valley. There were charges of Ranger brutality, of Rangers having shoved workers back into the fields and of Ranger participation strictly on the side of the farm owners and not in terms of keeping law and order in the area.

U.S. Senator Ralph Yarborough was the most bitter and vocal legislator to get into the battle. He promptly nicknamed the Rangers "John Connally's Strikebreakers." Yarborough's attack continued:

"Traditionally [they] were created to bring law and order to the wild frontier. . . . The role of the Texas Rangers in this labor-management dispute must be an unhappy one for the Rangers, who see their great reputation of searching out the most dangerous outlaws in the world lowered to that of pushing an unarmed girl carrying a picket sign. . . . However, in fairness to the Rangers, it should be noted that they did not order themselves into this duty. The Texas Rangers are under the command of the Governor of Texas. . . . I think the responsibility rests squarely upon the shoulders of the Governor of Texas for—instead of ordering the Texas Rangers to 'get their man'—he has ordered them to get a low standard of wages, and to keep wages low."

Yarborough's rhetoric inflamed an already heated situation in which the Rangers and Connally had been condemned by legislators, labor leaders, the Mexican-American Joint Conference, the League of United Latin American Citizens and even the North Dallas Democratic Women's Club.

State Senator Joe Bernal proposed a committee to investigate the situation and the possibility that the Rangers in Starr County were "acting as a partisan police force on the side of management and using unnecessary force." The committee went into the valley and returned with the impression that "the Rangers are vitally needed down there," according to Senator Oscar Mauzy.

A resolution introduced into the House asking the Governor to remove the Rangers from Starr County received blank looks from the legislators. After all, Connally was not the driving force, not the instigator of the legislation.

Through all this, the Governor remained staunchly noncommittal, but just as staunchly on the side of management and the establishment of Starr County and the rich fruit- and vegetable-growing area. Labor leaders asked his help in resolving the crisis, settling the dispute and removing the Rangers from the area. Connally declined. The secretary-treasurer of the Texas AFL-CIO asked him to consider making a request to the National Arbitration Association for an investigation of the situation and the establishment of procedures for legal union representation elections. Connally did not respond. Representatives from the United Farm Workers, then actively campaigning for union organization in California, and from the United Auto Workers, met with him and urged his support of a union election to settle the Starr County difficulties. Connally refrained from committing himself to any course of action.

Connally's stand put him foursquare on the side of the status quo.

But at the same time he publicly defended the Rangers at a press conference, though he pointed out that they had been assigned to Starr County without his knowledge. Connally said that the Rangers were under the leadership of Colonel Homer Garrison, a man in whom the Governor had "complete confidence," and they had been sent there because of the burning of a railroad trestle. Connally maintained that there had been no violence or bloodshed in Starr County and that the Rangers had not prohibited lawful picketing. He also praised them for assisting local authorities and described them as "the most honored group of law enforcement officers in the state."

Colonel Garrison also leaped to the defense of his Rangers, categorically denying all charges of brutality, especially those involving a union supporter named Dimas, who had been arrested by the Rangers and subsequently required medical treatment. Garrison pointed out that Dimas had been armed. He also said that "laws prohibit stopping trains and mass picketing, and they have been violated."

Connally, who had remained totally uninvolved in the dispute, then addressed the state convention of the League of United Latin American Citizens with vague words. He ignored the problems of Starr County and was critical only of "these itinerant, paid purveyors of division, distrust and dissension [who] would attempt to paint some of our people off into a corner, out of the mainstream of our society, by falsely convincing them that they're better off alone."

The Governor reached a personal nadir in his relations with the Mexican-American community some weeks later in El Paso when he, along with Senator Yarborough and President Johnson, attended a national conference on the problems of Mexican-Americans.

Connally was booed. His annoyance was obvious. Meanwhile, Yarborough received rousing cheers, even though he happened not to be in the hall. The President had introduced both men to the conference, which included delegates from several southwestern states and

Mexico. Yarborough, through a communications mixup, had remained on the bus under the impression that none of the traveling party was to enter the convention hall. He remained in the bus, but his introduction drew cheers from the delegates and high praise from Gustavo Diaz Ordaz, President of Mexico.

The reaction to the Governor shocked the delegates. Pancho Medrano, a United Auto Workers official, said with surprise, "I don't think in the history of the United States there has ever been anything like this, a governor being booed when the President introduced him." Equal reaction came from Dr. Clark Knowlton, head of the department of sociology at the University of Texas at El Paso, who said: "Most Mexican-Americans are very courteous and seldom, if ever, do anything like that. . . . I would say that Governor Connally is the one politician who is totally persona non grata to the Mexicans. On the other hand, Yarborough is their hero."

Reacting in standard political fashion, Connally said that he felt there was "no significance at all to the boos," a statement that is difficult to understand at all, especially in terms of the equal and opposite reception that Yarborough had received.

Again in standard political fashion, the Governor's staff got to work, reminding the people of how much Connally had done for Mexican-Americans. Reports and statements pointed out, for example, how many more Latin appointments Connally had made to governmental programs than Yarborough had made.

Nonetheless Connally, a solid member of the establishment, regardless of his party affiliation, remained unpopular with the Mexican-American community. For one thing, his behavior during the valley farm workers' march on New Braunfels in 1966 was remembered with bitterness. When the march ended, Yarborough had addressed a rally of the workers, but the Governor had declined to appear. This background is easy explanation of the subsequent reactions of the large minority and their feelings where both the Governor and the Senator were concerned.

Senator Bernal had accentuated the situation and pointed up the discontent by charging the Governor with a "cruel, if not stupid" act of appointing a commission for revision of the state constitution and leaving the Mexican-American community completely unrepresented. Connally promptly blamed the Senator for advocating "reverse discrimination" and then followed step number two in the politicians' manual by accusing his opponent of having written a "publicity-seeking" letter.

Bernal was not unprepared for a confrontation, and charged right back, using the fact that Connally had posed with two Mexican-American highway patrolmen for a campaign poster in the 1966 election. "If you can use Mexican-Americans during a campaign," Bernal asked, "why not let members of this ethnic minority share in shaping our future in government by naming at least one to such an important committee?"

Connally was not moved by the logic.

The Governor, hardly a liberal where civil rights and minority interests are concerned, was in even deeper difficulty later in the year when he attended a national governors' conference. On these extremely sensitive issues, he was quoted as having said, "These people will have to wait for what they want. They will have to learn to be patient."

When things are going badly for a political figure, they seem to gather momentum and everything becomes a questionable issue. A television appearance may appear to be a minor thing, but Connally's enemies leaped into the breach when he announced that the American Broadcasting Company had invited him on a trip to Africa for a hunting safari to be used as part of the network's "American Sportsman" program. Public figures in varying positions—athletes, entertainers and others—had taken part in the program in the past, though most segments were filmed in hunting areas of this country, many close to the homes of the celebrities rather than in the glamorous high country of Africa. It was very easy for skeptical non-Connally people to wonder, very loudly, why a major television network should be interested in taking the Governor of Texas to Africa and, more important, why the Governor of Texas should be happily accepting the largesse of a major corporation. Coincidental, of course, was the news of the merger between the network and the International Telephone and Telegraph Company (ITT), the world's ninth largest industrial concern. There was room for lots of questions, and lots of questions were asked.

Although the legislative session had ended, and a summer recess should have provided some opportunity for relaxation, it was not to happen for the Governor.

On his mind was the pervasive question of whether or not he should seek a fourth term, and this problem was compounded by deep and serious splits in the Democratic party in the state of Texas. These needed mending first.

Anti-Connally snipers had been peppering the Governor on the question of a fourth term all spring. The *Herald,* a weekly newspaper in the little town of Tulia, tucked neatly away in the Panhandle between Amarillo and Plainview, was shooting at Connally as early as February. An editorial writer dredged up Connally's 1962 promises in his campaign against Price Daniel. "One of the first things I shall do as your governor," Connally reportedly had said, "is to recommend that the legislature submit to the people a constitutional amendment preventing any governor from holding office more than two consecutive two-year terms. I would like for this to take effect during and to apply to my tenure. The last thing we need in Texas is one-man rule."

The *Herald* also had the splits in the Democratic party in mind, along with Connally's promise to "unite the party factions." The editorial writer kept firing from the hip, noting that "his promise to unite the party factions is even more incredible. Name one attempt the Governor has made to unite the Democratic party in Texas. The fact is, he has done more than any Governor in Texas history to widen the splits."

Whether or not the Democratic party of Texas could ever be united, regardless of leadership, was another question. The long tradition of one-party rule in the state had resulted in one party which had as many factions and fragments as two parties in a two-party state. With Yarborough as the leader of the moderate-liberal faction of the party and Connally as the leader of the conservative wing, that still left room for plenty of other leadership, ranging from far to the right of Connally to far to the left of Yarborough.

Through his two-and-a-half terms, however, Connally had made no obvious efforts to attempt a unification of the various factions of Democrats within the party. Perhaps he felt that a divided party was easier to lead, perhaps he felt that there was no use in wasting time and energy on an impossible task.

The relationship between the Governor and the Senator continued to be filled with tension and distrust, with periodic outbreaks of skirmish-line warfare. The difficulties over the springtime labor problems in the Rio Grande Valley and the sharply contrasting reception of the two men at the El Paso conference were revived in September on a different level, though the locale of the Mexican-American minority continued to be the battleground. Yarborough publicly accused Connally of poor handling of the flood emergency that savaged southern Texas in the wake of a hurricane. The region had a dense Mexican-American population, and the Senator accused the Governor of an "inexcusable" delay in declaring that part of the state a disaster area.

President Johnson, interested probably in both his home state and the problems of his Democratic party in the state, made a trip to Texas in September and included both Connally and Yarborough on his plane in a tour of the flood areas. The two men reportedly were cordial, though not friendly. The President talked privately, however, only with the Governor, and later publicly complimented him on his handling of the flood situation.

Even though it was more than a year away, the 1968 gubernatorial election rose to the top of the political milk again. After all, election day is the prime day for politicians, whether seeking office or seeking retention of office.

Connally maintained discreet silence where his fourth term was concerned, but Yarborough apparently decided to try to flush his opponent into the open. The Senator, his staff and friends began to let talk of Austin in 1968 come into the open, and the message soon became clear that the Senator might be interested in becoming Governor. When Yarborough spoke to a state convention of labor unions, he said, "I just might run, because Texas sure needs a governor." Yarborough was no stranger to running for Governor, however. He had been an unsuccessful Democratic candidate in primaries in 1952, 1954 and 1956, then turned to the Senate in 1957.

Yarborough's show of interest was a nifty piece of political gamesmanship, well calculated to keep Connally off balance and to keep himself with, so to speak, a foot in the door of both the U.S. Capitol and the Governor's Mansion.

Political analysts, however, began to question Yarborough's purpose. Did he really want to leave the exclusive club of the U.S. Senate to be Governor of Texas? Or was he thinking of entering the gubernatorial race solely to oppose Connally? Suppose Connally declined to run for a fourth term? Was Yarborough still interested? The obverse also was open to question. Was Connally really interested in a fourth term, or would he run simply to keep Yarborough out?

An easily predictable reaction came from conservative Democrats, who began urging Connally to seek a fourth term to keep "that man" out of the Statehouse. The Governor conferred often during the month of September with friends and advisers, but when he met with a very close group at a secret meeting in the mansion on October 4, he appeared blasé about seeking a fourth term.

Still, Connally was too experienced a politician to make a definite statement. Nor was he about to shed any of his support. He continued to keep the state's major daily newspapers in his corner, and he remained close to the major financial interests that had supported him in the past.

While Connally and Yarborough stood in the wings, each waiting for the other to make a statement or a decision, the other political factions in the state were busy seeking their own candidates and making their own plans.

Lieutenant Governor Preston Smith was the first to file as a Democratic candidate. He expressed his confidence that Connally would not run in 1968, since it would be a violation of "his expressed promise to the people of Texas." Smith, whose conservatism might have been a little stronger than Connally's, was a favorite of some of Connally's supporters. Other conservatives who were mentioned as possibilities were Waggoner Carr, former state attorney general; Dolph Briscoe, former representative; Joe Kilgore, former Congressman; and

John Hill, secretary of state for Texas. Young Ben
Barnes, speaker of the Texas House at the political
prodigy age of twenty-nine, was another to receive early
mention. Barnes was a favorite of Connally and had
often been praised by the Governor; reportedly, he was
securely in Connally's pocket and a prime force in prod-
ding legislation that the Governor wanted. Barnes, however, realizing the twin handicaps of his age and his lack
of exposure on a statewide basis, declined all invitations
and announced instead as a candidate for lieutenant governor.

Yarborough, of course, was the leader of the liberal
wing of the party, but he continued to debate with himself and his advisers whether he could do the most good
"as governor or as senator." He was extremely popular
in much of the state, and Texas liberals felt that he had
an excellent chance to win a gubernatorial race, regardless of conservative opposition. But Yarborough refused
to speak definitely about entering the race, though he
did make some vague references to a statewide platform
by saying, "The first thing I'd do . . . is move Texas
out of thirty-fourth place in education, try to move the
state into the twentieth century . . . and do something
about the minimum wage law." Don Yarborough, the
nearly successful candidate in the 1962 primary, was
another liberal Democrat who had some support.

Though the Republicans were down, they weren't
really out. Since the election of John Tower to the U.S.
Senate, the Texas Republican organization had expressed
hope, if not optimism, that it could become a force in
statewide politics. The party sought a strong candidate
who could oppose Connally or Yarborough and hoped
that the split in Democratic ranks was wide enough for
a Republican to sneak through. It was felt that Tower's
victory was created in that schism, and that a Democratic scramble among a liberal (Yarborough?), a conservative (Connally?) and someone just to the right of

that (the already-announced Smith) might hinder the party in a gubernatorial battle.

The key, of course, was John Connally. He had been elected to a third term with the largest margin of his three races, and his control of the party was such that he could probably succeed if he decided to run again.

Connally continued noncommittal. He made a few loose promises to announce his intention either before or after the National Governors' Conference opened on October 18, and he left for the conference, held aboard the S.S. *Independence,* without a word.

Once on board, however, the problems of a fourth term were lost in a political struggle on a national level, when Connally leaped into the breach to help his old friend, President Johnson, who was seeking endorsement from the governors of his policies in Vietnam.

Before the conference began, there seemed to be enough strength among the Democratic governors, with Connally in the forefront, to force a support resolution through the membership. Several Republican governors supported the President, and chances looked good.

But the unfortunate political tendency to seek over-kill of opposition on any matter promptly threw a massive monkey wrench into the Democrats' plans. W. Marvin Watson, the President's chief of staff, sent a telegram to Price Daniel, Johnson's political liaison with the governors of both parties. The telegram contained information concerning past Republican support of various Vietnam policies, and was to serve as intelligence and leverage on the resolution. It specifically mentioned several governors who could be used to help swing the Republicans into line.

Unfortunately, the telegram was intercepted by a press aide to Governor Ronald Reagan of California. Reagan informed his colleagues of this pressure from the

White House and promptly made sure it was leaked to the press.

The publication of the telegram solidified the Republicans, and when Connally presented the resolution, it did not even leave the resolutions committee with unanimous support. Obviously, the Republicans had joined to oppose any resolution on Vietnam, thus leaving themselves the privilege of second guessing any action by the Democratic Administration.

Connally snapped publicly at the leaked telegram, noting, "Every man has to live with his own ethics and morals. I don't read other people's mail and messages." The damage was done, however, and the Governor now strove to get the resolution to the floor of the conference. He proposed, as a last resort, that the rules be suspended and that the resolution be placed directly before the governors. He defended the action by saying, "I don't care how many votes it gets. I don't think this is a partisan issue. I don't think this is a political issue."

Obviously, he was incorrect.

The move to suspend the rules, which needed a two-thirds majority, didn't make it, in spite of Connally's most persuasive efforts. He then attempted to counteract the insinuation that partisan politics had been inserted into a conference of governors and wound up with a lengthy tirade on the history of American wars and the manifold difficulties caused by dissension and opposition to the forces of right and glory.

He neglected to include the Battle of the Alamo, perhaps because although there was no dissension in the building, neither was there victory.

Connally's actions at the Governors' Conference can be assessed at various levels. No one can know whether or not he conferred with the President before the conference, or, if so, what they said. There was speculation that the Governor would need the President to lead the national ticket in 1968, and equal speculation that the President would need the Governor to help him carry Texas. And then, suppose either, or both, decided not to run? What effect would that have on the Democratic candidates in both races?

Connally announced his decision first. He called a press conference on November 10 to state flatly that he would not seek a fourth term. His opposition, of course, was cheered. It was the end of an era, perhaps the end of one-man rule, since there did not seem to be anyone in the state who possessed the individual power of Connally. Indications are that he had enough support and enough financing to run for a fourth term, and probably to win.

The Governor himself said during the press conference that he had received much support from various sources and that a poll, which he did not identify, had placed him at the top of all prospective candidates.

While announcing his own withdrawal, Connally said he had not talked with Johnson about his intentions, nor had he informed him before the public announcement. His reasons were described as a lack of confidence in being able to "bring to the office for another two years the enthusiasm, the resilience, the patience that my conscience would demand, and that the state would deserve." He did not mention previous campaign promises about two-term governors or his legislative plans in that direction.

It is apparently as difficult for a politician as for a pretty young woman to refrain from being coy at certain times, so Connally refrained from endorsing anyone for the next election. He also declined to elaborate on any personal plans, leaving himself a completely open set of options.

Connally's decision cheered the liberal wing of the party and brought concern and some gloom to the conservative wing. The liberals began to move fast on an intensified campaign of voter registration and to plan strategy for the primary race. The conservatives, with House Speaker Ben Barnes as a spokesman, were worried. Barnes commented that "LBJ's running for reelection will make it a difficult election year. . . . The people are going to be upset and disappointed with things. We are going to see a new political era in Texas."

The Governor, now an announced lame duck, was back in the national news only a few weeks later as a possible Secretary of Defense. On November 27 President Johnson appointed Secretary of Defense Robert McNamara the new president of the World Bank. The next day Connally flew to Washington, ostensibly to discuss plans for the upcoming HemisFair '68. Again, what was said by whom to whom is hidden, but the Governor publicly did not acknowledge any relationship between the trip and the newly opened Cabinet post, though he did answer a reporter's direct question by saying, "If it [the Cabinet position] were offered, it would be very difficult to turn down."

Connally remained firm in his decision not to seek a fourth term, though there was immediate and amusing semantic discussion when he commented, "I do not intend to be a candidate for reelection as Governor of Texas." There were those who leaped immediately upon the use of the word *intend* and claimed that it left open the possibility that the Governor might feel forced—or maybe obligated to his party—to run again. Still playing coy, and still involved in word games with reporters, Connally said that he would not make a "William Tecumseh Sherman-type statement," which immediately was interpreted in print to mean that "Connally would not say he wouldn't run if nominated and wouldn't serve if elected."

* * *

The tradition of New Year's Eve parties and New Year's resolutions holds forth even in Texas. John Connally, Governor of the sovereign state, already having made his decision not to seek a fourth term in 1968, went to a gala function but kept his resolutions to himself.

After all, 1968 was a presidential election year. Lyndon Johnson, though battered and buffeted through his own term, was eligible to run for reelection, and John Connally was his friend.

Without state elections to worry about, or a primary to campaign for, the Governor was free to pursue a national reputation, to speak out on national campaigns and national issues.

Senator Eugene McCarthy of Minnesota was the first major Democrat to announce an interest in the 1968 nomination. He revealed in December 1967 that he intended to enter several state primaries against the incumbent. Senator Robert Kennedy of New York, brother of the late President, also was recognized as having aspirations for the nomination. He became a leading contender immediately.

Connally noticed both of them and promptly linked them together. He called McCarthy a "stalking horse" for Kennedy and elaborated during a press conference in New York. The Texas Governor said that McCarthy was "acting primarily as a catalyst for dissidents. It can't do anything but result in greater division in the party. It's clear if any Senator gives the prestige of his office and the force of his personality to coalescing the dissent in the Democratic party, it is going to be harmful to that extent."

It is interesting that Connally, who never seemed to worry about the divided Democratic party in his own state, was publicly concerned about it on a national level.

Dissent was about to become a national issue, and John Burns, New York Democratic State Chairman, promptly took Connally to task for his stand against it. Burns noted, "Perhaps Governor Connally does not fully appreciate the benefits which the Democratic party could derive from Senator McCarthy's campaign," and added, "Because of the dissension over the President's Vietnam policy, the Democratic nominee for President could lose the state [New York] if the party did not encourage a discussion of that policy."

The question of the right to dissent—who has it and how much?—became an issue that would shake the entire party and come very close to splitting it in half. The Vietnam war was the largest force for division, but it was closely connected with an increasing rumble from students and discontented minorities. Domestic problems continued to be unsolved, and the Democrats soon found themselves in the midst of a maze, trying to match up an emerging idealism with the political realities of financial support, party machines, ward heelers and the necessary acquisition of strategic votes.

Dissension among Democrats began to spill over. Connally was quick to try to jam it back under covers, behind curtains or any place else where it could remain hidden.

When Robert Kennedy criticized the role of the United States in Vietnam, Connally publicly accused him of attempting to undermine the country's foreign policies. Connally added, "The Senator's words and his actions have been a source of discord in this country. They've had a detrimental effect on the whole attitude of the people in this country and an even more disastrous effect insofar as Ho Chi Minh and the Communist world are concerned." And while foreign policy and dissent were one thing, party loyalty was a whole new thing, according to the Governor, who felt just as strongly that "obviously Senator Kennedy hasn't conducted himself in a manner designed to help President Johnson."

Whether or not it can be said there was a Johnson-Connally "faction" or "bloc," the Governor and the President were cut from the same socioeconomic mold and, more important, the same political mold. Political dissent, especially that aimed at the Administration's foreign policy, was considered as being disloyal and dangerous to the country, and, most of all, disloyal and dangerous to the party.

While Connally was busy moving as a figure on a national level, the Democratic party in Texas was absorbed in the search for a nice conservative gubernatorial candidate to succeed Connally. One anti-Connally Texas paper described thus the candidate that the Connally forces sought: "He wants one just like himself, one whose first love is oil, ranching, gas, utilities, big business and one with the proper 'philosophy' on how higher education should be financed." The liberal faction of the party was just as deep into a search for a candidate who could block the establishment and institute a new political order in the state.

Suddenly, a candidate emerged.

Eugene Locke.

Who?

Eugene Locke was a Texan whom President Johnson had appointed Deputy Ambassador to South Vietnam and previously Ambassador to Pakistan. Locke leaped full-tilt into the fray with the urging of Johnson and the silent cooperation of Connally. Locke had a long list of ties with both the President and the Governor. He had been Connally's college roommate and his campaign manager in the successful election of 1962, when Connally first became Governor. Locke had participated strongly in Johnson's 1960 campaign, and had been chairman of the Executive Committee of the Texas

Democratic party from 1962 to 1964. He also was
wealthy, a Dallas attorney who had vested interests in
oil, construction and real estate, including a 25,000-acre
ranch in the Big Bend country. His interests, obviously,
were aligned with the moneyed establishment and the oil
people. Locke also had been generous in his campaign
contributions to both Johnson and Connally.

Seeing in Locke a man who could hold the Texas
establishment together and make the state safe for Democracy (either large or small *d*) while protecting property for Johnson's eventual return to his home, the
President excused Locke from his post in Vietnam.

According to Locke, the President agreed that "the
situation in Vietnam had improved sufficiently so that
[he] could resign to try political campaigning for the first
time." Locke also said, "I have been in Vietnam nearly
nine months. During this time we have made progress on
every front—military, pacification, political, economic.
We have held village and hamlet elections where
thousands of officials have been elected by the people—
presidential and vice-presidential elections, and elections
to the newly created Senate and Lower House. With this
improved situation, I felt that I could appropriately
leave Vietnam and the President agreed."

Locke didn't wait long. He filed for office within
twenty-four hours of his return to Texas and immediately
began collecting the funds that began pouring into his
campaign headquarters. President Johnson was obvious
in his support of Locke for the Democratic nomination,
but Connally was less demonstrative. He did not openly
endorse Locke; and he privately was unenthusiastic
about the candidate's chances of gaining the nomination.
Still, he was represented in Locke's organization. The
Governor's brother Merrill I. Connally, of Floresville,
became Locke's campaign manager, a fact that was regarded as an endorsement from the Governor himself by

most people. Observers felt that the closeness to the
Governor could provide Locke with access to files and
mailing lists that would help him reach the moneyed interests that had backed Connally in 1962, 1964 and
1966.

Campaign manager Connally, trying to turn a disadvantage around, accented his candidate's lack of experience by describing him as a "clean candidate," which
could be a reference to his bathing habits, his mind, his
background or whatever.

Locke extended a Connally-oiled olive branch to
the establishment forces when he announced his candidacy, promising "to continue the elective, progressive,
creative government based on sound principles which
we have had under Governor Connally."

Money and media exposure were Locke's two great
needs before the May 5 primary election. After all,
Locke had spent most of the previous years out of Texas
and no one knew him. A fast-moving, expensive advertising campaign began, based on the simple slogan,
"Eugene Locke should be Governor of Texas . . . the
Governor of Texas should be Eugene Locke." A figure
of close to $3 million was mentioned in this massive
campaign, with some calling it the most expensive in the
history of the state. Later, campaign manager Connally
said that Locke's primary expenditures had been between
$400,000 and $500,000, still a hefty amount.

Locke also found himself immediately tarred with
the Connally brush, and even though the Governor still
had almost a year left to serve, there were those who were
eagerly awaiting his departure from the state capital.
Archer Fullingim of the Kountze (Hardin County) *News*
ripped into both Connally and Locke in a discussion of
potential Democratic candidates for governor. "No governor has talked more and done less than you," he wrote.
"You've blabbed day and night what you are going to

do and then you did nothing except favors for your campaign contributors. Now Connally wants to continue his inept administration in Eugene Locke."

As the filing deadline came and went, the list of candidates, which covered all possible areas of the political spectrum, with heavy emphasis to the right, narrowed down to Lieutenant Governor Preston Smith, the first to file; Don Yarborough, the liberal lawyer from Houston; John Hill, former Texas secretary of state and an ardent Connally supporter; and Waggoner Carr, former Texas attorney general and a loud proclaimer of the necessity for "law and order," along with Locke.

Senator Ralph Yarborough finally decided not to enter, perhaps thinking he could be of more use in Washington than in Austin. The Senator's family was reported pleased by his decision, and Texas labor supporters also felt he had made the correct choice. Labor leaders, speculating on his popularity in the state, felt he might win election as governor but then would lose his influential position in Washington. The Senator and Washington-based labor leaders had had an interesting series of struggles, pointed up by the splendid relationship between the Senator and Texas-based labor leaders. Yarborough and the Texans were mutual friends, aiding each other to whatever extent they, as the state's lesser financial and political powers, could. But it seemed that whenever Yarborough's position threatened establishment Democratic procedure, influential Texans in Washington would call on George Meany, president of the AFL-CIO, to lean on him. Finally, Yarborough had to threaten to embarrass the White House, since the President took sides with the establishment Texans, by promising to challenge Johnson at the Democratic Convention with a delegation of Texas mavericks. The Senator also had to confront Meany with the fact that friendship and loyalty between the two men would be a good thing since, after all, Yarborough was number three in seniority on the Senate Labor Committee.

With the Senator deciding to remain in Washington, the Texas liberal backing would go to his younger namesake. *The Economist* in London commented that "the possibility that Don Yarborough will win over all these is enough to terrify the state's economic interests, who have blocked all liberal legislation in the state legislature and have protected the big oil companies for a generation. But, even if a Republican were to defeat Mr. Yarborough in November, the establishment would no longer have a direct line to the governor's office."

With Yarborough the only liberal, and a quartet of conservatives aligned against him, the liberal wing of the party took faint hope in the possibility that the conservative vote would split widely enough for their man to slip through.

Hope was about all they could have. The establishment, wise in its long rule of the state, would never allow it. The power of the Governor was too strong and the significance of having the right man in Austin was lost on no one. For example, Hank Brown, president of the state AFL-CIO, said, "In six years, a governor can break the back of the corporate structure in this state. He can appoint more than 6,000 members of boards and commissions and councils—everything from wildlife to education—and they would control a billion dollars in annual expenditures."

Another string to the conservatives' bow was an unusual power written into the state political system in the days immediately after the Civil War. *The Economist,* in describing it, noted that it was provided "as a way of emasculating carpetbagging governors imposed by a victorious North." It allowed for the lieutenant governor to have a special veto power over legislation. The most powerful candidate for that race was Ben Barnes,

Connally's political child prodigy. Should he be elected, he could assume control over the Legislature, probably with advice and counsel from the ex-Governor.

What about Preston Smith, the lieutenant governor who wished to move up to the state's top office? He was a conservative, with a conservative constituency, perhaps even to the political right of Connally himself. But the two men did not get along. Smith was one of the first to point out Connally's broken two-term campaign promise, and he had blocked many of the Governor's programs in the Legislature.

Smith was the pre-primary leader, despite his extremely conservative views. They were views that most Texans supported, and they also had powerful backing from many status quo establishment interests. The strength of Smith was not lost on President Johnson, either. The President reportedly called Smith and asked if either he or Connally could name the organizational personnel for the party if Smith were elected governor. It was a good way for one of the men to keep some control over it. Smith reportedly replied, "Sure, Mr. President. I'll let you appoint them. I don't care about that sort of thing. I never went to a precinct meeting in my life."

With a political party and an election to worry about later in the year, Connally didn't seem overconcerned about matters at home, despite an internal problem that came right from Washington. Ramsey Clark, Attorney General of the United States, charged that there was "extreme brutality" in the Texas prison system. The Ellis unit of the Texas Department of Correction was singled out for its "heinous acts of discrimination and extreme brutality" and the Governor apparently took no action. The National Association for the Advancement of Colored People protested and Richard Dockery, regional director of the group, said on February 6: "We requested an audience with the Governor, and we were a little appalled at the five- or six-day delay to our request. We could not leave the problem unattended."

Connally's lack of action parallels his earlier statement that "these people will just have to wait."

More important than the Texas gubernatorial primary, even more important than the problems of the Texas prison system, was the growing national tension and depression surrounding Vietnam and this country's involvement in a costly and bloody war in Southeast Asia. Harry Truman had said of his own role as President that "the buck stops here," and President Lyndon B. Johnson was finding the same weight resting heavily on his own shoulders. After internal debate for almost a year, and discussions with close friends and family, including John Connally, the President dropped a bombshell on the nation on March 31 when he said he would not seek renomination or reelection in 1968. The announcement came at the end of a speech in which he informed the nation that he was reducing the bombing of North Vietnam.

Johnson's first discussion with Connally on the matter came during 1967 in a meeting at the LBJ Ranch, in which the political futures of both men were the subject of the conversation. At that time, the Governor apparently informed the President that he would not seek another term, but that he would run if the President needed him on the ticket to help carry the state. Even though Johnson was a Texan, he was not the state's most popular politician. A combination of both men probably would help both at the ballot box. So when Connally mentioned his own doubts about running again, the President confided that he was not certain he would seek reelection either, and he told Connally to make his own decisions based on that assumption.

Because of the long friendship of the two men, the

press had watched Connally during the months before his announcement not to run. News analysts were seeking clues from the Governor about the White House, and they also looked to the White House for clues about the Governor's Mansion. Johnson was cognizant of the relationship and of the fact that reporters were watching each man with an eye on the other. He commented about it in his book *The Vantage Point,* in reference to a conversation with Secretary of Defense Robert McNamara. "I told Bob I was convinced that once the announcement was made, the press would read significance into Connally's decision not to run, as it related to my plans." After Connally's announcement, the President wrote, "I was surprised and relieved, as I told Bob McNamara, that there was so little speculation in the press connecting Connally's plans with mine."

Connally's relationship with the President was such that the Governor helped draft the statement declining the nomination, and there were suggestions in some quarters that Connally's own political decision gave impetus to the President. In October 1967 Johnson and Connally had met at the LBJ Ranch and Johnson had asked his press secretary, George Christian, to outline his public statement. He directed Christian to include the fact that he didn't feel that he "could indulge the time and energy for a national political campaign and still be the President [I] felt [I] should be in these tense times. . . . Nobody was indispensable." Christian and Connally also met to discuss the ideas in the statement, and Connally helped the press secretary in the preparation.

Lyndon Johnson, always conscious of his place in the country and in history, was physically tired after four and a half strenuous years as President and emotionally bitter over the changes in his nation and the fact that he was being criticized continually for the Vietnam

situation and the problems in American society. Still, it
was uppermost in his mind to know how his decision
would be accepted overseas. Would it have an impact
on the morale of the American soldiers in Vietnam? He
also was prepared to change his mind if things began to
look better for the country and for the presidency. He
had originally planned to deliver his non-candidacy
statement as a closing paragraph to the annual State of
the Union message. By some strange circumstance, the
announcement, which had not been made part of the
printed text of the speech but which was to be carried
in the President's pocket and pulled out at the dramatic
moment, was not there when he reached for it. Still,
Johnson recalled later that he was convinced that an
earlier announcement would not have been appropriate,
even though there was not much change, either in the
United States or in Vietnam, between the date of the
State of the Union address and the night of March 31.
He pointed out that it might have weakened his ability
to handle national crises and to promote his programs
in Congress.

The television announcement, which was a well-
kept secret, dispersed shock waves in a variety of directions. A major impact was on the Democratic party,
which, like any political party, expected the incumbent
President to seek renomination and reelection. The party
also was left without leadership, especially conservative
leadership, and the race toward the White House was
wide open.

Texas Democrats went into action immediately.
They met the next day, with Connally, state chairman
Will Davis and national committeeman Frank Erwin at
the helm. The easiest tack was to support the Governor
as a favorite son candidate for the presidency. Connally
led a press conference in Austin on April 1 and immediately ruled out the thought of seeking the vice-presi-

dential nomination on a ticket headed by Vice President
Hubert Humphrey of Minnesota. Connally also ducked
any immediate question of endorsement of Humphrey,
saying he was not "prepared to announce support for a
man who is not even a candidate."

The next day the Texas Democratic Executive
Committee took action that came as no surprise to anyone. It endorsed Connally as a favorite son candidate
and also approved a resolution that would pledge support of all Democratic candidates "from courthouse to
White House." Though the move was encouraged as a
positive effort to display a united front by the party, it
was not as positive as all that. There was vocal opposition to the suggestion of support for Senator Robert
Kennedy if he were to become the candidate, and Frank
Erwin said, "I remain convinced that Bobby Kennedy's
cold ruthlessness, demonstrated opportunism and his
overriding personal ambition render him totally unfit to
hold any high office."

"From courthouse to White House" endorsements
might run into a few snags along the way.

As expected, Governor Connally accepted the man-
date from the party. He met with some 250 of his campaign workers at Austin on April 7 and announced that
he would actively seek the favorite son role. He pointed
out that this was the proper state response to the announcement by President Johnson and that he was acting "to fill the vacuum among Texas Democrats."

The unification of Texas' 104 convention votes behind Connally as a favorite son was a deliberate and
well-planned move on the part of the establishment
Democrats. Votes committed to Connally could not go to
either of the liberal candidates, McCarthy or Kennedy.
The number of votes had been determined with Connally's strong backing in 1966, and delegates for precinct, county and state conventions were chosen on that

basis. Therefore, the party regulars, led by the Governor, would have a valid claim to the delegates' support and obligation.

The united front of the establishment could not conceal, however, the disaffection of the labor and liberal factions, who vehemently opposed any endorsement of Connally, and who may have even more violently resented the tag "favorite" when applied to him. The youthful, long-haired and spirited supporters of McCarthy were out in force, working to find delegates to represent their candidate at any level of the selection process. August wasn't far away. The state AFL-CIO, which had been loyal to Johnson most of the time, mentioned possible support for Humphrey if the Vice President should decide to become a candidate. Although the regular Democrats were fighting to block Senator Kennedy at all turns, he was receiving more support in the wake of the Johnson announcement. His supporters, who felt he might have a better chance without having to face Johnson in his own state, also began to build strength on the precinct level.

Senator Ralph Yarborough, however, made the most direct and vocal challenge. He was encouraged by a large group of supporters and had solid backing in many parts of the state. He promptly challenged the Governor's claim by saying he was "not about to sit idly by" while Connally "poses as the favorite son of Texas Democrats." The Senator then accused him of being disloyal to both the Democrats and to the President's domestic programs, and the Governor fired back by saying that the Senator "doesn't know the meaning of the word *loyalty*."

It sounded like old times among the leadership of the Texas Democratic party.

Suddenly, there was a new club on the scene, posing as a political force, but more probably founded as

an irritant. It was called the "Connally For President—
Locke For Governor Club," and Locke himself told the
Democratic Executive Committee: "The immediate sta-
bility and health of the Texas Democratic party and the
long range interest of our nation will be dramatically
affected by Texas' choice of a favorite son for the presidential nomination. . . . No governor in modern times
has captured the hearts of Texas as has [Connally], nor
has any governor had a more perceptive eye for the needs
of this state."

The rhetoric was slightly short of dazzling, but
Locke's desire to climb aboard the Governor's bandwagon was impressive. If Connally was to be a favorite
son, perhaps Locke could be a favorite stepson.

With the President's declaration still fresh in everyone's mind, Democratic governors began to make plans
for an April meeting in Cincinnati. The gathering was
to be directed at assessing the situation for the upcoming
convention and planning strategy that would solidify
the party. Early indications were that a majority of the
governors opposed the candidacy of Robert Kennedy,
and there were reports that an alternative strategy would
be found. Still, with as many favorite sons as a governors' conference would feature, it was difficult to see
how the party would end up solidified.

Connally, speaking before the conference convened,
denied allying with the Vice President or trying to stop
Kennedy. He did say, however, that he "would like to
see Mr. Humphrey run for the presidential nomination,"
and he added that he could not "conceive of the situation" whereby the Democratic leaders would not find a
candidate to oppose McCarthy and Kennedy.

By the time the conference ended, the governors
had agreed on one thing—that they had been totally unsuccessful in agreeing on any unified position.

The governors adopted a resolution which said that

they would "observe the events of history as they develop in the next month and then reach a decision of conscience" on the Democratic nominee. In other words, the governors did not want to select a candidate, nor did they want to be committed to support any particular candidate. They wanted, as politicians always want, the free second guess. Connally tried a slightly different tack but again failed. He proposed that the governors agree to remain uncommitted for two or three months. The governors, however, preferred flexibility, or else already had made up their individual minds to run as favorite sons or to support an already announced candidate. There was speculation that Connally's suggestion was designed to help Humphrey, who had not yet announced for the presidency.

Humphrey received additional Texas support from Ralph Yarborough, who spoke in complimentary terms about the Vice President on April 16, when he also announced that he would not oppose Connally for control of the state delegation to the Democratic Convention in Chicago in August. The Senator had been urged by the Texas AFL-CIO to drop his challenge to the Governor on the delegation, and instead to seek the number-two spot on a ticket with Humphrey. Yarborough did not mention that at the time, but he spoke highly of Kennedy and McCarthy, along with Humphrey, saying he "needed the help of all three."

Connally returned from Cincinnati to open his pet HemisFair '68 project, and ran into a storm unleashed by his comments on the day after Dr. Martin Luther King, Jr., was assassinated. Connally condemned the act, but was criticized for his opinions of King's social philosophy and style of leadership. The Governor had said:

"This is a sad commentary on the actions and reactions of people in this country today. Much of what

Martin Luther King did and much of what he said many of us could violently disagree with, but none of us should have wished him this kind of fate, because the one thing we have to remember is that we have differences. We have a divergence of views for many, many reasons. He contributed much to the chaos, and the strife, and the confusion and uncertainty in this country, but whatever his actions, he deserved not the fate of assassination."

The Governor's message made headlines, and caused furor, in many areas. He accused the Associated Press of quoting him out of context and called a press conference at HemisFair to reinforce what he had to say. On the second time around, he said, "I said in the speech, as best I remember, that however much some people might feel that Dr. King had contributed to the chaos and confusion, he did not deserve this fate. The entire thrust of the speech was that in these troubled times . . . men and women must exercise a high degree of restraint, that unbridled emotions cannot contribute to lasting solutions."

When a videotape of the original speech was obtained, it revealed that Connally had indeed been quoted correctly by both the Associated Press and the United Press International. In the first talk Connally said, "He [King] contributed much to the chaos," and in the correction the Governor edited things to say, ". . . some people might feel that Dr. King had contributed to the chaos. . . ." The change was unmistakable, and when the Governor was told that he had been quoted correctly, he quietly dropped the issue. The NAACP was not so easily pacified, however, and a field representative in Houston said the Governor "owes the American people an apology for such a dastardly statement" about Dr. King.

Late spring had a firm grip on the state by May 5, when the first Democratic primary was held. Texas law provides that if a single candidate does not receive a clear majority, there will be a runoff between the top two vote-getters. So the first primary came and went and a runoff was set between Don Yarborough, representing the liberals, and Lieutenant Governor Preston Smith, representing the conservative-establishment wing of the party. Eugene Locke, fresh from Vietnam, was a solid fifth, and his defeat was a blow to the Governor's chances of retaining control in the Statehouse. The runoff was set for June 1, when the survivor would receive the opportunity to campaign against Republican candidate Paul Eggers of Wichita Falls.

On the same day another hat was tossed into the presidential ring. Supporters of Governor George Wallace of Alabama, seeking the nomination on the American party ticket, announced that they had collected 14,250 signatures and that their candidate's name would appear on the ballot in November. Wallace had many backers throughout the state, and conservative Democrats feared that his appeal might dilute the strength of their own conservative candidate, since the establishment felt that Smith could handle Yarborough when the next primary came due.

Connally's next task was the meeting of state Democratic delegates in Dallas on June 11, and he was fighting hard to bind all 104 delegates by the unit rule, with all committed to support him as a favorite son. Under the unit rule, a majority decision commits all the delegates, so that as close a vote for Connally as 53 to 51 would give him all 104 votes, no mean number to bargain with in the highly amorphous convention that everyone visualized.

In an effort to block Connally, the state liberals met in May, striving to find some sort of coalition that could challenge him. Unfortunately, the liberal Democrats were divided among Kennedy, McCarthy and Humphrey supporters. All were anti-Connally, and it was extremely difficult for the Humphrey backers to justify their feelings about the Governor, who still was backing the Vice President. Open discord erupted when Hank Brown, state AFL-CIO president, aligned himself with the Humphrey group. Brown, slightly wiser politically than some of the others at the meeting, had offered to join with the liberals if the three groups could unite to oppose Connally as a favorite son and on the unit rule. If successful, they could lead the state convention as a powerful coalition and then try to apportion the delegates among the three candidates. Brown's attempt for unity failed, and Don Allford, the McCarthy leader, seemed especially disturbed that labor would not support his man.

Actually, because of the adamant stands taken by the McCarthy and Kennedy forces, the anti-Connally Humphreyites were almost forced to join the conservative bloc.

The horrible assassination of Robert Kennedy in California only days before several state conventions created chaos among the Democrats. Those few who had carried the Kennedy banner in Texas quickly shuffled close to Connally in a last-ditch effort to be part of a winning campaign.

While the nation mourned, it was business as usual for the professionals, who now needed a new favorite since Kennedy's capture of the Democratic nomination had seemed assured.

Connally and the conservatives rode like Texas Rangers over the liberals and secured the delegation on the unit rule, firmly committed to Connally as a favorite son.

The liberals lost on their challenge of the seating of the delegates and their hands were tied on almost every issue.

They were heard on two counts.

"We want the nation to know that John Connally is no favorite son for all of us," said Mrs. Billie Carr, one of the leaders of the liberal group.

"In order for the party to represent the people, it has to represent not just the majority," said Lee Smith, another of the leaders.

The liberals resolved to challenge the unit rule in the courts and also to take the issue before the National Democratic Committee. The challenge was largely based on the U.S. Supreme Court's one-man-one-vote concept and how it was to affect political parties in their apportionment of delegations among competing candidates rather than allowing the majority, however slim, to have all the delegates.

As the summer grew hotter, George Wallace began to show more strength in Texas. Even Connally took notice, with a July 23 comment in Cincinnati that Wallace's support was "still growing. He's becoming more and more a factor." In an effort to blunt the Wallace attack, Connally said that he had advised Humphrey to pursue the "law and order" approach, since that seemed to be a key factor in Wallace's popularity. Texas House Speaker Ben Barnes, the Connally protégé, said the same thing in a meeting with Southern legislators. Barnes said that Humphrey could lose the South to Wallace if he were not strong on that platform.

Connally also took the time to comment on possible Democratic vice-presidential candidates. He was dubious about the abilities of Senator Edward Kennedy to handle the office of President, and he doubted that the Senator would really be an asset to a Democratic ticket.

"Many politicians and the press," said Connally, "have created the illusion, incorrectly I think, that the Vice President [Humphrey] might need a liberal on the ticket, someone with views that would appeal to the liberals." Connally felt that the candidate should be "someone of more moderate views perhaps than his own," though he did not elaborate on moderation. He did, however, deny any personal aspirations for the office.

On August 9 Senator Yarborough endorsed the candidacy of Senator Eugene McCarthy.

The next day Vice President Humphrey arrived in Texas. He was met in San Antonio by the Governor, and the two men toured the HemisFair. While Humphrey was trying to please all factions among Texas voters, he made the mistake of appearing in a Mexican-American area with Connally, still unpopular among that minority. A picket in the San Antonio crowd held aloft a sign that read, "Any friend of Connally is no friend of the Mexican-American."

Still, Humphrey was generally received with warmth by the Mexican-Americans, with a laudatory introduction by the Mexican-American Congressman Henry B. Gonzalez of San Antonio doing a lot to mollify a crowd of some 3,000 persons.

With the Democratic Convention ready to open in Chicago, Connally was described as "unhappy and sometimes even angry at the way everything was going." The way things were going was away from his friend Lyndon Johnson. It was evident that there was going to be dissent about Vietnam, dissent about the unit rule, dissent about a lot of things. Large gatherings of young people were arriving in Chicago, too, and it looked as if it were going to be a difficult convention. Connally was extremely defensive about the possibility of attacks on the unit rule, terming it "the very essence of pure democracy" when he was interviewed at the convention site.

Vice President Humphrey arrived in Chicago like a man on a tightrope, with Northern liberals growling on one side, Southern conservatives snarling on the other. It was going to be a difficult period for Humphrey, and his peace of mind was not eased by his boss, President Johnson. The latter had not given his Vice President much feeling of political security. In fact, when Humphrey told the President of his decision to run, Johnson reportedly said he was not surprised, but that the Vice President couldn't count on too much support because he was going to remain neutral "in order to devote all his time to ending the war."

National problems were compounded on August 22 when the Soviet Army invaded Czechoslovakia. An air of international crisis mixed with the already-present feeling of domestic tension. It was obviously not going to be a time to unite the Democratic party, no matter what leadership could be found. The President himself, following a meeting with the National Security Council over the Czechoslovakian situation, reportedly reprimanded Humphrey for his "inadequacy as presidential timber, charged him with being too soft on foreign policy, with leaning over backward to placate Eugene McCarthy's doves, and accused him of stretching the patriotism of John Connally and the Southern delegates to the limit."

Besides this obvious problem, Humphrey also was in an extremely delicate position on the unit rule. He needed to convince Northern liberals that he advocated its abolition while avoiding giving the appearance that he was breaking a pledge he already had given to Connally. He could only balance this compromise with the acceptance of the language in the Vietnam plank of the platform. It supported the position of the Johnson Administration, which Humphrey did not back, but the support was necessary to elicit any aid whatsoever from Johnson's cohorts.

Ironically, party debate on the Vietnam plank took

place the day after the invasion of Czechoslovakia. Connally emerged as a leading advocate of the Administration position, and at the same time he fought to belittle any candidates whose positions were in opposition to that of the President. Connally deplored the actions of McCarthy and Senator George McGovern. He urged the Platform Committee to "write a plank denouncing not our actions, but denouncing Communist aggression in South Vietnam, Czechoslovakia and anywhere else in the world."

When the peace-oriented wing suggested seeking cessation of the bombing of North Vietnam, cessation of aggressive combat action, reduction of American and Allied troops, peace negotiations and formulation of a coalition government, Connally responded by saying, "Let us assume for a moment that we follow these courses of appeasement and surrender. . . . What assurance do we have that any or all of these steps would result in anything other than North Vietnam sending additional troops, men, ammunition into South Vietnam in order to make a complete takeover?"

Connally's bitter denunciation of McCarthy followed the Senator's reaction to the Czechoslovakia invasion and his criticism of the President's convening of the National Security Council to discuss it. McCarthy also had been extremely critical of the Vietnam war policies, and the Governor went to work on him:

"Senator McCarthy's reaction to the Russian invasion is, in my personal judgment, a deplorable circumstance. . . . It is beyond any question that utterances such as these cannot do anything but hinder the negotiations which we have had under way for several months in Paris with North Vietnam.

"I would not request to appear before this committee in order to make a personal attack upon Senator McCarthy or Senator McGovern. . . . We should recognize certain very basic things and deal with them in general terms. This nation is the leader of the free people and those who hope to be free."

Connally even insinuated that those who dissented over the Vietnam war policy were doing so for their own political gain among the discontents and added, "These are strong words, I know, but these are times for strong words. The cause of peace should not be used as a vehicle for political favor or fortune. The cause of peace is not the personal property of any politician or political party."

The cause of war, however, might be something else again. Raymond, Morris, Knudson, Brown, Root and Jones, the Texas-based construction firm, had been working under Government contract in Southeast Asia for the previous seven years. The *Texas Observer* had looked into the situation with jaundiced eye, observing that the company's fortunes had "improved parallel to the political rise of Lyndon Johnson" and that it had had $1.4 billion in Government contracts. Senator Abraham Ribicoff of Connecticut had commented on the company, too, noting that it displayed large and un-traceable amounts of wasted funds because of "ineffi-ciency, dishonesty, corruption and foolishness."

When Connally had finished his speech, Pierre Salinger, onetime press secretary to President Kennedy, attending the Chicago convention as a delegate from California, said that the Governor had "practically called Senators McCarthy and McGovern traitors" and de-nounced Connally for resorting to "old-type Joe Mc-Carthyism."

The convention had barely started, and the battle lines were not only drawn, they were being hardened as rapidly as possible.

Connally's urging that the committee "support the determined fight of this Administration to preserve not only our own freedom, but to help provide the opportunity for freedom for peoples everywhere" was given impetus by the recent events in Europe and the Governor was cheered by most of the committee.

The majority plank, finally adopted by the vote of 1567¾ to 1041¼, called for the United States to negotiate with Hanoi "an immediate end or limitation of hostilities and the withdrawal from South Vietnam of all foreign forces—both United States and Allied forces and forces infiltrated from North Vietnam." It also included the American intention to work toward insuring "self-determination for the Vietnamese," which in itself was an area of contention between the Administration policy and the dissenting platform, which had no provision for peace talks.

The plank was the subject of lengthy debate on the convention floor, and the vote was extremely close until Connally stood tall and announced with triumph a solid bloc of 104 Texas votes for the majority report. The Governor had requested that the entire delegation vote together, and even if the unit rule had not been in force, the vote would have been 101 to 3. The three dissenters were visited personally by former Governor Price Daniel, who said that "the President had made a personal request that each Texas delegate vote for the majority report." Daniel also told the delegates that the entire group would be polled if the minority report lost by only a few votes. In that case, he assured them, they could change their vote. So the trio voted with the delegation as a unit and then tried hard to offer one another support in the upcoming battle for the nomination of their candidate, Senator McCarthy.

The vote had brought loud, out-of-tune and divergent demonstrations from the delegates as "Stop the War, Stop the War" battled to be heard against choruses of "Off We Go, Into the Wild Blue Yonder." Amidst the chaos, Connally personally thanked the three delegates who voted with the group and added, "The President will appreciate it."

The plank in the Democratic platform was far more than just an influence over foreign policy in the years to come, for whatever Democratic candidate was to be elected. It was a vote of confidence for the President and the Vice President. It was a decision on a question of principle, and it drew a violent and emotional response to the Vietnam war and the values it represented.

The adoption of the majority plank on Vietnam left a lot of open wounds, both inside and outside the convention hall and all around the country. The Harrisburg, Pennsylvania, *Patriot,* for example, asked, "If the administration gave us solemn assurance that the bombing would stanch the flow of men and supplies from the north, and Secretary of Defense Clark Clifford as well as Robert McNamara admit that the bombing does not really reduce North Vietnamese movements to the south, then what sense does it make to invest further in a bankrupt policy?"

Next arrival at the barricades was the issue of the unit rule, a situation that had inflamed minority Texans in the spring. Tempers had not eased.

The Rules Committee endorsed the "freedom of conscience" rule, entitling a state to use the unit rule but stating that the system would not be enforced if there were any delegates who protested. While it still awaited approval by the entire convention, the rule would unbind the Texas delegation. This was a matter of grave concern to Connally and his backers. They wanted and needed that bloc of 104 votes which they could wield with strength, and they were willing to fight for them.

Texas liberals had been sufficiently inflamed by the unit rule that they gathered a challenge delegation to appear before the Credentials Committee. The committee voted, 128 to 23, to seat the regular delegation, but it first had to listen to a brief that accused the Connally delegation of being "month of May Democrats" who turn Republican in November. It also stated that the liberal minority had been effectively disenfranchised by the unit rule and that the Connally Democrats had short-changed minority groups.

The ruling of the Credentials Committee did not stop the challengers. They termed themselves "Texas Democrats for an Open Convention—TDOC" and they went to work to gather petitions to bring their challenge to the floor as a minority report. They easily obtained the necessary signatures, along with promises of support from such liberal-laden delegations as New York and California. The Texans hoped that another state would second their motion for a minority position, thus insuring that their challenge be regarded as a "national issue."

With their foot strongly inside the door of the convention hall, the TDOC delegation challenged the Connally forces, claiming that they deserved seating on a racial basis. They recognized that this issue had legal grounds as well as strong popular appeal with the liberals at the convention. One of the TDOC leaders displayed affidavits by seventeen black precinct leaders whose requests to be on Connally's delegation had been denied.

The Governor, of course, opposed the liberal Texas group. An open convention is anathema to old-line politicians who prefer smoke-filled rooms and dark corners in which to make their deals. Connally's original argument, when the unit rule had been challenged in Texas, ran that "the unit rule has been a recognized, accepted, honored and enforced parliamentary device in Democratic party politics since 1948." He added, "There is absolutely no requirement, suggestion or 'hint' in the statutes of Texas or the Democratic party that the majority of a political convention must give the minority any representation on the convention committees, its offices, its platform or its delegates to a subsequent convention. . . ."

Committeeman Frank Erwin, a strong Connally and Johnson supporter, said in Chicago, "Relying on the unit rule, trying to unite our party in Texas, trying to prepare for November, we placed some delegates on this delegation who aren't for John Connally for favorite son." There may have been a hint of a tear in his eye as he went on, "We put them on there . . . because we knew that under the unit rule we could control how the votes at this convention would be cast. . . . If the unit rule was not going to be enforced, we would not have made that mistake."

Roy Orr, a regular delegate from the twenty-third district, added with ingenuous honesty, "The governor didn't want anyone on this [delegate] list who was not 100 percent pro-Connally."

Erwin, in his largesse, was perfectly willing to have a handful of non-Connally supporters on the delegation, but they were going to be bound to vote for the Governor, whether they wanted to or not.

Maury Maverick, counsel for the Texas Democrats for an Open Convention, denounced the unit rule, not because it opposed majority rule, but because "what we are against is having the alleged majority converted into a unanimous vote by hocus pocus, if not by pure force." The insurgents maintained that the majority should not use the unit rule to camouflage or to destroy disagreement within a single delegation.

The power of John Connally and his people through the unit rule is easily demonstrated. Nine states arrived at the Chicago convention bound by the unit rule. They totaled 415 of the 2622 votes at the convention. One state, Texas, had a shade over one fourth of those votes.

The TDOC kept fighting, claiming that blacks and Mexican-Americans were represented at a proportion that was far less than the strength of their Democratic voting power within the state. The Governor, of course, disagreed with fervor and patriotism, denying that there had been "one instance in recent history whereby a duly registered voter was denied the right and opportunity to participate in Democratic party affairs because of his race, color, creed or national origin."

Hank Brown, the Texas AFL-CIO president, fired back that "the bodies [of blacks and Mexican-Americans] were there [on the Connally delegation] but they were John Connally types for the most part." State Representative Curtis Graves, a black supporter of the rump group, said that only two of the six blacks were elected at the precinct level. The others, chosen by Connally, were "hand-picked, pledged 'Toms,' who guaranteed they'd shut up and wouldn't rock the boat."

Connally, never one to shy from a fight, reproached the challengers as "almost completely without merit." He defended his delegation, boasting of the state's seventeen black delegates and alternates, a number he had assumed was greater than in any other delegation except Michigan. Later—too late, of course, to be of any use—it was discovered that, in terms of racial composition, three states had more black delegates and nine had more delegates and alternates.

Things by now were getting touchy for the Texas establishment and its leader, John Connally. The battle over the Vietnam plank, followed by the strong efforts to abolish the unit rule and its resulting challenge of Connally's tightly controlled delegation, was causing pouts, if not panic, among the latter. In traditional Southern political style, there were rumors of a rebellion, of a walkout. The regular, old-line party members were alarmed over the events of the previous two days. They got no reassurances from Hubert Humphrey either, who continued to vacillate on both issues.

The situation so alarmed committeeman Frank Erwin that he felt it was time for some power politics, even brinkmanship. Claiming concurrence from Connally, Erwin said that if the unit rule were abolished, there would then be "a growing sentiment among those of us here in Chicago that Governor Connally should withdraw as a favorite son and we should nominate another great Texan who occupies the highest office in the land."

It was obviously time to play the trump card, to call for the President to reconsider his decision of March 31 and seek—or at least accept—the nomination. Erwin made his announcement on August 23, while preliminary business still was in order. Two days later, after there had been sufficient time for logical and coolheaded discussion and reflection, Connally squelched the draft-Johnson movement with the statement, "It is not in accord with his wishes, and we are not here to promote a draft."

Connally also said he intended to keep his delegates pledged to him until he himself decided to release them, a move which was pending the decision concerning the abolition of the unit rule.

Reports persisted that President Johnson had notified Erwin that he was most concerned over the Vietnam plank and that the party should work toward it, since it was strong support of his position. When that plank was approved, another draft-Johnson move arose, but this one came from the opposite end of the political spectrum and perhaps was offered more as a sardonic statement than as a real intention. William Vanderhooven, McGovern's campaign manager, and Richard Goodwin, a key worker in the McCarthy organization, announced on television that they would renominate President Johnson if his war policy was included in the platform.

"It's his platform," said Vanderhooven. "Let him run on it."

The two men, following their television statement, informed the Texas delegation. Connally promptly told them that if they tried to do it, he would have Alabama or Alaska yield to Texas, putting that state in control of the nominating speeches so that Texas would be able to remove the President's name from the list.

Regardless of how serious the threat by Goodwin and Vanderhooven might have been, Johnson never was nominated.

The floor challenge from the rival Texas delegation for seating was scheduled for August 26, despite a motion to delay the conflict over credentials to the following day. The preliminary motion, made by Jesse Unruh, speaker of the California House, was defeated, 1691½ to 875½, and speakers from the opposing sides each were given fifteen minutes to discuss their case. Appeals that the "regular Democratic party of Texas had deliberately excluded Mexican-Americans and blacks from the delegation" were teamed with the anticipation that this delegate challenge would demonstrate that the new Democratic party was "ready to deal with Mexican-Americans throughout the Southwest."

Chairman Will Davis took a far narrower and more traditional approach as he defended the position of the Texas delegation. He simply explained that "the opposition got beat, got beat badly. We have two groups in Texas, the ins and the outs. The ins want to stay in and the outs want to get in. You've heard from the outs. Now you're going to hear from the ins."

TDOC supporters booed loudly, but the minority

report was defeated, 1368 to 955, upholding the credentials of the regular delegation to be seated on the floor of the convention.

Still, the vote represented a number of larger issues, and a promise for the future.

Senator Yarborough described the close vote as "a great moral victory." The liberals, predominantly supporters of McCarthy, did not get their seats in Texas, or in Georgia or Alabama, which also had challenges, but there were signs that the principles of proportional representation among minorities were moving toward becoming party doctrine. The Credentials Committee voted to present the convention with a request for "sweeping rules changes" and for a standing committee to help establish guidelines and state cooperation. The committee decided to leave the process of delegate selection open to challenge at every convention, that the unit rule be reexamined or abolished at all levels of delegate selection and that hand picking of delegates by party leaders be outlawed.

The day of decision also gave some indications of Vice President Humphrey's support against that of Senator McCarthy. The Vice President himself said that he would have "supported the majority position on the Texas case. There isn't any doubt about that." The Southern states were joined by Humphrey's strong supporters in Pennsylvania and Michigan to bring about victory for Connally and the Texas establishment. Strong McCarthy states like New York and California gave almost unanimous support to the TDOC. Texas AFL-CIO president Brown, a strong, if lone voice, said that he, though an anti-Connally delegate, would have upheld the regular delegation and the unit rule so that strength for Humphrey would not have been diminished. The reasons for the decisions of politicians come in wondrous ways.

The TDOC, beaten on all fronts, remained in Chicago to support other liberal causes and to express their anger against Connally. They distributed flyers in the lobbies of hotels where delegates were staying, passing on information about the Governor's confrontation with the Mexican-American farm workers on their way to the Statehouse, his position on the minimum wage, poverty programs and other legislation pushed hard by liberals round the country, and of course his comments about Dr. Martin Luther King on the day of his assassination.

Another major battle was yet to reach the Texas delegation. With all the delegates bound to Connally on the first ballot, outright support for Humphrey was slow to appear. Texas regulars were not too enthusiastic about him anyway, especially since he had promised Connally that he would oppose any abolition of the unit rule. When a letter was circulated that indicated the Vice President now favored the discarding of the unit role, a lot of explanation was due the Texas delegation. Connally accused Humphrey of "ignoring" the Texas delegates, and there were apologies and recriminations from both sides. Humphrey had offered some vague support for suspension of the unit rule in 1968 and had recommended abandonment in 1972. His staff, however, moved rapidly, if weakly, to move the Vice President out of this morass by saying that Humphrey, "very tired, had signed the letter without reading it and without realizing its implications."

Connally had been a speculative subject as a possible vice-presidential candidate ever since Humphrey had announced his candidacy on April 14. The Texan clearly had political ambitions, but he refrained from any active—or at least publicly active—endeavors in that direction. But even speculation about Connally was having its effect on Humphrey. He asked Senator Walter

Mondale of Minnesota to be his campaign manager, but Mondale was reluctant to take the post, both because of his poor estimation of Humphrey's chances of nomination and because he was disturbed over the fact that Connally might become a vice-presidential candidate. Humphrey, however, assured Mondale that it was not his intention to ally with Connally.

By July, the liberal *Texas Observer* was hinting that Connally was eyeing the position, or that, perhaps, the position was eyeing him. Connally already had suggested to Humphrey that he include a moderate on the ticket, someone more moderate than the Vice President, but Connally also saw no reason for choosing a liberal, especially Edward Kennedy. And, of course, there was always the speculation that President Johnson was interested in having Connally in the office so that he could keep his own interests in the White House.

As the convention slowly proceeded, Humphrey was the obvious front-runner, and more obviously began to show that he was the only candidate behind whom the party could show any semblance of unity. Still, he was not very satisfactory to many of the influential factions that were battling through Chicago. Mayor Richard Daley of that city, who was not interested in McCarthy and not confident in Humphrey, began to lead a surge toward Kennedy, whose presence was a real threat to Humphrey. Apparently he was a threat to Lyndon Johnson, too, because the President began to move. His influence showed strongly as Southern states, led by Connally and Texas, began to solidify in Humphrey's corner. The Vice President held the support by his pledges to both the unit rule and the administration war policies.

On Tuesday, August 27, Connally, along with Governors Buford Ellington of Tennessee and Robert McNair of South Carolina, withdrew their names as favorite sons and put their delegations behind the Vice President. Later that evening, Senator Kennedy made a number of telephone calls to people at the convention, telling them he would not be a candidate. The nomination was assured.

During the balloting, there were two dissenting Texas votes, one for Senator McCarthy and one for the Reverend Channing Phillips of Washington, D.C. Apparently Connally and Erwin instituted "freedom'of conscience" and did not ask the entire delegation to vote as a bloc. It was an easy and generous, and an obviously politically motivated, move since Humphrey was locked in by that time.

The unit rule itself was dead, having been abolished by voice vote, with six of the Texas delegation joining the majority. Ironically, the pre-vote debate pointed out the fact that unit rule had first been initiated in Texas in 1831, and that it was about to be abolished on a Texas challenge.

The action was momentous and changed the structure of the political system in a real way. It also increased friction between conservatives and liberals all the way down the line. In the future, conservatives and the power structure vowed, they would be far more careful in their selection of delegates so as to avoid dissent. The liberals, on the other hand, cheered the end of the rule and said that it presaged more debate, more open conventions and more opportunities for them to challenge the power structure right out in public.

Connally continued to show some power in the choice of a running mate for Humphrey, though he himself was not considered by the Vice President, nor did President Johnson show a real interest in having his old Texas crony on the ticket. An August 30 poll revealed that Senator Kennedy was the favorite choice, with Connally desired by 12 percent of the Democrats and 11 percent of the independents.

Humphrey himself narrowed his choices to three senators, Fred Harris of Oklahoma, Edmund Muskie of Maine and Richard Hughes of New Jersey. It was time for Connally to make one last move. He led a delegation of Southern governors to a visit with the Vice President at one-thirty in the morning and they insisted that Hughes be dropped from further consideration. Humphrey agreed.

Southern Republican governors had made a similar move in insisting that Richard Nixon drop any consideration of liberal Republican John Lindsay, then flourishing as mayor of New York, as a running mate.

The final choice of Muskie was considered acceptable to all, which meant that while no one actively hated him, no one actually loved him, either. Connally's comment was probably the opinion of many people, both in and out of politics: "I don't think anyone knows him in Texas. I don't think it will affect us one way or the other."

The 1968 Democratic Convention was more than floor fights, credential challenges, the Vietnam plank and the unit rule inside the building. It was a week of clamor in the streets, when student demonstrators of all shades of political leaning were facing Chicago police in open combat, and a nation, watching on television, was shocked by what was going on. The blood that flowed across the screen was real blood, and the beatings were real beatings, and there was not a Hollywood stunt man to be seen.

The Texas delegation, backing the establishment wherever it appeared, left for home displaying pro-Daley stickers to indicate that they felt "the Chicago mayor and his police treated demonstrators as they deserved." Connally assessed the situation by saying, "I must say the almost overwhelming charges of police brutality are not quite fair. Several thousand demonstrators tried to take over the hotel and under those circumstances, the police have to use force."

Although the convention had left many persons bruised and bitter, both inside and out, there still was unity to be displayed, a campaign to be run and elections on all levels to be won.

Humphrey sought the help of several Texans, including Congressman Jim Wright, who had served on the Rules Committee, and young Ben Barnes. Humphrey sought Wright for assistance on the national level and he was interested in Barnes as state campaign coordinator. Connally, in giving casual advice to the candidate, suggested that his campaign managers not be involved in their own election campaigns so as not to divide their energies, though he was interested in Barnes's acceptance of the Humphrey offer even though Barnes was a candidate for lieutenant governor of Texas. It also was decided that the various factions of Texas Democrats would manage their own campaigns because of the divisiveness between the liberal and conservative wings. Along with that, however, was a feeling that the liberals would work much harder in a Humphrey election fight because of strong support from labor ranks.

One of the first steps in running a campaign is to raise money—lots of money. Texas oilmen have been a starting place in many campaigns, and members of the Humphrey campaign team and members of the Democratic National Committee met with a group of oilmen at the Houston Petroleum Club. The first question from the oil barons was about the depletion allowances, a special tax loophole that oil, gas and hard mineral people have maintained for many years. The candidate, however, had been a strong opponent of depletion allowances, and his aides knew it. When they admitted they could make no promises, the oilmen admitted they could make no gifts or loans to help run the campaign.

Neither Connally nor Lyndon Johnson appeared to offer much help to the Democratic candidate, even in their own state. Bob Short, a Humphrey fund raiser, went to Austin to meet with Connally and discuss a series of fund-raising dinners, a standard method of obtaining money for politicians. Afterward, Short said, "We decided it wouldn't do any good to have a dinner in Texas because we just couldn't get any cooperation from Connally." Short also felt that the President "never used the power of his office to help us. We got damn little money from Texas. I don't think the word had been passed from on high."

Another controversy arose over the use of some $700,000, raised through a 1965 Democratic party advertising book. Johnson did not release those funds for Humphrey's campaign, amid rising speculation that the President was using punishment by denial, especially after Humphrey spoke out in disagreement—very slight disagreement, but enough—with the President's Vietnam policy.

September was a bleak month for Hubert Humphrey, practically ostracized by his own party. He arrived in Texas on September 11, and Connally turned down an invitation to campaign with the candidate in Houston. Preston Smith, the Texas gubernatorial candidate, was too busy with his own race to meet with Humphrey, and Connally remained at his ranch, failing to see Humphrey at all. The snub was so obvious that it may have been a cause for a Humphrey statement that irritated the President. The candidate said, while in Texas, that "troops already were being pulled out [of Vietnam], that probably they would continue to be pulled out later this year and in 1969." Johnson immediately called Humphrey on the carpet, questioning him on his sources, belittling him on his predictions, reminding him that only Secretary of State Clark Clifford was supposed to make such statements and sarcastically informing him that the troops being pulled out were merely a temporarily assigned marine regiment.

Only Ben Barnes showed any loyalty to his party during the month of September. The young candidate for lieutenant governor publicly encouraged support for the Humphrey-Muskie ticket. Other Texas Democrats avoided the subject as if it would produce hives. They campaigned vigorously for themselves and some of their associates and spoke broadly of the Democratic ticket without mention of the presidential candidate.

Texas was not alone in its attitude toward Humphrey. When the candidate reached California, he was avoided by Jesse Unruh. When he got to Connecticut, he was avoided by Abraham Ribicoff. When he reached Massachusetts, on September 19, he was shouted down by college students, and Ted Kennedy, sharing the platform, shared the boos. It finally became too much for Humphrey. When he stood with another liberal Senator, George McGovern, to receive his endorsement while students shouted angrily, Humphrey finally reached the point of anger. "Look at their faces," he said, "filled with hatred, bitterness, bigotry. Look at their faces, filled with violence. They will never live long enough to run us off the platform because basically they are just cowards."

September was the winter of discontent for Hubert Humphrey. Shunned by party regulars, attacked by students, he was facing an apathetic public and a more apathetic group of fund raisers. Neither money nor support was visible, while the polls showed Richard Nixon leading, 43 to 28 percent. The firebrand independent, Gov. George Wallace, had a substantial following of 21 percent.

It became obvious to the candidate that he had to do something, and the Minnesotan did. He revised his own position on the Vietnam war to one that was not offensive, not constricted by the Administration policies and one that could be a sign of encouragement to those who opposed the war. As Humphrey said, "I don't care who it pleases, I'm going to write this speech the way I want it, and if people don't like the speech, that's the way it's going to be."

Humphrey's moment came on September 30, in his speech from Salt Lake City. He spoke strongly, presenting a three-point program where he "would risk a complete bombing halt in the interests of peace, and then see what response might develop, reserving the right to resume bombing if no such response was clear." It was a long way from his earlier statements in which he attempted "to signal a desire to end the bombing, yet simultaneously not yield entirely to the enemy in the first stage of negotiations."

The candidate had called the President before the speech to alert him to the statement and had assured the President that he was not straying far from the Administration position. It was not enough for Lyndon Johnson, for whom the war had become a violent crusade. Johnson was not happy with the speech and he showed his dissatisfaction shortly afterward. Two Humphrey workers visited the President to seek his help in border state campaigns, and they were told, "You know that Nixon is following my policies more closely than Humphrey."

Still, Salt Lake City was a turning point for Humphrey. The Democratic National Committee, desperate even for the funds to televise the speech, suddenly found money coming in. The atmosphere changed rapidly and markedly. Student protesters subdued their anger and some even expressed some faith in the candidate. The McCarthy organization and other liberal and reform groups openly endorsed his candidacy. The public responded strongly and, by the next Gallup Poll, he trailed Nixon by only 5 percentage points (35 versus 40). Press comment was largely favorable, and enough money came in so that television appearances were guaranteed right up to Election Day.

Even Connally finally got around to a public endorsement of Humphrey on October 18, and even more strangely, he offered to introduce Senator Ralph Yarborough to the candidate when he made his return visit to Texas. Why Humphrey and Yarborough had not campaigned together the first time is a strange and unanswered question. Texas labor was solidly behind Yarborough; national labor was strongly behind Humphrey. Senator Ribicoff of Connecticut joined the fold the next day as Humphrey support grew.

While Connally was speaking for Humphrey on one side, he also had been privately helping Nixon, recruiting a number of influential Texans, members of both parties, to work for the Republican candidate. It was a forecast of things to come.

When Humphrey returned to Texas on October 22, both Connally and Yarborough were at the Fort Worth airport to meet him. Lady Bird Johnson also appeared at a Humphrey rally later in the day in Dallas, and the crowds were large and enthusiastic.

Two days later Connally guided Humphrey through the state, accompanying him at many rallies and meetings. Congressman Henry Gonzalez headed a fine crowd of Mexican-Americans in rallies in San Antonio, including one at that most hallowed shrine in Texas, the Alamo.

Yarborough spoke with enthusiasm, adding, "We have never in twenty-four years had as united a Democratic party as we've got today." The togetherness lasted through the month. Muskie arrived in Texas on October 29, accompanied by Yarborough, and while Connally pleaded "prior commitments and the press of business" as reasons for his absence, he sent telegrams promoting the entire ticket, especially the top two men, and insisted they be read at the various meetings.

On November 1, with the election right around the corner, Connally spoke in Fort Worth and referred to Humphrey as "a man of candor . . . a man of courage. . . a man who is a fighter . . . a man who speaks his convictions even though they may be unpopular."

Humphrey fever rose throughout the country, and indeed many experts feel that if the campaign had lasted another fortnight, the results might have been different. Strength grew for the Democrat in New York, Pennsylvania and Ohio, all following the strong lead from Texas. President Johnson leaped to the side of the Vice President, perhaps hoping for some of the overflow of support, and joined him at a mammoth rally in Houston's Astrodome.

It was enough.

Humphrey won Texas, though by the very narrow margin of 39,000 votes out of a total of 3,100,000 cast in the state. The last few weeks of solid support had done it; the vote reflected one of the few occasions in Texas political history when liberals and conservatives reached a temporary peace. Connally had been privately welcomed by Nixon's supporters, and Yarborough had originally endorsed both Robert Kennedy and Eugene McCarthy.

Where Texas fell short was in fund raising. Reports were that Democratic leaders raised less than 10 percent of the amount collected for Lyndon Johnson in 1964, and that the disparity should not have been so great. In addition, Texas was the only Southern state to go to the Democratic side, supporting, for the first time since 1924, a losing presidential candidate.

On the Texas level, Preston Smith was elected Governor and all statewide offices went to the Democrats. The Legislature was maintained as a one-party structure, with the Democrats holding at one time a crushing 148–2 edge in the House, 29–2 in the Senate.

Connally himself announced that when his term expired in January, he would join the prestigious law firm of Vinson, Elkins and Searls. The Governor's own name would be added to the door of the Houston firm, and the new structure would be Vinson, Elkins, Searls and Connally.

There was more than just a legal partnership, however, in the offing for Connally. He was named a director of Texas Instruments, Inc., on November 27 and, as a post-Christmas gift, became a director of the Gibraltar Savings Association on December 29.

In 1969 public citizen John Connally returned to private life. Big John's doings appeared seldom in the press for the short period after he left the Governor's Mansion and returned to the lucrative but relatively routine practice of law in Houston.

If his name appeared at all, it was as a new member of a board of trustees or a board of directors of a usually expanding business or banking firm. For example, on February 14 the multimillion-dollar Halliburton Company announced the election of John Connally to its board of directors. Halliburton provided extensive and expensive oilfield services and owned a research subsidiary that manufactured explosive devices in Arlington, Texas. The Brown and Root Construction Company was a key subsidiary of Halliburton Company. Only a few devout Connally watchers remembered that Big John had been a Brown and Root supporter against the Texas unions in the 1950's. Connally had remained an unofficial corporate adviser while Governor and now it was reward time. Big John has been accused of chasing corporate directorships the way lesser men pursue women.

Meanwhile, back at the ranch, the political prophets were second-guessing Connally's next move in their arena. Election manipulation and projection is the favorite "Monopoly" game in the Lone Star State. The late columnist Drew Pearson in *The Nation* once said that Big John would run against Ralph Yarborough in the Texas senatorial primary to promote himself for the 1972 Democratic presidential nomination. Pearson's position was endorsed by political writers in New York and Dallas despite regular Connally denials. Pearson and his then unpublicized aide, Jack Anderson, also said Connally's unofficial campaign manager would be Lyndon B. Johnson.

But Big John wouldn't admit to any political plans, though in "imagining" a possible contest between himself and Yarborough, Connally said, "You never know what a man is going to do. I don't want to be coy or evasive. You never know what you are going to do." Connally also claimed to be happy "leading the private life of a Houston lawyer."

On December 9 John Connally was elected a trustee of the United States Trust Company of New York.

The year 1970 was another important election year for Texas, and the new political rivalry ignited. Senator Yarborough's campaign for reelection to the Senate meant both an intraparty fight and a battle with the Republicans. His Democratic opponent was not Connally but a lesser known politician, Lloyd Bentsen, who apparently was supported by Big John. Senator Yarborough accused Connally of "running by proxy" through Bentsen. The incumbent liberal Senator said, "I read in the papers that one of them [Bentsen] is Connally's man and the other [George Bush, Republican candidate for the Senate] is Nixon's man. Friends in Houston tell me they belong to the same club and spent a lot of time conferring there before they got into the race."

Bentsen's appointed campaign director, Austin business executive John Mobley, was John Connally's former executive assistant. Bentsen's father, who owned several banks in the Rio Grande Valley, was using his influence by leaning on prominent Texans for contributions to his son's campaign; most of the key financial backers had also paid for Connally's successful gubernatorial campaign.

Connally attacked Senator Yarborough for having criticized LBJ's war effort after having supported the Administration's policy in earlier years. But Big John had arranged for former President Johnson to avoid involvement in the campaign—or so he thought; and in an effort to avoid appearing too much involved in the anti-Yarborough campaign himself, Connally kept busy with speaking engagements about his favorite subjects, oil and money.

Connally lectured to the twenty-first annual Institute on Oil and Gas Law and Taxation at the Southwestern Legal Center in Dallas on February 4, 1970. He avoided political questions and discussed the federal regulation of operations on submerged lands. He elaborated on the responsibility of the operator for non-intentional pollutants. "I am disturbed," he said, "by the idea that an operator who conducts his operations in a non-negligent manner but who nevertheless causes harmful pollution can be held liable for the cost of cleanup."

The oil barons loved this, but the Texas consumer groups were outraged. They felt Connally had sold them out despite the fact that many of them had supported him because of his early ties with President Kennedy.

By May the state primary campaigns were getting more intense. Although John Connally was not personally running for any office, the family name had not disappeared from the ballot. His brother, State Senator Wayne W. Connally, another LBJ crony, was facing a serious challenge by a Mexican-American, Erasmo Andrade.

With the increasing vote of minorities in Texas, Andrade hoped to get enough support to win in the primaries. He argued to the poor whites and Chicanos that Senator Connally had voted "against a minimum wage law, against a raise for teachers and in favor of a sales tax on food." He linked the Connally brothers together as anti-poor.

But more than anything else at that moment John Connally, private citizen, was frustrated. After having reached minor martyrdom via the Kennedy tragedy and serving an unexpected three terms as Governor, Big John was bored with his non-public career. The law firm was making more money for the tall Texan than he ever imagined he would see. His personal investments were going well, and America's leading corporations were competing for his services, either as a lawyer or as a director. Yet he missed the clamor of the media and the power of position.

John Connally was, in fact, at a turning point. He had pushed his way to the top of Texas politics and been able to influence elections from councilman to Congressman.

He walked with presidents of nations and billion-dollar corporations. He had picked up an ulcer, a flurry of rumors about his personal life, a medium-sized fortune and a small but near-fanatic fan club. If he was ever to move to the highest plateau of Government service, he would have to begin now. It would mean sacrifice, discipline and some luck. Big John believes that with the first two you can make your own luck.

John B. Connally and some faithful political allies—the first dollar bills bearing his signature as Secretary of the Treasury. April 20, 1971. *Credit: United Press International Photo.*

[6]

Nixon's Economic Guru

I came in as a Democrat and I'll leave as a Democrat.

SECRETARY JOHN B. CONNALLY, JR.

Richard Nixon is the ultimate partisan. He has never hesitated to proclaim his views with respect to political patronage, its values and its aims. Throughout his Checkered career, Nixon has argued strongly for the right of any President of the United States to appoint only those who share his philosophies to the Supreme Court, the Cabinet and major ambassadorships.

But even a one-party thinker, perhaps especially a one-party thinker, like Richard Nixon knows and understands the realities of political life. There must be some token representation at various administrative levels of the opposition, regardless of its loyalty. The solution of such potential presidential problems is to appoint these representatives in areas where they can be closely watched and exposed much more conveniently to failure than to success. So when Nixon promised in his campaign to have a bipartisan Cabinet, it was interpreted by most political observers to mean that he would give a second-echelon administrative job to the most conservative Democrat he could find, who he hoped would be opportunistic or ingenuous enough to accept.

Every contemporary President has been surrounded by a large variety of advisory commissions and boards, most of which are designed to study an agency or project and counsel the President on how to operate it more efficiently. There are also several commissions and boards whose major function seems to be to issue reports agreeing with the President's ideas. Most of these austere bodies are composed of outstanding men and women whose leadership and personal resources enable them to take such appointments for a dollar a year plus expenses. They get little out of them and usually put less into them. The end result is a picture taken with the President and a framed certificate of appreciation of as much significance as a Boy Scout merit badge when scouting days are past. And then there are the occasional commissions and boards that work diligently and issue meaningful, progressive reports which happen to disagree with the Administration's announced plans. These are immediately forgotten.

Most of these commissions and study groups, especially the cost-saving ones, expend a great deal of money; in fact, they usually spend more money than they might save. This turned out to be the case with President Nixon's first such appointment: an Advisory Council on Executive Organization whose goal was to reexamine the organization of the President's office and find ways, in the great political cliché, to "trim the fat." The chairman of the group was Roy L. Ash, president of Litton Industries, so the council soon became known as the Ash Council. Other members included George P. Baker, former dean of the Harvard Business School; Frederick R. Kappell, former chairman of the American Telephone and Telegraph Co.; Richard M. Paget, president of a management consulting firm in New York; Walter N. Thayer, president of the Whitney Communications Corp.; and John B. Connally, whose most recent job was as Governor of Texas. It was a group of high prestige and big names, one which would allow the President to boast of his high-caliber advisers.

John Connally was the only Democrat on the council, but his political and social philosophy was very close to that of his Republican cohorts. There were no true academicians (Baker was primarily an administrator), no members of Congress and no one who could be considered anything less than affluent.

A sarcastic *Wall Street Journal* reporter suggested that perhaps the President needed some smaller businessmen, or maybe some housewives, people who were more concerned with and more experienced in cutting costs. The group that President Nixon named had been responsible for collective expansion totaling millions of dollars in their respective fields.

The duties of the council were threefold: to examine the organization of the Executive Branch as a whole in light of the changing needs of government; to present solutions to organizational problems that arose from among the more than 150 departments, offices, agencies and other separate executive organizational units; and to examine the interdepartmental relationship between the Federal Government and the nation's states and cities.

The Ash Council took eleven months to issue its first proposals to the President, who quickly approved them. They delighted him. The report proposed the reorganization of the Bureau of the Budget into a division to be called the Office of Management and Budget which would emphasize the office's responsibilities in areas of management as well as in the budget itself. It also suggested the formation of a Domestic Council, which would include all Cabinet members whose duties related to domestic affairs as well as an enlarged White House administrative staff. The suggestion was designed to dilute the power of individual members of the Cabinet and to centralize authority in the White House, close to and directly under the President.

The latter proposal especially pleased Nixon, who had long felt that the best way to keep the machinations and machinery of government out from under congressional inquiry or media eyes was to take as much as possible from the Cabinet and hide it somewhere in the halls of the White House. For example, the appointment of Dr. Henry A. Kissinger as Assistant to the President for National Security Affairs—in effect, chief foreign policy adviser—with more power than any previous Secretary of State was a calculated effort to retain control of the Vietnam war in particular and foreign policy in general without having to worry about congressional inquiries. A presidential adviser could be cloaked with Executive privilege and could avoid the often arduous routine of testifying before Senate or House committees, thereby keeping his budget and his mobility intact. The Kissinger technique was applied at all levels, both domestic and foreign, and led to awesome authority given to such men as H. R. Haldeman, John Ehrlichman, and John Dean, who were able to prevent even Cabinet members from having access to the President. It took the Senate Watergate hearings to reveal the extent to which the Administration had centralized its power.

The ordinarily powerful State Department post was given to Nixon's loyal ally and old friend, New York Attorney William P. Rogers, with the at least implicit understanding that the role would be token insofar as policy making was concerned. It took five years of Vietnam war, the many lies about the Cambodian bombing and, finally, Watergate to convince the Nixon Administration that the public and its Congress will not be circumvented.

Although it may not have appeared as such, Nixon's nomination of Henry Kissinger as Secretary of State in August 1973 was a conciliatory and apologetic move to the people and the Congress of the United States. Kissinger had been Secretary of State in fact, if not in name, for a long time. Now he would have to be properly confirmed by the Senate and would have to answer to the nation's elected officials.

Cabinet officials felt justifiably threatened when the Advisory Council on Executive Organization plan was presented to them on March 4, 1970, and their hostility was open. But the President was ready with his new number one Answer Man. John Connally stood up and quelled their fears, explaining the policy to them with the suave and consummate eloquence that he had learned from many years with Lyndon Johnson. It was Connally who also lobbied for the plan in the Congress and gently guided it toward passage. Connally successfully convinced leaders in both the Senate and the House of Representatives that their power to oversee the Government would not be weakened by the proposed changes.

Again President Nixon was impressed by John Connally's handling of a delicate situation. The Texas Democrat had accomplished an almost impossible task. He had convinced a skeptical and stubborn Congress and an experienced group of Cabinet members to approve a plan that would both diminish their authority and stifle their stature in terms of running the American government. That kind of salesmanship obviously had a strong effect on the President.

On December 1, 1970, the President rewarded Connally by appointing him to the Foreign Intelligence Advisory Board in the State Department. That board was

headed by Admiral George W. Anderson, Jr., a retired
Chief of Naval Operations, and had ten members. This
was the sort of position that was a delight to John Connally. He was involved in the intrigue of foreign affairs,
and, as a former naval officer and onetime Secretary of
the Navy, he was comfortable talking about foreign intelligence. It served another need for Connally. Always
the masterful long-range planner, he understood the need
of a broad international background and an image of
extensive knowledge for anyone who might be seeking
public office, especially a very high office. It was the
same ambition that would push Connally and Nixon
closer together in the following years, and eventually
would involve Big John in a campaign to become Secretary of State. Ironically, the Jewish, German-born Henry
Kissinger would prevail over the tall, suave WASP.

The John Connally who said he was going to become a private citizen after leaving the Texas Statehouse
had never become a private citizen. He was becoming a
big man in national and international policy decisions.
His Texas law firm prospered, and the corporations that
had named him to their boards were delighted.

Nixon's promise to name a Democrat to his Cabinet
finally was kept on December 14, 1970, almost two years
after his inauguration, when he named Big John as his
money man, the Secretary of the Treasury.

Nixon never had been unaware of the national
sensitivity of economic issues. Hundreds of thousands of
Middle American voters, worried about welfare give-
aways and foreign over-aid, had been convinced by the
Republican organization that Hubert Humphrey represented the worst of all economic possibilities. With prices
rising rapidly, pocketbook politics took over.

In any given election, the Wednesday morning
quarterbacks will try to analyze the vote and the lack of
it. When Humphrey was defeated by Nixon, most pundits

agreed that the economy had been the critical domestic issue, despite the more publicized problems of civil rights, labor disputes and law and order. Moreover, during 1969, large and very dark economic clouds rose on the horizon. Top-level New York Stock Exchange executives met with the President during the year in an effort to save a Wall Street that was threatening to collapse because of its own incompetence and mismanagement. Brokerage firms were facing failure and wise market executives of both political persuasions feared major—and depression-causing—problems.

Nixon needed a high-level huckster on his staff who could sell his "dynamic, new, expansive economic program [along with his new legislative proposals] to the press, the Congress, the business community and the nation."

John Connally was a natural.

Early in December 1970 the President had invited his new Texas friend to the Oval Office with no particular reason given for the invitation. They chatted amicably about a number of topics, then began to speak more seriously about the Vietnam situation. "I am determined," the President told Connally, "to extract this nation from Southeast Asia, but the United States must carry on its role of leadership. We must not withdraw into a state of isolation and turn our backs on our responsibilities of world leadership." This was obviously more than just a comment to a private citizen, or even to a well-known and affluent lawyer.

As the discussion of war and peace went on, the President told Connally that Secretary of the Treasury David Kennedy was resigning. Then he asked Big John if he wanted the job. Perhaps the Oval Office is not as dramatic a spot as the San Clemente swimming pool, where Nixon later asked Kissinger about becoming Secretary of State, but a job is a job.

Connally, surprised, rejected the offer. "You'll anger both the Republicans and the Democrats," he said. "It's not a winning proposition."

Connally, almost legendary for his innate sense of political timing, believed that the critical exposure he would receive as a Democratic Cabinet member in a Republican Administration could be fatal to his own career.

But Richard Nixon has always been persuasive, and at the President's request Connally returned to the White House a few days later. Outwardly, he was groping for reasons to decline, but there was a magnetic pull. As one friend says, "Washington holds a great fascination for him. It just seems to hold some sort of spell over him." Connally told the President, "I don't believe I can afford it. I need to make some money in my law practice in Houston."

Nixon replied, with a wide presidential smile and strong presidential sincerity, "But, John, this is an opportunity to do something for your country."

At the end of the second four-hour session, Connally had agreed to take the Cabinet post, saying, "If the President wants me to do it, I'll do it." Nixon immediately called the LBJ Ranch to introduce the former President to the new Secretary of the Treasury. Since the negotiations had been a well-kept secret, Johnson was reportedly miffed because matters concerning his own political protégé, John Connally, had been arranged without him.

When the President's decision was announced, even his friends wanted to know why, of all people, John Connally had been the Democrat selected. Robert Finch, counsel and friend to the President, said the idea was "pure Nixon." One presidential aide, after receiving the message directly from Nixon, said, "The old man's decided to do something about the Texas situation, and you won't believe who he's got to help him do it." The comment related to worries among the President's campaign advisory staff that unless Nixon could carry Texas and California in 1972, he could lose the reelection attempt. Finch tried to show, however, that there was no collusion involved and that the President was merely trying to select the best man for the job when he said, "There was no deal with Connally to carry Texas."

President Nixon reminded the critics of how impressed he had been by Connally's participation on the Ash Council. Connally, always smooth, slick and articulate, presented himself and his ideas with such authority and confidence that he particularly endeared himself to the President, who never seemed to have quite as much confidence as the Texan. In addition, the President would have a Democrat in his Cabinet, true to his campaign promise. Added bonuses to the appointment were the facts that Connally was a conservative and that he was a politically strong figure in a key state. His fiscal qualifications to be Secretary of the Treasury were weak, but they were heavily outweighed by his positive qualities of "leadership and experience as a lawyer, businessman and governor," according to the President's press secretary.

Not everyone was quite so impressed. A high Texas official who had known and worked with Connally for many years described him as "by far the best political song and dance man in America, and for the time being he belongs in the Nixon Administration."

When Nixon told the nation of his choice, he explained it as "a desire to approach American problems in a bipartisan manner." He emphasized former Governor Connally's special qualifications in dealing with the issue of revenue sharing, the distribution of federal monies to states and cities. Connally had favored such revenue sharing when he was Governor. Big John's

tough position on the Vietnam war was spotlighted by
Nixon. Connally's views on foreign relations certainly
were closer to Nixon's than to those of segments of Big
John's own Democratic party.

Once the initial shock had subsided, reactions to
the appointment were generally favorable. Banking
leaders throughout the country expressed modest pleasure
at the selection of a conservative whose primary interest
would probably be in preserving the status quo. David
Rockefeller, chairman of the Chase Manhattan Bank,
said that Connally was "an appropriate choice." Clifford
Sumner, president of the American Bankers Association,
added that Connally's "broad experience in the governmental process" would be "invaluable to the new post."
At Democratic party headquarters, however, the men
who make the decisions scratched Connally from the
starting lists in future party conventions.

Those who questioned Connally's qualifications to
handle the nation's economic problems sided with *The
New York Times.* In an editorial the country's most
powerful newspaper said, ". . . but there is little in his
background to suggest that he has the financial experience, insight or creativity that the nation so urgently
needs in its Secretary of the Treasury." There was little
reassurance when an Administration spokesman described Connally as "a quick study" and "easily edu-
cable." There was also the retelling of an incident in
Connally's student days. Cast in the lead of a campus
stage production, he had blown his opening lines, yet
rebounded to receive a standing ovation by the end of
the evening. Besides, the Department of the Treasury
was filled with unknown and unsung experts who could
solve the problems while Connally spread the Nixon
gospel.

Connally's real strength lay in his alleged ability
to work within the Democratic party-controlled Con-

gress in support of the President's programs. Senate Republican leader Hugh Scott of Pennsylvania went along, saying, "He knows all the Indian trails on Capitol Hill." Robert V. Roosa, a senior partner in the important New York banking house of Brown Bros., Harriman and Co., said, "It is more important to put in a strong man whom the President has confidence in, rather than grope around for a strictly financial type." In other words, the conservative philosophy of politics was far more important than a man with great economic qualifications. Even Connally's experience with the Texas Legislature during his three terms as Governor was not to be discounted. A Houston banker described Big John by saying, "Everything about him conveys the impression of fiscal responsibility. He and Nixon are cast from the same mold. They are conservative, and both basically espouse the balanced budget."

The money men obviously were more interested in the "impression" of fiscal responsibility than in "real" fiscal responsibility. *Image* was the key word. Connally was a marketable commodity, neatly packaged in expensive suits, and he could be sold to the nation like a box of soap flakes.

Back home in Texas, politicians expressed concern and skepticism about the position Connally would have in the 1972 state elections. The former Governor always had been a party man. State officials raised the question of whether Connally could support or campaign for a Democrat in opposition to Republican Senator John Tower, a conservative who was very close to a Republican Administration in which Connally now held a key post. Nixon wanted the Tower seat preserved for the GOP. Connally said that he had intended to continue to support Democratic candidates and that he had "won Mr. Nixon's pledge to let him do so." Connally emphasized, "I came in as a Democrat and I'll leave as a Democrat," a statement that is not featured in any official biographical material about him. Big John refuses to discuss any possibility that a deal already had been made for him to jump to the Nixon bandwagon in 1972, first as chairman of what would be called Democrats for Nixon and later as a convert to the Republican party itself.

One of Connally's close friends described the unique opportunity which had presented itself to the new Secretary of the Treasury by pointing out, "John knows the economy can't get much worse. He has nowhere to go but up. If the situation improves, he can get the lion's share of the credit. It is a situation that appeals both to his political instincts and to his rather roomy ego." Former President Johnson saw the situation from the other end of the political spectrum and with the astuteness of an old-line campaigner. A Johnson-Connally ally noted, "The President [Johnson] feels that Nixon could be had on the economic issue, and the last thing any Democrat should do is identify the Democratic party with Nixon economics."

Washington being the capital of the rumor mills as well as the capital of the nation, there was the traditional speculation about upcoming presidential campaigns in the wake of the President's appointment. The prophets raised the possibility of Spiro Agnew's being dropped from the ticket in 1972 to be replaced by John Connally. In fact, one Democrat predicted with amazing astuteness, "To my dirty mind, this appointment means only one thing: the start of 'Democrats for Nixon' in 1972." He was perfectly accurate.

There also was a certain amount of kidding on the square, as in the question asked by Massachusetts Governor Francis Sargent, not completely in jest, "Can John add?"

Connally's responsibilities as Secretary of the Trea-

sury would be monumental, including administration of
the tax laws, collection of more than $200 billion a
year in taxes and other revenues, handling government
payments, managing the public debt, directing the proces-
sing of imports and customs duties, overseeing the Secret
Service and the Bureau of the Mint, supplying the Office
of Management and Budget with official estimates of
revenues and supervising some 90,000 employees. He
also was to be a member of the Oil Policy Committee, to
sit on the President's Domestic Council and to be a part
of the Committee for Natural Energy.

There were continuing rumors, encouraged by enemies of both Connally and Nixon, that the Cabinet post
was Connally's reward for being of underground assistance to Nixon in the 1968 presidential campaign. Even
though Hubert Humphrey carried Texas, the Democratic
party was unable to raise much money during the campaign, and there was much speculation that this reversal
of past contributions was largely the work of John Connally. William Chapman of the Washington *Post* described a conversation he had with a "reliable Texas
source" who had attended a gathering of conservative
supporters of both parties in the Sheraton-Dallas Hotel
in October 1968. "We made it clear," said the source,
"that we wanted to see Nixon elected and that we wanted
to know where he stood. Connally told us he thought it
would be best for the country if Nixon were elected President. We talked about people who would be helpful
politically and financially to Nixon—friends of Connally
who were Democrats." It was a matter of record that
neither Connally nor Lyndon Johnson did much for
Humphrey until the final weeks of the campaign. When
Connally went to Washington in 1969 and remembered
to mention that he had done "all he could" for Nixon in
1968, the appointment to the Ash Council suddenly appeared. Connally's later appointment to the Foreign In-

telligence Advisory Board also was considered a quid pro quo, so why not the next step up the ladder, an appointment to Nixon's Cabinet?

From time to time the press would revive the story of Connally's onetime role as a lobbyist for natural gas legislation that ended in a major scandal in 1956. The issue had been widely aired again when Connally ran for his second term as Governor of Texas in 1964, and his opponents had tried to use the scandal as campaign leverage.

On January 8, 1971, Marquis Childs, the nationally syndicated columnist, revealed that John Connally had been given a retainer fee of $50,000 by the Government of Algeria for advice concerning the oil industry. It was suggested that his services had been sought and obtained because of his "Navy experience in Algeria, combined with his knowledge of the oil business."

Connally appeared before the Senate Finance Committee on January 27 as hearings began to set the way for the vote on his confirmation as a member of the Cabinet. He informed the committee of President Nixon's directive that he develop a broad tax reform program. Connally did not outline any specific plans for these broad reforms, but he did raise the possibility of a national sales tax. The would-be secretary also relayed the President's reluctance to set high property taxes and high income tax rates "at all levels." When Connally was questioned by Senator Fred Harris about the effect of a national sales tax, which would impose similar and, in fact, far heavier burdens on the poor than upon the wealthy, Connally responded that "Everybody ought to pay some tax. It is wrong to have a democracy in which all the people don't contribute."

It was a mixed committee that would be voting on the Connally nomination the following week. Senator Russell Long, the Louisiana Democrat who was chairman of the committee, praised Connally at the first session. Long was impressed by the fact that the prospective Secretary of the Treasury would be "incurring a heavy loss of income by accepting the appointment." Connally had told reporters that he would be selling his equity in a number of business and banking firms so as to avoid any "potential conflicts of interest." Connally said that he would "assume a loss of income totaling several hundred thousand dollars." Big John would retain his several ranches in his home state. Connally deftly avoided revealing details of his financial holdings, but did mention, with a jab at the liberal press, that his "vast wealth" in oil and gas holdings "reached the magnificent sum of $7,240."

Long's concern for the financial well-being of John Connally was so unnecessary as to be amusing. No Cabinet post could possibly be a better guarantee for future income and security for a lawyer-executive. Even without any taint of conflict of interest, and without the slightest violation of the strictest construction of legal ethics, Connally was assured of new—and much higher—levels of corporate income when he completed his government service and returned to private industry. The name of a former Cabinet member looks prestigious on the letterhead of any firm and is a strong addition to any board of directors. Besides, the contacts made at such a high level of government are invaluable when it comes to settling even the stickiest problems that a firm could acquire.

When he was questioned about wage and price controls, Connally said that he would suggest to the President "in the strongest terms" that he pressure both labor and management to hold down wages and prices. Connally said he was in favor of instituting a wage and price board to keep controls on any inflationary trends as a result of either labor or management action, but he did not advocate strict controls at either end of the potential spiral. Senator Vance Hartke, Democrat from Indiana and a member of the committee, called Big John's testimony "jawboning."

There had to be a question as to why Connally, a Democrat, would take a post in a Republican Administration, and of course it came. Big John had the opportunity to deliver a quip, and he did. "Mr. Nixon had persuaded me that I could be of service. I suppose I was vain enough to believe it and silly enough to try it."

Congressman Wright Patman, a powerful member of the Texas delegation and chairman of the House Banking and Currency Committee, was surprised and not pleased by the Connally nomination. He had hoped that the Nixon Administration would move toward lower interest rates and a more liberal monetary policy. The *Texas Observer,* the longtime voice of Texas liberalism and persistent foe of Connally, picked Patman as a potential stumbling block for Connally's programs in the House of Representatives.

"Patman doesn't like Connally," noted the publication, "is opposed to revenue sharing and can't abide party turncoats."

There would be many confrontations between Connally and the Democratic Congress, but the real economic battleground on which the Texan would fight would be in the high-echelon private club composed of Nixon's top economic advisers. There the new Secretary of the Treasury would be up against the chairman of the Federal Reserve Bank, Arthur Burns; the chairman of the President's Council of Economic Advisers, Paul McCracken; and the director of the Office of Management and Budget, George Shultz. Connally would be the only professional politician, which gave him an edge in one area. The others were experienced economic and fiscal experts, which put Connally at a disadvantage. Would Connally, no matter how convincing, be able to dominate the confident Shultz? The President assured his new Cabinet member, "Don't worry about Shultz. You report to me directly, not through any intermediaries."

On February 1, when the hearings on the Connally appointment were about to be concluded, *The New York Times* carried a front-page headline which read, "Foundation Paid Connally $225,000 While Governor." The *Times* story was based on extensive investigation and raised a series of questions surrounding the fact that Connally had received $75,000 a year for services while he was Governor from the Sid W. Richardson Foundation, which had huge oil and gas holdings throughout Texas. The Richardson-Connally link was no secret, but Texas law prohibits a governor from receiving any "salary, reward or compensation or the promise thereof from any person or corporation for any service rendered or performed during the time he is governor." Big John was in an embarrassing spot. To be sure, Perry Bass, director and spokesman for the Richardson Foundation, explained that the payments to John Connally were for his services as an executor of Sid Richardson's estate. "Those were executors' fees," Bass said. "That was a helluva long time ago." But the aura of opportunism that continually surrounded Connally glowed even brighter.

Other newspapers picked up the story and raised questions about whether Connally had received extra compensation while he was Secretary of the Navy, in 1961, and what the specific services were that Connally had performed as an executor of the Richardson estate.

John Connally did not hesitate to defend himself. On the day that the *Times* article appeared, he asked the Senate Finance Committee for a public hearing to explain his role as a Richardson executor. He had been asked by President Nixon to refrain from any press conferences until the Finance Committee had passed on his nomination. Senator Long granted Connally the hearing and said that, as soon as it was concluded, the committee would move into secret executive session for discussion and its vote.

In his testimony to the committee, Connally explained a number of things about his payments from the Richardson Foundation. The bulk of Richardson's estate, finally valued at $105 million, had been left to the foundation, which assumed the executors' fees as debts; as his share, Connally was entitled by Texas law to receive approximately $1.2 million. But when he was offered the job of Secretary of the Navy, in late 1960, he made an agreement with the other two executors (one was Perry Bass) to accept a total fee of $750,000, to be paid to him over a ten-year period; before the end of 1960 tax returns for the estate were filed and Connally's job as executor was essentially finished. (The *Times* had pointed out that, when he testified at hearings on the Navy job, he said that he had given up at least $450,000 of the executor's fee legally due him but he did not mention that he was to receive the remainder over a ten-year period.) Indeed, annual payments were made to him while he was Governor—but for services rendered several years before he was elected. Connally emphasized that fact for the senators: "I think it important to realize that . . . as of the time that I agreed to accept the $750,000 as my total fees, those fees . . . —they were mine."

If Connally had chosen to be entirely candid with the Senate Armed Services Committee in 1961, there would have been no newspaper articles and no reminders of his fortunate connections with Richardson and Bass in 1971. But the whole affair gave welcome opportunity for others to express their support.

Connally's fellow Democrat, Senator Lloyd Bentsen, victor over incumbent liberal Ralph Yarborough in the 1970 election in Texas, commented: "A careful reading of *The New York Times* story shows the lengths to which these opponents will go in their attempts to discredit Governor Connally. There are no facts in the story which would indicate that the payment is anything more than installment payments for a debt incurred." Connally responded personally to the Texas publication which had quoted him as saying he had "performed no services or received any compensation" during his term as Governor. Obviously piqued, he snapped, "The last thing I would do before this committee or any other responsible body in this Government is, very frankly, to vouch for what appears in the *Texas Observer*."

Robert Griffin, the GOP minority whip, leaped to the Democrat's support when he said, "If there is a problem of ethics, it's ethics in journalism."

The Senate Finance Committee accepted all of Connally's explanations about the handling of his finances and the Richardson Foundation fees and approved his nomination, 13 to 0. The Senate confirmed him by voice vote, without debate or opposition, on February 8.

John Connally was sworn in as Secretary of the Treasury on February 11, 1971. President Nixon, applauding his own appointment to the nation's top economic post, said, "He is a man who is qualified because of his years of experience in state government, national government and private enterprise." The President noted that he had fulfilled his "bipartisan pledge" and spoke with great enthusiasm and high hopes of the federal revenue sharing programs and the welfare programs with which he would be working in his new post.

Having officially taken over as Secretary of the Treasury, Connally now began openly advocating particular economic policies. He began to discuss them be-

fore the public and in testimony to congressional committees, always, of course, pushing the Nixon view of
economics.

Connally's early statements included:

"We think we have to have a fairly liberal policy
with respect to the availability of money, and unquestionably, low interest is essential to the restoration of
vitality to this economy."

"We think we have every reason to encourage and
stimulate the economy even if deficit spending is involved."

"I think it [an unemployment rate of 4 percent] is
a goal we have to strive to reach. I do not think it is impossible to attain. We may have two percent, three percent inflation, with full employment. I would hope we
could achieve that in the fairly near future."

"You do not need to fear any imposition of a value-
added tax unless and until it is a part of a sweeping
change in the whole tax structure of the Federal Government. . . . It is going to be in lieu of some existing
tax."

Of course, with his Texas background, he "opposed
further cuts in the oil depletion allowance," but, echoing
a word usage made familiar by his old mentor, Lyndon
Johnson, he would "certainly recommend" an increased
utilization of "jawboning."

Throughout all the statements and comments, the
Texan was effectively selling the Administration line to
Congress, to government officials, to the public and to
the world. His smooth approach and convincing manner
made him an ideal economic spokesman for Richard
Nixon.

The Connally personality emerged rapidly in its
new surroundings. The glory that Washington promised,
the fascination that big government held for him provided the optimum condition for the man. Democratic

Senator Herman Talmadge of Georgia had admonished Connally during the Senate confirmation hearings, "I hope you will undertake to fulfill your responsibilities in accordance with the duties of your office and not in accordance with the dictates of a White House staff member, and I hope the flow of power will be down from the President rather than up from his staff." Connally, pleading that he was "new in this town, at least on this visit," replied, "I think, without in any sense appearing to be arrogant, Senator Talmadge, that you can be sure that so long as I am Secretary of the Treasury, I shall be Secretary of the Treasury. . . ."

Talmadge's words were an interesting and prophetic prelude to his questions during the Watergate hearings.

Connally soon had friction with the White House guard and the men who felt it was their "duty" to protect the President, both from his enemies and from his friends. Connally sent a memorandum to Nixon and it promptly came back with a note attached asking the Secretary of the Treasury why he wanted to "raise this particular issue" with the President. It was a bureaucratic act and it was insulting to a member of the Cabinet. Big John flew into a rage and sent another memo to the White House aide asking why the aide had taken it upon himself to rudely obstruct his personal communications with the President. The aide apologized, and Nixon's personal reply to the memorandum came soon thereafter.

Still, the battle lines were being drawn, with Connally on one side, Haldeman and Ehrlichman on the other.

Regardless of this one interruption, Connally still had far more personal attention from the President than many other people in high government circles. Cabinet members and advisers went weeks without talking to the Chief Executive, but Nixon regularly sought Connally's advice and companionship. "The President doesn't just admire Connally," said one top Administration official. "He stands in awe of him." Another, trying to describe the blossoming relationship, said, "Connally is the kind of physically impressive and commanding guy who inspires a certain awe in Nixon. He sees great strength in him, the same as he does in [John] Mitchell." The admiration that Connally seemed to feel toward the President was increasingly more apparent and more a mutual feeling. When Connally spoke of Nixon, he called him "a man who fully understands some of the very basic problems of his country. . . . His ideas in foreign policy reflect an unusual awareness of the uses of power in the broadest sense." And the admiration, in the same tone, swung back again when the President described John Connally as "one of the few men in this country who understands the uses of power." The mutual admiration society went on as jealous White House staffers fumed privately and plotted devious schemes to dethrone the tall Texan who was replacing them in Nixon's trust and confidence.

Down the street from the White House, in the Treasury Department building, Connally's new aides spoke of him with admiration and loyalty. "He's enthusiastic. He lights people up," said one of his assistant secretaries, adding, "If Connally's optimistic about something, so am I." Connally brought an earthiness and a common touch into the department that was reminiscent of Lyndon Johnson. When an associate came in poorly prepared, Connally would snap, "Go run your traps," which was his way of saying, "Go get some more facts and give me a proper presentation." Connally's enthusiasm stemmed from his eagerness to be directly involved in the entire workings of the department. His predecessor, David Kennedy, "delegated a great deal of authority," Connally said one day. "I frankly like to be a part of nearly everything that goes on. . . . I'll be more of an activist." In one way, it was a splendid attitude for a new boss. In another, it was a method of holding a tighter rein over the department. When a reporter quoted an anonymous, high-ranking Treasury official on the matter of interest rates, Connally immediately responded to what was taken as the "alleged Treasury position" and said, "If a fellow has anything to say, he ought to say it on the record."

The comparisons between Connally and Lyndon Johnson were drawn every day. One wit described him as "LBJ with couth." Connally's physique, accent and general presence were direct reminders of his friend and mentor. Connally, when he approached Democratic Congressman George Andrews of Alabama one day to seek his support of revenue sharing, was met with this comment: "You look like an arm twister to me. . . . In fact, some say you look almost like his twin brother."

And Maxine Cheshire, the salty columnist of the Washington *Post,* described his appearance at a White House function in the following vivid way:

"John Connally's attire attracted a lot of attention at the White House party. He wore an outfit that can best be described as 'Midnight Blue Cowboy.'

"His Tex Ritter tuxedo was two-tones of azure and delphinium, with piping around the double-breasted jacket and four large mother-of-pearl buttons.

"His shirt was two different tones of blue and so was his large bowtie.

"His wavy white hair is shorter, but otherwise, he looked so much like his close friend, former President Johnson, that some guests were startled.

" 'He found Lyndon's tailor,' someone whispered, 'Now if he just finds his barber, they'll be twins.' "

During his first few months in his new post, Connally turned down numerous speaking engagements and ceremonial functions until he felt he was on solid ground and able to discuss economic realities with intelligence. No one had ever accused him of being less than intelligent. He was aided by the fact that he was a fast learner and a hard worker. To the great annoyance of his staff, he scheduled briefing meetings early every morning. Previously there had been one a week. Even Connally foes, or neutral observers, had compliments for his work habits. Connally "does his homework," commented Paul McCracken of the Council of Economic Advisers, adding that it was a good thing because otherwise the sessions would be "three guys talking Greek and one Latin."

From the day that Connally moved into the Nixon Cabinet, political commentators had been whispering and speculating about the 1972 vice presidency. The Texan taunted them by saying, "All of you seem so well informed, I'll just sit back and listen." Connally never would commit himself to any campaign intentions or ambitions for 1972, especially if they involved a switch of party, but he did drop a hint of interest in the presidential race of 1976 if his age, which would then be fifty-nine, was not a deterring factor. One Republican, impressed by his leadership, said, "I'd vote for him for President on either ticket." And Big John smiled and said that was good. At another time he noted, "I'm not an arm twister at all. I would like to think that I'm an advocate or a spokesman. I'd like to think that I'm not forcing people to do what they don't want to do because I don't think you can do that anyway. . . . I've been called an opportunist, and I do move from place to place and from thing to thing and I enjoy it. I'm also called ambitious. In all due humility, I might say that I had several opportunities to run for the U.S. Senate and was considered to have a fair chance of winning and I passed them up. I just didn't want to spend the rest of my life in the Senate simply because I felt there were too many other things to do, to see, and too many other ways in which I could make a contribution. I have an insatiable curiosity about just about everything. I don't have the education to understand a whole lot about some interests like astronomy—but I do know a little about many. I'm just interested in everything."

"Including the vice presidency?" someone asked, and Connally replied, "Now, you just picked out the one thing in which I have no interest whatsoever."

Indications began to grow that if Connally were interested in a top government position, he was interested in the very top, and second best wouldn't be enough.

Connally was recognized in Washington for his unusual habit of chewing on unlighted cigars. He had smoked them for many years, but stopped lighting them after having been wounded in the automobile with President Kennedy in 1963. No one understands the connection and Connally does not explain it. He also braves the Washington winters without a topcoat, in the style of former Presidents Kennedy and Johnson, and he refrains from any more alcohol than two before-dinner Scotches.

A Connally work day at the Treasury Department began promptly at eight o'clock with a breakfast meeting and ended late that evening as he worked at home from a briefcase bulging with Treasury documents that needed review and examination. For all his faults, Big John is not lazy. He would work at his Washington desk until six, and three nights a week he would take his wife, Idanell, on the Washington social circuit. The family lived in a six-room suite at the Sheraton-Park Hotel, a few doors from two members of the Supreme Court.

Connally's knowledge of congressional intricacies and the backroom dealings of Washington quickly became evident, especially in his handling of the difficult 4½ percent interest-rate ceiling which placed him head-to-head against the powerful Wilbur Mills of Arkansas,

Democrat and chairman of the House Ways and Means Committee. Mills had not intended to compromise, but finally did, noting, "Any time he opposes you, you've got trouble." At first Connally was aggressive, though diplomatic and persuasive, in his relationships with Congress, and he earned the respect of men on both sides of the aisle. Soon, however, he became known for a set of standard responses that he used in the many congressional hearings that he was forced to attend. He evaded specific questions and tried diligently to circumvent any congressional inquiry into President Nixon's economic plans. Big John's favorite response seemed to be, "I couldn't agree with you more," yet more and more rhetoric and fewer and fewer facts came from the Secretary of the Treasury.

One Treasury aide told me that Connally "doesn't suffer fools gladly." His office door was rarely locked, but it was seldom open, and there seemed to be few close Connally friends. One was a mysterious friend from the Houston police force named Pat. He claimed "excellent access" to President Nixon through Secretary Connally and revealed this access in a conversation with another Texan whose signed affidavit was being used to help free convicted Teamsters leader James Hoffa. The affiant had learned that Nixon wanted to pardon Hoffa, but was afraid of a bad reaction from press and public. What the President wanted was the financial and political support of the powerful Teamsters Union in the 1972 campaign. If Connally's friend of a friend would sign the affidavit that he had committed perjury in Chattanooga, where Hoffa had been indicted, then the President could pardon Hoffa and the helpful friend would receive immunity. The friend was Ed Partini. He signed the affidavit and Hoffa was released.

When the 1972 campaign rolled around, Frank Fitzsimmons, successor to Hoffa as president of the Teamsters, was an active participant in the "Democrats for Nixon" organization.

One of the President's first requests of his new Secretary of the Treasury was to represent the Administration in the delicate negotiations between the Lockheed Aircraft Corporation and the British Government. Lockheed was to have used Rolls-Royce engines in its new L-1011 Tri-Star commercial aircraft, but the British engine maker suddenly went bankrupt. Unless the British Government could assist Rolls-Royce, Lockheed also might fail, and the loss of one of the manufacturing giants could critically impair the American aerospace industry. A side effect would be a heavy political loss to the Nixon Administration since the aircraft industry could always be counted upon for some substantial political contributions and for a large number of votes.

Since the monetary difficulties involved a commercial plane rather than a military aircraft, the issue technically could be placed under the Department of the Treasury rather than the Defense Department. It never became very clear whether Connally was actually overseeing negotiations or merely keeping in touch with the complex situation in order to advise the White House of developments.

As the discussions went on, Nixon and Connally were seen together more and more. Big John gradually was replacing Henry Kissinger as the day-to-day confidant of the Chief Executive. Nixon relished Connally's well-groomed, big-man, easygoing manner, and he also enjoyed the score he'd made when he named an LBJ Democrat to a key position in the Administration. He felt as if he had dealt a major blow to the Democratic party while strengthening his own. Kissinger, unused to seeing someone usurp his position, bristled at the invasion of his exclusive preserve as Nixon's mental baby-sitter and the number one choice of Washington hostesses as an honored guest. But Connally stayed close to the Oval Office in the White House and kept expanding his role.

After numerous consultations with the President, Connally took a hard line with the British officials who came to the United States and requested an American guarantee to repay British Government advances on the Rolls-Royce engine if the Lockheed program should be scrapped. Connally, who monitored the discussions between the parties, said it was impossible for the Administration to make such guarantees. The British, after all, were seeking American funds as a security against Lockheed's potential bankruptcy.

Still, Connally presented to Congress a plan asking for authorization of guarantees of $250 to $300 million in loans to Lockheed as part of government efforts to keep the company from folding its labor tents and adding to the employment problems that already were plaguing the Pacific Northwest. Big John began more than just monitoring; he had begun to actively suggest financial alternatives and to chart the Administration's course in the affair.

Congressional support for the guaranteed loan was a particularly sensitive issue, especially in light of the recent dramatic decision to deny government funding for the supersonic transport plant that was supposed to revolutionize the transportation industry. Connally had spoken before the Senate Appropriations Committee the previous month to encourage the allocation of $190 million for the SST. He had predicted that the successful American production of the plane, before European competitors could get theirs into the air, would produce a gain of "$22 billion in the nation's foreign trade account over the next twenty years." George Meany, president of the AFL-CIO, said the plane's development and construction would involve 42,000 immediate jobs and 150,000 potential new ones.

Connally was accused of "numerical science fiction" where the international balance of payments was concerned by the chairman of the Council of Economic Advisers. But John Volpe, Secretary of Transportation, urged the completion of the prototype models of the plane so that it could go into production, and he too spoke strongly for congressional action to help fund the project.

Without the SST program, the aerospace industry would continue to suffer from massive unemployment problems, and it was hoped that Congress would not add to the decay of the industry by refusing the Lockheed loan. Since Congress had established a ceiling on loans to companies involved in critical defense work, the legislators had to approve all loans that would exceed $20 million.

Some congressional leaders stood firm against any part of the Connally plan for aiding the desperate Lockheed Corporation. Senate majority leader Mike Mansfield said, "I don't think we ought to pick up the tab for any more than we have." Senator Proxmire, the outspoken Democrat from Wisconsin, wrote directly to Connally, saying that the "Government has no business forcing the [Lockheed plane] on the market" and the loan guarantees were "just one step away from outright subsidy."

Connally made his first major response to this opposition on April 21, marking the occasion of the first press run of dollar bills bearing his name. Big John requested and got the first hundred of them from the Bureau of Engraving and Printing, and he paid for them with a personal check. They will, of course, have later value as collectors' items, but that is a point not worth concern. After all, astronauts and others have similar thinking where souvenirs are concerned.

Connally argued that it was up to the President as to whether the Administration should ask for congressional approval of loans to be guaranteed by the Government. But, he was quick to point out, Britain's financial support of the Rolls-Royce engine for use in the "airbus project" would depend solely on the U.S. Government's guarantee of the financial survival of Lockheed. The Secretary made it abundantly clear that he spoke for President Nixon when he again testified before the Senate Appropriations Committee. The pressures from above were increasing and a decision was expected by the following week. At that hearing Connally was asked by Senator Joseph Montoya, a New Mexico Democrat, if, in fact, a government guarantee for the Lockheed airbus was not "in effect, a subsidy for a British concern, Rolls-Royce, that competes with General Electric and Pratt & Whitney, American engine makers?"

Senator Montoya is one of the quiet members of the world's most exclusive club, the one composed of one hundred U.S. Senators, many of whom are unknown to the general public. It is traditional to know the names of the two Senators from one's home state, or to be able to discuss the glamorous stars like Kennedy, Goldwater, Percy and a handful of others. But a man like Joseph Montoya was relatively unknown outside his own state until recently. The Watergate hearings have elevated a handful of members of the Senate, including Montoya, to sudden national personality status. Years ago Montoya might have asked a question of the Secretary of the Treasury and it would have been unnoticed. If Montoya had had the stature then that he has recently acquired, Connally might have crumbled in his presentation to the committee on behalf of Lockheed, and on behalf of Nixon.

Connally responded to Montoya by saying that "it would cost $50 million to redesign the plane to take substitute engines made by either of the American companies" and "I don't think the airlines are going to wait around long enough for redesigning." Since Lockheed was the only major manufacturer even close to production status, there wasn't much else the airlines could do but wait, but Connally didn't get around to discussing that angle. Instead, he added that $1.2 billion already had been invested in the program, that 25,000 to 30,000 jobs were on the line, that Great Britain had a major investment in the engine development, that bank commitments had been made and that airline customers were practically waiting in line at the ticket counters. All these things were about to collapse unless the Government guaranteed the loan for Lockheed.

Montoya, however, was not impressed.

President Nixon finally decided to make a personal request for congressional approval of the $250 million loan guarantees. Connally had been the blocking back for the project, but Nixon likes to quarterback his own victories. Connally was given the task of facing congressional lions like William S. Moorhead, Pennsylvania Democrat, who described Daniel J. Haughton, Lockheed chairman of the board, as a man who "by sheer guts and baling wire has kept his group of incompetents afloat by intimidating the Federal Government with threats of corporate suicide and then walking out with the taxpayers' money."

Connally kept on selling. He urged support of the program by saying that he did not see any costs to the taxpayers arising from the loan guarantee, which would provide federal backing for banks and other major lenders who would be supporting the corporation. Both he and the President predicted the rehiring of the 7,000 Lockheed employees who had been laid off, and they spoke strongly of the effects of the Tri-Star program on restoring the proper balance of payments in the nation's foreign trade. Connally added, "The impact on the economy by the bankruptcy of Lockheed would be enormous in my judgment."

A quick look at Connally's activities might make it appear that the Secretary of the Treasury was spending all of his time arguing the Government's position and sifting through the federal bureaucracy in an attempt to help sell the Nixon program of economic salvation. Still, Big John was able to find time each week for meetings with key political leaders on all levels throughout the nation. It might be a dairy millionaire from Florida named John MacArthur or an obscure mayor from a northwestern city, but the men seemed to have in common an ability to help groom Connally as a national candidate. The worst-kept, and most discussed, secret in Washington became John Connally's political ambitions. At a party attended by several staff members and friends from Texas, the hostess requested that the orchestra play "Hail to the Chief" when Connally crossed her Georgetown patio. Connally loved it, and though many guests cheered, others laughed quietly into their hands, or bit their lips in embarrassment.

Next, Connally tackled the Joint Economic Committee of Congress in discussions of domestic economic issues like tax revision. He opposed possible action by Congress to authorize additional taxes on the oil and gas industries beyond the increases enacted in 1969. The gas and oil companies felt that they deserved relief. Connally knew the economics of the oil and gas industry better than almost anyone else in Washington. After all, he had been their lawyer, a corporate director, a lobbyist and an international negotiator for several oil giants, and if he couldn't deliver some sort of reasonable plan to the oil firms, then he would risk sacrificing a large part of his personal power base and the chance for major financial contributions to an election campaign.

In his tax revision testimony, Connally said he was only "concerned for our basic fuel supply" and added, "We ought to turn our attention not to ways of discouraging further oil exploration, but to encourage it."

When the tax was increased in 1969, the oil companies had paid $700 million extra. But as is often the case, a compromise was worked out that would be politically expedient and publicly acceptable. The oil industry would not be clobbered too badly, and the taxpayers and little people would think that the rich and powerful oil interests had been somewhat regulated.

With his work on the Lockheed loan problem and his taxation meetings with congressional committees, Connally was flexing his muscles on and around Capitol Hill, and dealing from strength in Cabinet meetings. White House spokesmen kept reminding the media that, when Nixon appointed Big John, he was putting the Administration's economic and fiscal leadership back into the Treasury Department with a man who would push his programs, even before a defiant Congress. Nixon also had said he was putting the department into the hands of a man who would put "full employment ahead of sound money." Connally, with his tax cuts and spending increases, was aiming at a gross national product of $1.065 trillion by the end of 1971. Since putting more money into the economy by spending than is taken out in taxes was the general theme of Nixon's economics, Connally continued to be secure.

Connally's activities of "easy money, budgetary deficits and government spending" were basically Democratic tactics, but Connally, able to work on either side of the party fence, was in an ideal position. As one aide said, he "doesn't have to pick sides, and he's not trapped by any theoretical dogma or by position papers he wrote twenty years ago."

While Connally's stature grew in Washington, to the discomfiture of many Nixon confidants who had been shuttled into more obscure positions, there were problems in the Secretary's home state. Some Texas Democrats kept referring to Big John as a "former" Democrat, while others fanned the speculative embers about his interest in the vice presidency. Connally kept repeating the standard comments about "premature" decisions, but he never silenced the conjecture. It appeared to many that he really did not want to.

Connally went before Congress again in June 1971 with an issue that both President Nixon and his economic advisers were strongly promoting—a federal revenue-sharing plan. Secretary Connally outlined the plan to a House Ways and Means Committee that was anything but receptive. Only four of the committee's twenty-five members, all Republicans, expressed any favorable comment on the Nixon plan. Chairman Wilbur Mills had a rather backhanded compliment for Connally when he said he had made "a very fine statement for a very weak case."

Most of the political opposition to the plan was based on questioning as to why federal revenue had to be distributed to "every town and village in the nation." Connally defended it by saying, "Podunk is part of America," and Michigan Democratic Congresswoman Martha Griffiths attacked it by noting that the plan was "a political formula, designed to get the vote of every mayor." She added that the revenue-sharing money, raised by taxpayers throughout the country, would go partly to localities that "just won't raise" their own taxes. One of the targets along the way was Connally's home state of Texas, one of twenty-two states without an income tax. There was more artillery leveled on the extremely wealthy Los Angeles suburb of Beverly Hills, which, according to Connally, would receive a higher percentage of shared revenue than a poorer community, since Beverly Hills could afford to vote for higher taxes and could also afford to pay them.

Mayors of large cities were split in their reaction. Some didn't want to be beholden to the Federal Government. Others were excited because they could see a welcome source of revenue, or because they had problems similar to those of cities like New York, whose money-raising abilities were constantly hamstrung by an anti-city state legislature.

Committee Chairman Mills, however, saw the revenue-sharing plan as "the most dangerous proposal that has ever been developed" and while he compared it to a "Trojan horse," he anticipated that the program could produce greater federal restrictions on the authority of state governments.

Testimony over revenue sharing almost got the Secretary of the Treasury into a public relations knot, but he managed to break it. He was responding to testimony by a number of mayors in front of the Ways and Means Committee when he said that revenue sharing was "not a bill to relieve the urban crisis." Congressman Charles A. Vanik, an Ohio Democrat, promptly snapped, "Say that again. I'd like to get that message out to the people," and Connally, thinking fast, attempted to correct himself by the insistent addition of "not alone, not alone."

Connally testified that revenue sharing was "not an anti-riot bill, not an unemployment bill," and he tried to impress upon the committee that the use of the money would rest with state governments which were "closer to the people than the Federal Government is." Others continued to express the opinion that the program would merely "put the money where the wealth is."

The Secretary made a further pitch in a speech to

a National Tax Association seminar on July 22. Connally expressed the philosophy behind revenue sharing by saying, ". . . we want to give you a little [tax revenue] back because we think frankly that you can spend it a little better and a little more wisely, and in a little better way and for the purposes that you think you need it and, frankly, we think your judgment is better than ours."

Connally obviously was thinking of his own six years as Governor of Texas when it would have been very nice to have had uncomplicated access to federal funds. It was easy for Connally to empathize with state officials on the matter of revenue sharing.

Mayors of larger cities were carefully examining the federal formula for distribution and the amount of funds they might be eligible to receive. The Administration specified a grant of $5 billion the first year, with the total rising to $10 billion by the tenth year. A similar plan, proposed a month earlier by Senator Muskie, had considered an allocation of $6 billion, with monies to be apportioned according to need. Communities with large numbers of low-income residents and welfare recipients would receive extra funds. Supporters of the Muskie Plan said the Administration would have to double its own ante and begin with $10 billion.

Though tax reform and revenue sharing now were the hot issues, the spectre of Lockheed still remained on the Northwestern horizon. Connally admitted he did not foresee "a panic" if Lockheed went bankrupt, but he was still representing the Administration at hearings by the Senate Banking and Currency Committee. Connally assured the group of his actions in attempting to safeguard the loan, and he spoke of the sure footing of the corporation. He did not seem to make much of an impression on the committee, and it appeared partic-

ularly disinterested in his plea that the bill be passed in
"no more than forty days," a pace which represents
breakneck speed to members of Congress.

Connally's testimony revealed that the Government
would get first call on Lockheed's assets if it should go
under. He also said that he "will not use the authority
to guarantee loans unless and until all the major purchasers have signed firm new contracts renewing their
original commitments." Connally said he would not want
to jeopardize the jobs of those working on the Lockheed
program. He went on to speak of a "deep-seated fear,
the opposite of confidence" that could have an eroding
effect on a nation's economy. Connally eyed the possible
"failure of the nation's largest defense contractor" with
great uneasiness, and he said with immense gravity that
the prospect of the failure of Lockheed bothered him a
great deal more than it bothered his detractors.

There were those committee members who questioned Connally about the free enterprise system, and
whether government support for a company that could
not make a profit on its own was not contrary to the
American way of life. The Secretary replied that some
defense contractors had become so large that regular
banking systems could not meet their needs.

Connally was most displeased when some Congressmen, and some political commentators, referred to the
Lockheed bill as "welfare legislation" for a large company. When Senator Proxmire suggested it, Connally
retorted that it wasn't welfare legislation when Congress
provided a $20 million tax break for American Motors,
a large employer in Proxmire's home state. The Senator
replied that his concern was over competition in the
automotive field, and a failure by American Motors
would reduce the industry to only three major corporations. Connally then had the chance to drive a winning

point home when he noted that a Lockheed bankruptcy would leave only two major American aircraft producers, Boeing and McDonnell-Douglas.

The Secretary of the Treasury worked hard in his congressional testimony. He was fighting for a cause that was unpopular with a large portion of the American public and a vocal portion of the American Congress. It took all of his long-time political experience and composure to keep cool through the hearings, but he generally did an excellent job. He was angry one day before a Senate committee when it was mentioned that the replacement of Lockheed management might be a condition for congressional approval. There had been considerable discussion that the company had been poorly managed and had been hampered by fiscal irresponsibility. Senator Alan Cranston, a Democrat from California, had suggested a bill requiring all present directors and the chief executive officer to resign.

Connally was earning his Cabinet member's salary with his work before Congress, and he was doing the bidding of his boss, the President. What else was in it for him?

John Kenneth Galbraith, the noted economist, remarked that Connally's proposed legislation was intended to "increase his political stock" and Galbraith added sarcastically that the bill for guaranteed loans proved that "the military-industrial complex is alive in Washington and doing well." The President was on Connally's side, the economist pointed out, but Arthur Burns, chairman of the Federal Reserve Board, and David Packard, Deputy Secretary of Defense, did not receive the Connally ideas with great warmth. Galbraith himself portrayed Connally "as a new boy in town and a Democrat in a Republican Administration . . . needing to prove himself with the President."

As the Lockheed battle grew hotter, the Secretary found himself inextricably linked with it. It was not only a Lockheed proposal, but a Connally proposal. It was not only a Nixon desire, but a Connally desire. Success would be a strong factor in helping future political ambitions, and total failure would be a severe blow. There was sufficient middle ground so that Connally was generally secure, but it was becoming a major battleground for his ambitions.

Another anti-Connally spokesman was Senator Birch Bayh, an Indiana Democrat who saw inherent dangers and a perilous precedent if the Government continued to rescue "a few giant and persistently shaky" corporations. What about "financially ailing" hospitals, colleges and medical schools, Bayh wanted to know. Why couldn't the Government underwrite loans for such institutions as well?

Congress was nearing the summer recess, and the Lockheed fight was entering its final innings. Connally pressed harder for immediate congressional measures to insure the continuance of the company. He addressed the House Banking and Currency Committee and expressed "high hopes" that Congress would reach a favorable decision and thus help quell the fears that Connally predicted would arise if some action was not taken immediately. He predicted that without Lockheed's survival there could be "market repercussions that could severely dampen and perhaps thwart the business recovery."

Chairman Burns of the Federal Reserve Board came up with a broader concept of handling the Lockheed situation, suggesting legislation that was vital to "provide better protection against the risk that a temporary problem of one business enterprise may grow into a major national problem."

Connally immediately put higher priorities on the

Administration's original Lockheed-only bill, which also happened to be the Secretary's bill, but admitted he could accept the broadened Senate version.

Connally's meteoric rise from a rookie member of the Cabinet to President Nixon's "chief economic spokesman" was capped in June when he appeared at a meeting of the Cabinet and laid before it the economic policies that he and the President, along with a few other top economic advisers, had discussed the previous weekend. Though the plan was the work of a number of men, the President chose Connally to represent him and to make the case to the Cabinet. The Secretary told the Cabinet that the President had acted only after seeking advice from a wide range of persons both in and out of government, and that it had required much consideration on the part of the President. Nixon had decided not to pursue an active part in artificial stimulation of the economy at the moment, and Connally's presentation to the Cabinet was basically a set of decisions not to do anything. In other words, the President had decided not to institute a wage-price review board, not to impose mandatory wage and price controls authorized by Congress, not to seek any form of tax relief and not to increase federal spending.

As Nixon's spokesman, Big John announced Nixon's policies on June 29, saying that the economy is "perking up," but sagely adding, "Frankly, we are going to require some degree of patience on the part of the American people." Connally expressed the President's personal dissatisfaction with the fact that the nation's unemployment rate was at 6.2 percent, and he was again talking for the Chief Executive when he said, "He [the President] feels that to reduce unemployment on a short-term basis would jeopardize their gains, their jobs and the jobs and gains of millions of other Americans by adding a thrust to inflation that would be unacceptable

and unfair." Part of the explanation of the unemployment rate included the fact that the figure would be only
5.5 percent if it had not been for servicemen released
from active duty. The remark, which also included the
comment that the President was "reducing the size of
military forces and bringing down defense spending,"
could be taken several ways—a demonstration of the
President's desire to bring the nation out of its Southeast
Asia dilemma, or a jab at those who wanted it so with
the comment that increased unemployment really was
their fault and not the fault of the Administration.

Early in his career as the top Democrat in a Republican Administration, Connally had said of the President,
"We are close, but not intimate." The relationship was
showing signs of change. With Connally's promotion to
top economic spokesman, he was apparently doing a
recognized and excellent job of outlining the President's
economic policies to those who could be considered his
opponents. As his success increased, and his services were
more in demand by the President, the feeling of presidential trust grew. As one observer said, "He [Connally]
talks and the President listens." The Texan and the Californian were in almost constant contact, often together
at the White House for "breakfast, lunch, dinner and in
between." When a presidential aide branded one of
Connally's ideas as a good one and offered to "pass it
along to the President," Connally's calm response was
that the aide shouldn't bother since he was "seeing the
President this afternoon—I'll pass it on myself."

Nixon himself continually expressed enthusiasm for
Connally's performance in presenting economic policies
and, more important, in convincing those who needed
convincing. During a briefing for Congressmen on the
necessity for government reorganization, Connally was
remembered as being so intense that when he finished,

even the President commented, "I'd vote for that." The Secretary of the Treasury, always candid and completely at ease before congressional hearings, could quip as well as talk seriously. He told the Joint Economic Committee at one point, "I'm just an old country boy. I learned a long time ago that I'm just not smart enough to be devious."

The tall Texan continued to grow in stature and importance. He was now listening to the complaints of bankers and industrialists, as well as confronting the press and Congress in his role as Nixon's spokesman. A financier once told him, "You're the only man we believe." After all, they knew he spoke for the establishment, for conservatism, and that he was living proof that, regardless of party, the establishment always took care of its own.

One question that emerged as Connally became more aggressive, more visible, more of a public figure —"he's not going to run the Treasury, he's going to run the country," was one comment—was whether or not the country was looking for another Lyndon Johnson. Connally's earthy manner and Texas drawl kept him under the shadow of Johnson, but differences in style began to emerge, and observers soon began to notice habits and mannerisms that were exclusive to Big John. "Connally laughed better and he talked better," noted one observer. The Secretary was more reserved, less offensive. Big John once said of Johnson, "Want to know what's wrong with Lyndon? He's ashamed of being a Texan, and I'm not." Connally held his pride high.

Internal finances were not Connally's only worry as Secretary of the Treasury. He had begun to openly discuss the American financial situation relative to burgeoning European and Asian economic powers. The balance of payments deficit was becoming more and more a matter of concern, and the President was beginning to worry about maintaining the economic strength necessary to support the nation's military and political position in world affairs. It was a worry that reached crisis status in 1973. Connally, testifying before a Senate committee, opposed any reduction of troops in Europe, a move that had some congressional support. Connally did admit that other countries should assume a "more fair" share of the responsibilities of defense that the United States had undertaken ever since the end of World War II, but his background of dealing from strength kept him firm in his feeling that national defense was a vital part of any budget.

While the President spoke to the nation's newspaper editors on the economic situation, his spokesman, John Connally, was urging positive action with members of Congress. Connally said it was up to both labor and private industry to "help redress the decline in our competitive position and improve our economic position in foreign markets." This would be an essential step for the American people, said the President, for them to "regain their competitive spirit and moral strength and stay ahead in the race for world leadership."

Connally's strength and individuality—and the fact that he could get away with being his own man, even in the administration of another party—were dramatically shown in late May. The President had asked his Secretary of the Treasury to represent the nation in Munich at the International Monetary Conference of the American Bankers Association. Many of Europe's top financial and business leaders would be present, and it was obvious to Big John that it was a perfect place to display his strength and his abilities. Suddenly, there were some changes. Chairman Mills wanted the Secretary of the Treasury to testify on revenue sharing before the House Ways and Means Committee. Senator William Fulbright wanted him to testify before the Senate Foreign Relations Committee. The President sent word that it would be nice if Connally could testify for the revenue-sharing plan before Mills's committee. But Connally, always his own man with his own thoughts and plans uppermost, turned down both powerful Arkansas legislators and went to Munich. He obviously had decided that it was better for his own future, if not for the nation, if he went to battle for the position of the dollar in the world of international finance. Connally, with unusual bluntness, told the world bankers exactly what was on his mind. He felt that they should "share more fully in the cost of defending the free world," and he told them that they should strongly consider liberalizing trading arrangements so that American exports could expand. "No longer can considerations of friendship or need or capacity justify the United States carrying so heavy a share of the common burdens," he said.

Ambitious politicians have to have both national and international scope, and trips like this were just the thing to give Connally an international reputation and the ability to talk like a world leader.

He hadn't been back from Munich very long when he spoke before the Texas Bar Association and said, "No one is going to look after these United States unless we look after them," and he added, "We have competition around the world in unprecedented intensity from the very nations that were destroyed twenty-five years ago." The obvious references were to Japan and Germany, and Big John had an eye on mainland China as well.

Connally's worldly eyes looked in all directions. Turning south in response to the threat that some South American governments were posing to American-owned companies, Connally summed up the situation with the realistic comment, "We don't have any friends there anyway." With Big John's position of influence over American lending power, he could express his disturbance over the expropriation of American holdings in Latin American countries. The unspoken threat was that the Treasury Department could withhold loans until, using Chile as an example, there were "satisfactory" assurances on compensation to American copper industries being nationalized under new Chilean laws. President Nixon was equally sensitive to the Latin American situation. He had friends among the powerful industrialists whose firms were being taken over, and the friends made important contributions to the nation's economy and the Republican party's war chest. Since he was sensitive, his "chief economic spokesman" also was sensitive. Connally's get-tough policy with countries whose governments were swinging to the left carried a two-edged sword. The hard line could perhaps frighten other countries that were thinking of instituting a policy of expropriation, and it certainly would demonstrate the Administration's readiness to listen to the cries of American business interests and respond with all possible help.

The hard-nosed policy, however, struck an altogether different chord in the U.S. State Department. One department official moaned audibly about "the effect that Connally's get-tough attitude will have on relations with the whole Western Hemisphere. There are 230 million Latin Americans, and we have other important interests besides copper." Besides, there had been no American policy of preventing the issue of loans to expropriating countries as long as it appeared that the country was ready to pay fair compensation within a reasonable period of time. In the case of Chile, the obvious if unspoken target of Connally's ire, that country's controller general needed six months to assess the expropriated interests and reach mutual agreement with the former owner. The United States Government was denying a

loan which Chile had pledged to repay. Nationalization
had been in effect only twenty-seven days.

Many observers of the international scene were
wondering how and why this infringement of the long
established "Good Neighbor Policy" was being pursued
by the President. Was Nixon's increasing trust in John
Connally overriding the value of advice given by Secretary of State Rogers? If so, how would this affect Nixon's
future attitude toward Latin America? The Secretary of
the Treasury was well known for his personal attitude
toward Mexican-Americans, a feeling he had shown
during the Starr County farm labor disputes of 1966,
and he may easily have considered the remainder of
Latin America just an extension of Mexico.

The President continued to place Connally in increasingly vital roles for developing and defending American economic policies, abroad as well as at home. Things
weren't going as well as expected in the latter area, since
the battles still raged over the President's desire to guarantee a loan to the Lockheed Corporation, plus the
revenue-sharing plans which were a basic part of his
economic program. In these struggles, Connally was the
man between the President and the populace who would
have the chance to reelect him in 1972. The Texan said,
"The President knows there's an election in 1972, but
he also knows that we have to continue this fight against
inflation, that if we don't do that, then you're not going
to get the economic expansion . . . that's going to provide these jobs for American working men."

It became extremely difficult to tell where the President's proposals left off and Connally's own policy-
making influence began. The Texan, wise in the ways
of the political world, always spoke guardedly about
any advice he might offer the President. He would say,
"It is immaterial what position I take. I am not the
President. He is." Connally also was wise enough not

to consider himself an experienced economist. But he became attentive to the advice of other men, usually wiser men, and he watched their attitudes as well as their statements.

"What I'm going to do, very frankly," he said early in his career at Treasury, "is get advice from all sides . . . and then there are other considerations, I think, that have to be applied. There are instincts that have to be applied, and they're not mine alone, but they're the President's." Although Connally confessed to lacking the "capacity to create the [economic] models," a special assistant to the Council of Economic Advisers referred to his capacity by saying, admiringly, "It's more than an inch deep. He sees the relationships."

On the issue of unemployment, Connally could not accept the theory that 4 percent represented "full employment." He labeled its achievement as "a myth. It has never happened . . . saving a wartime, not in the last quarter of a century." He felt that 4½ percent was as close as anyone was going to be able to achieve.

Secretary Connally and his fellow Texan, Democratic Congressman Wright Patman, chairman of the House Banking and Currency Committee, came to grips over the issue of the long-term interest-rate ceiling, which Patman was striving to keep intact. Connally pushed through $10 billion worth of long-term securities bearing interest rates above the ceiling (4.25 percent), and Patman commented, "Connally makes some excellent public statements about the need for low interest rates. It is still my opinion that it is unwise for an Administration to select a lifelong Democrat to carry out age-old Republican policies on interest rates and money matters."

Connally would disagree with Patman's assessment of the situation and would illustrate by telling one of his favorite parables, one he often used to demonstrate his position as a Democrat in a Republican administration. The story dealt with a preacher being interviewed by the deacons for a church in the Texas hills. The deacons asked whether the preacher believed in the Divine Creation or in the Newtonian theory of man's descent from monkeys, and the preacher replied solemnly, "Deacon, I can preach it either way."

When the Treasury Secretary presented what later was termed President Nixon's "Four-Point, Do-Nothing Plan" to Cabinet members, many of his suggestions were not visible in the final drafting of the language. Connally had urged the President to push forward with scheduled federal tax cuts and to reinstate the 7 percent investment tax credit for businessmen. One of the President's four points was the decision against requesting any tax relief from Congress.

Connally also advised the Chief Executive that his Administration should become more directly involved in monitoring major wage and price decisions. The President's announcement offered no suggestion of imposing any type of wage-price controls, nor did he ask for the institution of a wage-price review board. Arthur Burns of the Federal Reserve Board took issue with Nixon for not moving toward a review board, but Connally did not openly express disappointment or dissatisfaction over the fact that his suggestions were not heeded. The importance of watching wages and prices was not completely ignored by the President. Although he did not specifically mention it, jawboning was not eliminated as a tactic for keeping closer rein on industries or unions that were threatening the Administration's "battle against inflation." Nixon, influenced by either Connally or Burns, or both, revealed that he intended to meet with representatives of both the steel industry and the United Steelworkers Union at the White House on July 6 to discuss their plans and to dictate to them the necessity for holding down both wages and prices.

Conditions were changing rapidly in the summer of 1971, however. On August 4 the President held a press conference and indicated a major change in the course of the nation's economic policies. Mr. Nixon said that he would consider "a recommendation on wage-price boards, an idea which had been frequently suggested by Burns." At the time of the announcement Nixon also noted that he and Burns "then and always had been in agreement on the big issues."

Less than two weeks later, the President announced a "new economic policy for the United States," and Connally commented, in the aftermath of the August 15 decision, "There's nothing, as the wise saying goes, there's nothing constant except change." The President issued executive orders that initiated a ninety-day freeze on wages and prices, added a 10 percent surcharge on dutiable imports and suspended the convertibility of the dollar into gold. The next day Connally had his own televised press conference to defend the President's new program, which also included proposed tax reductions to be presented to Congress when it returned from its summer recess on September 8. When Connally was asked if the new program represented "an admission that the Administration's policies up to now have failed," he called upon his longtime restraint and political background to note, "Oh, I don't think we did it in terms of an admission of anything. I would characterize it as a new policy, a new economic action." The Texan spoke at length in defense of the program, emphasizing that the President had deliberated a long time before deciding on this type of action. The decisions, Connally said, had been "long in the making," but many observers felt that an impending international monetary crisis, with lessening confidence in the U.S. dollar, seemed to spur the President into a more active economic course. The Office of Emergency Preparedness was busy making preparations for the operation of the new program, and would administer the wage-price freeze, but compliance with the new order probably would be effected by the force of public opinion.

The tax relief program, which contained some facets of relief for individual taxpayers along with repeal of the automobile excise tax and incentives for businesses, received strong support from Chairman Mills of the House Ways and Means Committee, a key legislator in rapid approval of the President's plans. Mills termed the economic plan "an excellent one" and anticipated speedy House approval. Since Congress was in recess until early September, Connally announced that the taxes could be retroactive to the time of the announcement. On the other side, several liberal Democrats criticized the tax-relief program, suggesting loudly that the major relief should go to lower-income persons rather than auto-mobile manufacturers (or buyers) and other business-men.

The President, finally moving toward more active economic policies, realizing certain failures in the old programs and a rapid lessening of public confidence, seemed to be taking the advice of Connally. The latter, in turn, predicted, "I think the President is prepared to take whatever action is necessary to maintain a stable economy in this country."

Still, neither the inquisitive press nor the acquisitive politicians, all of whom had their own vested interests, dared to take their eyes off the possibilities of a Nixon-Connally ticket for the Republicans in 1972. Ben Barnes, now lieutenant governor of Texas, predicted that Con-nally was not likely to seek elective office "ever" again. Barnes had met privately with Connally in June and had left with the strong impression that "he's going to come back to Texas a Democrat." Barnes himself was carefully studying the contest for Governor and weighing it against a race for a seat in the U.S. Senate. He felt that Connally's position in the Cabinet of a Republican administration would make it difficult for the Democrats in the upcoming statewide elections.

Connally still had not come out directly to refute any interest in the vice presidency, but he left little hints that could be found, examined, reexamined and interpreted almost any way at all, depending on the finder's own political views and his thinking about Connally. He once remarked that he "never knew a vice president who was not frustrated." In mid-June, however, the Dallas *Times Herald* reported that a clipping had appeared on the desks of Washington reporters in unmarked envelopes. The clipping was supposedly a statement that Connally had made to a group of Texas businessmen, telling them that under no circumstances would he run for vice president as a Republican. If so, that was his first positive denial of rumors that had begun at the time of his appointment as Secretary of the Treasury. The cloak-and-dagger technique of unmarked envelopes and "high, unimpeachable sources" is the sort of glorious nonsense that reporters—and especially Washington reporters—dearly love.

Later on in the year Connally put the final quietus on 1972 vice-presidential rumors when he was featured on a television panel show moderated by Nancy Dickerson of the National Broadcasting Company. "I don't think it [replacing Agnew] is in the cards," said Connally. "I don't think it is something the President will want to do. I don't think it is something the Republican party wants to do. I personally have no ambition."

Of course, with the extreme closeness that had grown between the President and Connally, it would have been very easy for Nixon to have explained that it was in the best interests of the country and of the party that

Agnew be retained in 1972. Connally would have bought
at least one of the reasons.

In Texas, Barnes had been leaning toward the
Senate race, but with Connally holding strong and getting
stronger in the Cabinet, he decided to withhold any announcement until the end of the 1971 legislative session.
Everyone knew that all national power hovered over
Washington, but there remained some rich and influential
Texans who felt comfortable with an ally in the Governor's Mansion. Some said that Perry Bass had threatened to hold back on any campaign assistance unless
Barnes ran for Governor on the Democratic ticket. Looking over the broader political picture, the strategy seemed
to be part of an overall plan to secure the state and avoid
any bitter fights. With Barnes running for Governor,
Republican John Tower would easily win reelection for
the Senate. That would leave a Senate seat in the hands
of the Republicans (Lloyd Bentsen was not due to defend his own seat) while the establishment Democrats in
Texas would have Barnes in the Governor's chair and
the state in good hands. This also would make things
much easier for Nixon to carry Texas in 1972 and would
also leave a place for Connally as Vice President if Nixon
decided to dump Agnew.

Ronnie Dugger, the guiding spirit of the *Texas
Observer,* questioned in his *Atlantic* article the Nixon-
Connally alliance and its significance to American society, observing: "Like other Texas Democrats in the
last twenty-five years, Connally may have decided that
he has no future as a national Democrat and can do
better for himself on the other side. Nixon's and Connally's thinking may have converged into one political
strategy, the creation from the Republican side of 'a new
American majority' of Republicans and Southern Democrats, conservatives and moderates, funded by oil and

other big business, that can finally reduce the liberals to a minority."

Washington observers had noticed that Nixon and Connally shared common ground as fiscal conservatives, but there were other similarities that drew the men close together, one as the admired adviser and the other as the admired advisee. They shared a great respect for politics as an art form and both played the game continuously, for fun as well as for profit. Their personal values converged on the basic issues of order, hard work, self-discipline and moderation. Their politics and their personalities, along with their ambitions, could easily bind them into a powerful political force.

Comments continued, despite the Connally denial, on his possibilities as a vice-presidential candidate with Nixon in 1972, then, perhaps, succeeding him in 1976. Connally's wife, Idanell, echoed her husband when she commented on the speculation as "silly—we came as Democrats and we'll leave as Democrats."

Another friend of the Connallys explained things in what he considered a politically pragmatic manner, noting, "You just don't take an outstanding Democrat and present him at a Republican convention as your vice-presidential nominee. They took Wendell Willkie for president in 1940 and spent the next twenty-five years fighting about it."

An ironic linking of Connally and Senator Kennedy came up in September when Kennedy defeated Connally in an election: Kennedy was voted the nation's best dressed politician by the Custom Tailors Guild. Connally finished second. The Secretary was noted for his pride in his good looks, termed excess vanity by some, and his devotion to careful dress. *Newsweek* magazine, in reporting the story, quoted a Connally friend as saying, "He believes strongly in appearance—in looking the role of a leader, in looking right for a job and having the right setting." Connally had been known to tell Treasury Department colleagues to "sharpen up" when their appearance began to sag, and his own appearance was considered a welcome relief from what the magazine described as a "decidedly dull Republican inner circle."

John Connally is in fact a total professional. He has a perennial candidate's instincts. In years to come he could be another Harold Stassen but with spats. He believes in the entourage, the advance man and the bumper strip. One of the worst-kept secrets of 1972 was a campaign tactic in which airports in every city that John Connally visited would be telephoned every few hours and asked to page John Connally for an urgent message. He was never there at the time.

There have been occasions when reporters were invited to participate in press interviews on the run. Connally likes to leave his office with one or two aides and build the group up so that it becomes a more noticeable crowd when he arrives at a television station or campaign headquarters.

An openly anti-Connally staff member in the Office of the Vice President claims "he wouldn't go to the men's room without sending an aide ahead to check out the crowd." Connallyites defend their idol's perfect professionalism by the logic that the public likes their stars to act like stars.

President Nixon's fateful August 15 announcement of new international trade and monetary policies was still controversial news when the annual meeting of the International Monetary Fund and the World Bank opened in Washington on September 27. The President's action had not been well received by the other countries of the world, and feelings for the United States were not good when the meeting began.

John Connally, of course, stood by the actions, rationalizing that other countries were getting too used to living on the balance-of-payments deficit supported by the United States and that this free ride was going to end even if the withdrawal symptoms left a bitter taste for some other countries. There would be fewer exports, more imports and a possible loss of jobs in those countries. The 10 percent surcharge on import duties was one of the more severe tactics for trying to bring about a swing of some $13 billion in the nation's balance of payments. One Administration critic argued that Connally's target of $13 billion was an overestimate of between $3 and $5 billion, that the figure was impossible to attain and would threaten American trade relations with many countries. Connally, however, seemed committed to the hard course of action and was taking an extremely firm stand with other countries.

He also felt that former allies should show more appreciation for past American aid that went all the way back to President Harry S. Truman's implementation of the Marshall Plan following World War II. Connally expounded on "unfair" exchange rates, trade rules and defense burdens, but always failed to mention the American commitment in Southeast Asia, the huge expense of the unpopular war and the abysmal condition of the economy of Vietnam. He also was a roadblock to any negotiations on the exchange rates for currency and gold, and wanted undefined trade and defense concessions from other nations before he would discuss a change in the 10 percent surtax.

Connally addressed the IMF meeting on September 30 and continued to pursue his course, insisting that other countries make "tangible progress" toward "dismantling specific trade barriers over the coming weeks" and allow "market realities freely to determine exchange rates for their currencies for a transitional period" before the

United States would move toward lifting the surcharge barrier. Despite the President's attempts to assure other countries of the nation's continuing role in world politics, questions were being raised about an American return to strict isolationism.

The new economic policies and trade barriers were causing irritation, confusion and then anger throughout Europe, and Connally was invited to discuss details and explain the American position in international trade at a meeting of the Organization for Economic Cooperation and Development. Connally, not surprised over the confusion, explained, "I had a choice between being considered mysterious and being considered overbearing and demanding. I chose to be mysterious."

Connally did feel that other countries were beginning to understand the background and the rationale of the American moves. He optimistically felt that they soon would take a positive response to the American demands that barriers to American exports and investment be lowered before there was reciprocation on trade barriers or negotiation on new relative currency values.

Connally's hard line continued throughout the IMF meetings. He spoke to a closed council session and, in words obviously addressed to Latin American nations, spoke critically of countries which "first entice and then expropriate American business interests without adequate compensation." He urged that the United States "reappraise its policies with these countries."

The Texan's attitude in the IMF meetings left disturbed feelings all over Europe, and many financial experts considered the American image to be badly soiled, but Nixon apparently felt Connally had done a perfect job because the Secretary of the Treasury next was on his way to South Vietnam. If the President couldn't attend the inauguration of President-elect Nguyen Van

Thieu, he would send one of his most trusted advisers. Connally now was not only the President's chief economic spokesman, but an international political figure and a direct representative of the President at a major state function of another nation.

Connally's visit was scheduled for the end of October, tying in with Thieu's inauguration, and the visit to South Vietnam was only a part of the entire journey. Connally would represent the President in stops in a number of countries in the Orient and Southeast Asia, a task which would enhance his prestige inside the Administration and broaden the base of his experience for future years. There was speculation that Connally would consult with South Vietnamese leaders on the country's economy in the wake of the departure of American troops, and there also was the opportunity for Connally to suggest to the South Vietnamese Government what steps should be taken for the emerging nation to gain a strong base for its own operation.

American foreign policy may have reaped benefits from the Secretary's trip, but an incident along the way proved a definite embarrassment for Connally among a group of American tourists. Connally, on his way to Tokyo and Manila for economic discussions, stopped for a rest on the island of Bali, and the government-owned Bali Beach Hotel had an enthusiastic welcome for him. The management even substituted American-inspected water for the native water in the interest of Connally's health and because he was suffering from a minor stomach ailment. The management also went so far as to ask a group of American tourists to vacate their rooms for Connally and some of his party. The Americans moved out, but they were none too gracious about the experience, even going to meet him at the airport and telling him, "We came eighteen thousand miles just to be thrown out of a hotel for you." Connally apologized, but the damage was done and a handful of votes probably had been lost forever.

When Big John returned from the Far East, he reported on the great advantages that Japan was gaining in trade opportunities compared to the United States. He also described an American banker who was enthusiastic about the fact that he had made a small deal in Japan, but who had no knowledge of what Japanese bankers were doing in America. "That feller," said Connally in deepest Texan, "thought he had killed a hog." When the group, which included the President, had stopped laughing, Connally added, "The Japanese looked at me like I was a cowboy. But a cowboy has got to learn to ride, and I'm going to ride with this."

Even though he now was an international diplomat as well as an economic force in the world, Connally pushed strongly for tariff and investment concessions from America's trading partners. His stubbornness was met with sharp remarks from angry Europeans, who described his demands as "boorish" and "arrogant," words that no doubt were of great kindness when compared to the ones they used in private meetings. *The New York Times,* for example, acutely aware of the sensitive position the nation was taking in relation to world economics, described Connally's international policy as "vague, outsized demands for worldwide concessions in return for eliminating the surcharge" with potential "economic and psychological damage." The newspaper pointed out that the Secretary of the Treasury seemed determined to rebalance the trade deficit, which it described as "Mr. Connally's determination to get the extra five to 10 percent—and to get it in advance—in the form of unilateral concessions from the allies in trade and defense-burden sharing."

Connally kept insisting that the allies share the cost

of defending the free world, and again the *Times* pointed out, "The bulk of the defense drain is due to unilateral American policies in Vietnam," a military endeavor in which America's European allies were not even consulted. Moreover, most of them opposed the American position.

Critics also were quick to point out that Europe had become both politically and economically stronger through an East-West security system and the involvement of Great Britain in the Common Market, and added that it was to the interest of the Secretary of the Treasury and to the United States not to threaten the Western European and Atlantic unity that had been forged over the years since the end of World War II.

Another critic, Francis M. Bator, professor of political economy at Harvard University, described President Nixon's August 15 announcements as "a declaration of economic war on the rest of the world." Dr. Bator continued the analogy by calling it a phony war, with no one shooting back, but he pointed out that if Connally kept waving a gun in someone's face, the other side would eventually take some action.

A key question, of course, was whether Connally was defending his own policies or was serving as a loyal and trusted defender of the President's own course of economic action.

The question came up again when Nixon scheduled business meetings with leaders of France, Canada, Great Britain, Portugal, West Germany and Japan in December and January 1972. These meetings were preliminaries to the upcoming visits to Moscow and Peking, but why was Nixon meeting with the countries who had taken the brunt of the economic blows leveled in the August 15 speech? It was easy to speculate that the direct meetings would give the President the "opportunity to pull back from the extreme positions" taken by Connally at the IMF meetings and use his own diplomatic abilities to repair a few fences.

It was almost as if, on a worldwide level, Connally and Nixon were selling cars. Connally came through with the hard line, boosting the price of the new car and flatly saying he could not go lower. Nixon, posing as the sales manager, then came to the buyers, smiling broadly, and cut a couple of hundred dollars off the price, sending the buyer home happy and the seller home even happier.

Even though Connally had been on the firing line at the IMF meetings and others, it had been Nixon who made the speech on August 15, when he outlined economic policies for the coming months. It also was Nixon who had imposed the surtax and hinted at its repeal when his demands were met by trading nations. Nixon did not want to repudiate Connally's brash actions, since he agreed with them, but he met with foreign leaders at the suggestion of Henry Kissinger. The latter also agreed with both Nixon and Connally, but also did not want to see the policy become a regular fixture in American dealing with international allies who also were trade partners.

When Connally was listed as a member of the President's official party for the trip to Paris for talks with President Pompidou, it was recognized as a positive step toward closing the international gap which Connally had opened. C. L. Sulzberger, foreign affairs specialist of *The New York Times,* commented, "It is necessary that Connally understand the degree of irritation here with the policies of which he has made himself the flamboyant symbol."

When Dr. Henry Kissinger made his major television appearance, on November 30, to announce the plans for Nixon's trip to Peking, he threw in a good word for John Connally. Kissinger spoke in defense of Connally's handling of the international monetary problems and excused his often blunt tactics and hard-nosed approach. He said that Connally was "doing everything just right" but that the secretary, in performing the wishes of the President, was embroiled in difficult negotiations and was "using rough tactics for a noble end."

Experienced economists and experienced writers on the subject still could not resist questions and criticisms of the Secretary of the Treasury. Paul Einzig of the *Commercial and Financial Chronicle* could not understand the importance that Connally was giving to the price of gold. He wrote, "No statesman or economist or banker has ever paid such supreme homage to the power and prestige of gold as is implied in this attitude," describing Connally's feeling that the gold parity of $35 an ounce of fine gold should be maintained at whatever cost. "To give A–1 priority to the maintenance of $35 gold parity," Einzig went on, "implies recognition and admission of its immense importance. If it were as unimportant as Mr. Connally claims it to be, then what difference would it make whether its prices were $35 or $70 or $140? If I thought gold unimportant I could not care less what its price would be."

As to Connally's importance and influence in Administration economic policy, as well as his strength as a major adviser to the President, Einzig said, "I simply cannot understand how President Nixon, who is in most other respects a shrewd politician, should allow himself to be dominated by a charlatan."

Einzig's attack on Connally also brought up the man who created the Treasury Department, Alexander Hamilton. What would he have thought? Einzig answered, "Is a man like this fit to occupy the chair of Alexander Hamilton and his many distinguished, intelligent and public-spirited successors?" Meanwhile, at the Paris economic conference on December 10, a high official whose name was not given described Secretary Connally as "the best secretary since Alexander Hamilton"!

Connally, still leading the world in economic unpopularity, met with the so-called Group of Ten members of the International Monetary Fund in Rome during December. Connally was the chairman, in a position to demonstrate not only the power of his nation but his own political strength and cleverness. The United States presented its economic proposals at the beginning of the meeting, seeking reevaluation of the world's major currencies averaging 11 percent against the dollar. The Europeans countered with a suggestion for a devaluation of the dollar through an increase in the price of gold. Connally took a stubborn stand against the European idea and a French delegate snapped, "If this is your position, we can all go home." Connally, waiting patiently for an American advantage, then let down the barrier of opposition. When Valery Giscard d'Estaing, French Finance Minister, asked pointedly, "What is to be the American contribution to realignment?" Connally answered, "Well, we leave that up to you. What change in the gold price do you want—eight, nine, ten percent?"

The sudden turnabout shocked the gathering. An English representative called Connally's negotiations "not economics, but jujitsu. You resist, and then suddenly yield so that your opponent falls flat on his face." A Belgian diplomat summed up the meeting by saying, "They'll be studying Connally's tactics at foreign service institutes for a long time to come."

When the session was adjourned, Connally scheduled it to be reconvened on December 17, in Washington. As a meeting place, he selected the Smithsonian Institution's "castle" because it was "a wonderful American equivalent" of Lancaster House in London and of the setting for the most recent meeting, the Palazzo Corsini of Rome.

Meanwhile, President Nixon was making headway in his series of small and individual summit meetings with heads of state. The President was easing a little the heavy-handed economic tactics of his major spokesman, and he was slowly resealing the European bonds. Support was vital before Nixon went to Peking and Moscow. Connally's attitude had aroused resentment and distrust, and Nixon and Kissinger worked overtime to soothe angered diplomats. In fact, at the Azores Conference with President Pompidou of France, the United States agreed to devalue the dollar in exchange for minor trade concessions and a hazy agreement to discuss long-term issues at a later date.

At home Connally continued his severe outlook where expropriation of American industry was concerned. Testifying before the House Committee on Interior and Insular Affairs, he advocated strong government involvement in these situations, so that other governments would realize "you don't negotiate just with American business enterprise. You negotiate with the United States government." In discussing American foreign economic diplomacy, Connally urged this backing from the Government because "no American business enterprise can operate on a par with a foreign government."

Another witness was the outspoken Admiral Hyman Rickover, father of nuclear propulsion for warships. Rickover discussed both the energy shortage and the population explosion, and came up in head-to-head confrontation with Connally on both issues. Rickover suggested that tax laws be designed to discourage large families and Connally commented, "I hate to see the government get into its tax programs these types of social surges and social impulses." On energy, Rickover warned that the United States was consuming its natural resources at a dangerously rapid pace and Connally disagreed, saying, "Our oil and other hydrocarbon resources are not scarce. We have vast resources of hydrocarbons. We need not fear running out of these resources physically."

That song, too, had different words in the summer of 1973. The words then, in front of many gasoline stations around the nation, were, "Closed—out of gas."

Connally's growing role as an international spokesman, to go with his role as an economic spokesman, was causing increasing friction and controversy between the Department of the Treasury and the State Department, especially as outspoken economic foreign policy continued to weaken normal diplomatic relations. Connally reportedly had implied that the State Department was a nest of "ponderousness" and "in some sectors, innocence." Connally even was said to have expressed to associates a preference that the State Department be sidestepped in cases of international trade and economic conferences. The State Department reacted strongly to what it felt was a power play on the part of the ambitious Texan. One senior diplomat said, "Connally is trying to dominate U. S. foreign economic policy. He is a very strong man, but he has tunnel vision. Economic policy is just one aspect of overall American relations abroad; it is not an end in itself." Another saw the tampering with traditional European allies as particularly dangerous, adding, "All this talk that we've been taken in by our allies, all this behavior as if we're blind adversaries, is just unprofitable posturing. It's worse, because it gets everyone mad."

Still, Connally seemed to be receiving a free rein for all economic negotiations, directing both trade and monetary policies with the apparent approval of the

White House while the State Department remained in the shadows.

As a result of Nixon's August 15 policy statement and his own subsequent actions, Connally soon found himself fighting a two-front war. He was involved in disputes abroad over his high-handed tactics concerning trade barriers, and he began to get plenty of heat at home over the President's wage-price controls.

Organized labor took a stand in a hurry.

President George Meany of the AFL-CIO spoke strongly against the controls, saying that the unions had "absolutely no faith in the ability of President Nixon to successfully manage the economy of the nation. We're not advocating defiance, we're just not cooperating. If they can put it over without our cooperation, I guess they will."

Connally leaped to the defense of the President, accusing Meany of making a blatant political move in withholding his support. The Texan appeared on the NBC "Today" show to defend the program and to attack Meany's stance as being politically based. Connally even managed to display some humor: "I used to think of M&M as . . . a chocolate-coated candy that doesn't get on your fingers. But I'm afraid M&M is about to take on a new meaning, the Muskie-Meany line." He also condemned both men for having been early advocates of wage-price controls but "turning 180 degrees" when the President instituted them.

Senator Muskie reacted blandly, noting that the President should have acted "earlier and more effectively" and that he should also have offered further tax reductions for low- and middle-income families.

Meany's response was stronger, directed more at Connally when he said, "I think he's looking for the enforcement concession. He wants the horsewhip concession so he can sell horsewhips. Connally doesn't know anything about the people's problems. He has no poor friends as far as I know."

Among the many defenses of the August 15 wage policy that he had to make, Connally had to respond to charges that the freeze was uneven because of the arbitrary deadline. Connally said that the timing had to be a surprise and therefore probably would involve some inequities. "It is significant that most of the bargaining on major labor contracts has already taken place," he pointed out. "I don't know of any period of time that you would pick when less inequities, less hardships would result." When Connally elaborated on the controls, he said that the freeze on wages was all-pervasive, but that, where profits were concerned, business income had not been "all that big" anyway and controls of prices would necessarily affect the rise of profits.

The AFL-CIO Executive Council responded by saying it had supported such controls as long ago as 1966 but felt that restraints should have been levied "across the board" including corporate profits and executive benefits.

One of the first major acts of defiance came from Connally's own state. Governor Preston Smith had ignored the controls on August 20 when he paid teachers and government workers their scheduled increases. White House press secretary Ron Ziegler responded sharply, accusing Smith of disregarding a freeze "which was imposed to cure a basic problem in this country—inflation. . . . The governor of Texas, for motivations which only he is aware, is seeking to single out a group of Texans for preferential treatment. We don't think any Texan wants that, particularly when all of the nation is joining together to defeat inflation."

The Governor, not impressed by the statements of the press secretary, replied, "This flagrant violation of Texas law and the Constitution must be challenged, and that is exactly what I am doing. I am refusing to obey the President's order to scrap our appropriations bill which was signed into law months ago."

The President, not overexcited by the challenge, responded calmly from the Western White House at San Clemente, "I think Governor Connally can take care of him."

Connally predicted some of the future course of the American economy when he said during an interview on August 28: "It will be the disposition of the American people to have as few constraints as possible after the ninety-day freeze period, and if we can get voluntary compliance now we can avoid stringent controls later. But it would be unwise to think we can go back to where we were before. American business and labor may have to get used to the idea of living within certain parameters."

The mechanics for the new economic system included the Cost of Living Council, composed of the nation's top economic advisers and Cabinet members, including Connally, which met for the first time on October 5, before the beginning of economic Phase II in November. Two other control councils were to be the Price Commission and the Pay Board. Controversy arose over who had the power to do what to whom. For example, the Pay Board was to have fifteen members, five each from labor, management and the public, but it could be "vetoed if we [the Cost of Living Council] consider them inconsistent with the purposes of the program," or so said Herbert Stein, a member of the council.

Meany was less than enthusiastic about the limits being placed on the authority of labor and threatened to resign from the board. James Hodgson, Secretary of Labor, tried to reassure Meany with a slight change in the wording that covered the council's authority: "It will not approve, revise, veto or revoke specific standards or criteria developed by the Pay Board and Price Commission." The wording was a little different but the limitations remained practically the same.

With the veto situation still a bone of contention, George Shultz, director of the Office of Management and Budget, suggested that Meany watch a news conference on October 8, when Connally was scheduled to set out all the details.

When the conference was over, Meany said, "So we watched the press conference and three times Mr. Connally was asked point blank to clear up the question about the Cost of Living Council's veto power over standards set by the Pay Board. But Mr. Connally did not clarify and did not answer the question."

The battle between Connally and Meany continued, with both sides firing verbal broadsides. Meany spoke late in 1971 and said Connally "is a proven expert in Texas politics and knows quite a bit about the oil companies and their needs and the banks and the insurance companies and what they want. I'm not sure he knows much about the national economy and I am certain he doesn't understand the problems of American workers. . . . This shocking lack of faith in the ability of the American people and the American system to reach and maintain full employment . . . sounds like acceptance of Communist propaganda."

President Nixon attended the AFL-CIO Convention on November 19 and received a rather rough reception. Connally cited Meany's actions as deliberate sidestepping of protocol and rudeness toward the President; there was no band, a cursory introduction and only slight applause, which "reflected an arrogance and a boorishness and a discourtesy that ill becomes a leader of the American labor movement." Meany violently denied the charges and said that the President himself had tried to "stage-

manage" the labor convention for political purposes.
"We were not discourteous," he said. "There was no
booing and there was no jeering." Meany admitted
there was some laughter when the President spoke optimistically, but the labor leader held strongly that "we
have a Constitutional right to laugh."

Connally also made a strong point, while speaking
bluntly against Meany, that the latter's salary increase
from $70,000 to $90,000 a year was "a flagrant con-
tempt for the program of anti-inflation controls."

The Secretary of the Treasury did have one success
during November. His longtime project of securing government guarantees for loans to the Lockheed Corporation moved ahead with the approval of a series of loans
from the Emergency Loan Guarantee Board. On November 17 Lockheed received permission to borrow an
additional $25 million, which brought the total to $75
million. Congress had approved the entire loan guarantee of $250 million, which was the amount submitted
by Connally. It had been a fight lasting more than six
months, but the Secretary had steered the bill through
unimpressed congressional committees and a less-than-
enthusiastic Congress. It was a moment of triumph for
John Connally.

These moments were not too frequent, as Connally's
name kept popping up in odd and not always favorable
contexts.

For example, a tax bill already approved by the
House Ways and Means Committee and pending before
Congress was discovered to have beneficial implications
for a company in which Connally had a substantial
amount of stock. The company, Insurance Securities,
Inc., wanted to start a new type of mutual fund whose
shareholders would be limited to tax-exempt organizations. Connally, whose holdings in the company
amounted to $50,000, said he didn't know the bill was

under consideration, though the Treasury Department had approved the bill earlier.

For another, a Los Angeles environmentalist noted that John Connally was a director of Texas Instruments, Inc., and became interested in a large oil spill that resulted from an open valve on a barge loading diesel oil from a Texaco refinery. The oil had swept out into North Puget Sound, and the Environmental Protection Agency awarded a $45,000 contract to Texas Instruments to study the effects of the spill. The environmentalist also discovered that Texas Instruments had large interests in offshore gas and oil; a quarterly report had told its stockholders, "Another market force impacting our current operations is the geophysical exploration budget of the world petroleum industry. TI has a leading position in this market and opportunities will grow dramatically as the worldwide energy shortage becomes increasingly critical."

Connally's last official act for 1971 was to receive a medal, a traditional gesture to the Secretary of the Treasury. Connally joined the list of former secretaries on December 16, when his medal was added to the series produced by the United States Mint. Big John's was the twenty-fourth in the set. The medallion was struck in bronze and showed a full-face portrait on one side. The seal of the Treasury Department, centered over an outline of the state of Texas, was on the other, and the inscription listed the various public offices that Connally had held in his career.

As 1972 opened, Connally predicted that the economy for the year would be excellent. After all, it was an election year, and a good economy brought out the voting populace to keep the incumbent party in power. "I define that as moving forward on all fronts," Connally explained. As a criterion, he discussed the Dow Jones

Industrial Average, predicting that it would top 1000 "without any question" and might rise over 1100.

The optimistic announcement came as Connally and the President were flying from San Clemente to Washington after talks with Eisaku Sato, Premier of Japan. Much of the conversation had been economic, and Connally commented, "We will not get all we want, not all they should give. We know there are things they can't do but we are setting up further negotiations in 1972 and 1973 on a broader scale."

As Secretary of the Treasury, Big John was deeply involved in the budget and in the budget deficit. He spoke of it to the U. S. Chamber of Commerce on January 20, presenting the group with the figures for the expected deficit. Earlier estimates had placed it at $28 billion, but Connally was far more realistic and reported that it would be between $35 and $40 billion. "This is a political world," he added in explanation of the large deficit. "We have to have some fiscal stimulus" at a time when some five million people were unemployed. Connally also confronted the group with the Administration's defense of profits and the proposed reenactment of the investment tax credit on a permanent basis, pointing out, "You asked for it. You got it. What have you done with it? Nothing."

Once again, the Texan's high-handed attitude and strong speech had caused injured feelings and affronted a powerful group. Connally's talk to the Chamber of Commerce, telling the members that they "ought to applaud the deficit" was another chance for Administration critics to turn on Nixon and Connally. An editorial in *The New York Times* pointed to the deficit as "evidence of the Administration's poor forecasting and worse policy decisions" and suggested that Connally should reevaluate "the trickle-down tax cuts to business." The cuts were instituted to stimulate the economy by encouraging business investment, but nothing had been done to strengthen capital spending.

Connally continued to be placed in the unenviable position of defending Nixon's economic policies to a nation that was growing more and more hostile. His next stop on the firing line was in testimony before the House Ways and Means Committee on January 31, when he was trying to defend the Administration's request for a $50 billion increase in the debt ceiling. Connally tried to convince an openly angry committee that a tax increase in the near future was "not inevitable" if spending did not exceed the President's proposed budget. A number of the legislators, however, were firmly convinced that a tax increase was in the offing, though the Administration would probably try to hide it until after the forthcoming elections. Connally was questioned about the possibility of a value-added tax as a form of national sales tax, but he replied, "We don't accept the theory that you do—that we will have to have a tax increase," and he said that there had been no decisions about any particular form of tax. The committee appeared unconvinced.

The same day, the Secretary made the disclosure that legislation raising the price of gold and formally devaluing the dollar would be sent to Congress later in the week.

It was about the same time that the Washington rumor mill, always active, began circulating reports that Big John was thinking of resigning as Secretary of the Treasury. Connally reacted with amusement to questions by saying he had "no plans to leave my present job," but the reports persisted and there was no formal denouncement or denial.

Despite Nixon's variety of economic guide lines and phases, prices continued on a steady upward course, and food prices were a major concern to the housewife, the voter and, of course, the President during an election year.

"Like an army," commented a columnist, "an electorate also travels on its stomach."

Still handling the difficult role of the President's economic spokesman and leader, Connally met with the heads of major supermarket chains on March 29. William Mitchell, president of Safeway Stores, Inc., introduced him with the comment, "Secretary Connally is a very persuasive person. I think you will see prices going down."

Connally, who had spoken calmly of the Administration's having an "acute awareness of the problem of keeping food prices down," spoke with optimism at the close of the meeting. He predicted that beef prices were expected to fall and that the supermarket chains had agreed to prepare weekly reports on meat costs for the Cost of Living Council, though what another mass of paperwork in Washington was expected to achieve was never really explained.

"I did not threaten them," Connally said of the meeting, though he added with a tight smile, "I did not eliminate any possible action" by the federal government in the future.

In the spring of an election year the skirmishing of the candidates begins, and 1972 was no exception. The upcoming election was gradually moving into national focus, and several Democratic presidential hopefuls were advocating tax reforms. Connally attacked the reforms as a weapon that could drive the Dow Jones stock average down to 500 or lower, and he spoke in defense of what often were considered "loopholes" in taxes. The Secretary also condemned the Democrats for stepping into taxation issues with little or no real experience. A year as Secretary of the Treasury had done wonders for

Big John's economic knowledge. Connally refrained from seeking heavier taxation of capital gains, always a sore point, and he explained it in a speech to the American Society of Newspaper Editors by saying, "I don't want to destroy the real estate industry and the securities industry."

The Connally-Lockheed relationship, which had been a major battleground for Big John throughout 1971 as he fought for—and succeeded in gaining—government guaranteed loans for the aircraft giant, came to the fore again in 1972, and this time there were accusations of Connally's being "in clear violation of the law" in regard to the Secretary and the executive board which he directed as the monitoring agency for the $250 million guaranteed loan.

Controller General Elmer B. Staats of the General Accounting Office started the fireworks when he spoke before the Senate Banking Committee's Subcommittee on Housing and Urban Affairs. Staats said that the Connally board was obstructing the authority of the GAO by refusing to disclose various Lockheed documents and records. The GAO, an investigative arm of Congress, felt these records were needed, but Connally, in a letter to Staats, said that "it was not the intent of Congress that the decisions of the board be reviewed by the GAO." Connally headed a three-man board called the Emergency Loan Guarantee Board, which had been established to make sure that Lockheed handled its guaranteed loan properly and avoided further embarrassment to an Administration that already was rather red-faced over the aircraft company.

One of Connally's most consistently outspoken critics, Senator Proxmire, spoke concernedly about Connally's defiance of Congress and the possible jeopardy which the Government would face as a creditor if Lockheed should fail.

By the beginning of May, John Connally was fighting a lonely battle against an unconquered balance-of-payments problem and a still-rising inflation. He seemed to spend much of his time defending unpopular issues before hostile audiences, and he was rapidly losing credibility as government plans began to show signs of strain and failure. Connally felt he had been stranded by the nation's big banks and multinational corporations. "I don't think they are being good corporate citizens," he said sadly at one point, though he had to admit that the international giants still had "to get along with all the governments with whom they do business, so they're not going to get up and defend us." Inflation through the first quarter of the year, he admitted, was "not only unpleasant but undesirable," and he dodged the issue over the necessity or the possibility of tightened economic controls by saying, "We need a little more time" before a decision could be reached.

Tax reform continued as a major topic for the Secretary of the Treasury and for the Administration, and Connally agreed that some tax reform would be satisfactory, but "I don't think the last half of an election year is the appropriate time to do it. I think it's probably a two- or three-year study." All the Democratic candidates had their own comments on the necessity for tax reform, and Connally reluctantly admitted that they "all have something to recommend them." Still, his conservative premise against immediate change was, "If you change the whole fundamental social structure in this country when you do it [revise tax laws], . . . it ought to be a very conscious decision in a calm, reasonable atmosphere."

Mr. Secretary also had come to the realization that the various and complex issues of trade, foreign aid, overseas military spending and reform of the monetary system should not be examined separately. He advocated the position of taking an "overall perspective on the problem," but he was no longer about to challenge the entire Cabinet as he had done in the fall of 1971. Connally's actions at that time, when he reached his arms wide for more power to affect Administration policy, had brought criticism from the State Department and threatened the entire American position in international diplomacy. He had gone a little too far, and he realized it.

Talk of the possibilities of the Texan as a 1972 vice-presidential candidate continued, and he even received a boost from a California astrologer who said Connally "is under marvelously good aspects this year and can do anything he wants to do. Everything is at his fingertips." Connally's response was, "I'm glad to hear that. I've got a lot of secret ambitions I'd like to fulfill."

Although there was continuing questioning, especially in Texas, of what role Connally would take in the 1972 campaign if he were not a candidate for office, it began to appear that Big John would not only be a spokesman for the President's economic policies, but would actively endorse him for reelection. Still, he continued to express loyalty to the Democratic party, a rather confusing stand.

Connally's link with the Committee to Re-Elect the President was formalized in late March when he addressed a Lincoln Day gathering of the Middlesex Republican Club of Boston. Connally praised Nixon's wage and price controls and it appeared that the two men would be inextricably tied through 1972.

A high Republican party official commented after the Boston appearance, "We won't ask him to speak before party rallies in the primary states, but this was the signal for more activity on his part."

There was a real hum of activity on April 30, when the President made his first visit to the home of a Cabinet member. Of course, it was Connally's Floresville, Texas, ranch home. Big John had invited some two hundred guests to meet the President, and there were few welfare recipients among them. The group comprised lawyers, businessmen, bankers and newspaper editors whose help might prove valuable in an election campaign. Nixon addressed the guests on a number of key issues, including Vietnam, where he could not "in good conscience permit a Communist takeover," and the oil depletion allowance, a topic with which the guests were extremely familiar and intimately involved. Nixon also talked about school busing and about the health of his predecessor, Lyndon B. Johnson.

He also used the occasion to burst any potential Connally bubble and announced that Spiro T. Agnew was again his first choice as a running mate.

After the furor over the announcement had subsided, the President went on to speak of John Connally, telling the crowd that he had demonstrated that "he could hold any job in the United States." Another of the President's favorite topics, the work ethic, was reiterated to the wealthy guests when the President decried an "increasing tendency in this country to turn down jobs just because they are so-called menial jobs. I say that any job that puts bread on a man's table to feed his family is not menial."

The cheers were loud, but what response came from the serving help was not recorded.

Connally had described the evening as a "nonpolitical" social gathering, but added, "I have never learned much in politics, but I always learned that you have to fish with live bait. And we are not without some in this gathering this evening."

During Richard Nixon's Texas visit, he met many influential and powerful men, both Republicans and Democrats, but the guest list at the Connally ranch

crossed party lines and was decided more on economic
and establishment lines. As one guest pointed out, "There
are no Republicans and Democrats any more, just liberals
and conservatives. We're all just Texans and we're all
here."

Less than a week later, on May 4, John Connally
bore the President's wreath in tribute to FBI Director
J. Edgar Hoover. The importance of Connally's service
as the President's prime representative at Hoover's funeral
was not unnoticed. The President's feelings for Hoover
were well known, and obviously Connally was now in a
similar position of esteem as far as the President was
concerned.

Connally, despite the knowledge that he would not
be a 1972 vice-presidential candidate, remained extremely close to the President. He and Kissinger, for example, were close to Nixon when the Chief Executive
debated the decision to expand the Vietnamese war by
mining Haiphong harbor, among other tactics. Secretary
of Defense Melvin Laird announced the decision on May
10, but the President, Connally and Kissinger had held
several lengthy meetings in the previous days, and the
strategy obviously was high on the agenda. Connally,
long a super-hawk on the Vietnam situation, obviously
had reinforced the President's decision.

Big John Connally also served as an unofficial public defender for the Nixon action. He told reporters that
the Chief Executive's decision was "not in any sense a
confrontation, a throwing down of the gauntlet" to the
Russians. Speaking with authority and confidence on
foreign policy, he added that the Soviet Union has
"enough self-confidence that they don't have to wildly
react. The United States did not treat the Soviet invasion
of Hungary as a challenge."

The eloquent Texan continued optimistic in terms
of economic issues and the nation. He sponsored a

luncheon for reporters at the Treasury Department and
reviewed some of the issues, still strongly optimistic
about the Dow Jones average reaching 1000 during the
year. He said the President might propose some tax reform, but it would be "basic and fundamental, not a
few isolated cases that have a little political porridge in
them." He discussed the possibility of a value-added tax
but said it would be "a tax of substitution, not an additional tax," which was a stand he had taken for some
time on the issue. He discussed possible termination dates
for wage and price controls, looking at the spring of
1973 as a tentative target date, and he commented on the
European Common Market and the jump of a price in
gold.

Finally, he got to politics, and Connally told the
reporters that he would submit his resignation after the
election because he had "no interest or expectation of
serving" in a second Nixon administration.

On May 16, however, President Nixon announced
the sudden resignation of his closest Cabinet member,
the man who had been his economic spokesman and who
had come to have the most powerful position among
Cabinet officials.

Connally, surprising everyone with the resignation,
announced his intention to return to private life. He
heaped praise on the President, and the President responded by describing Connally as the "dynamic and
skilled" architect of the nation's foreign and domestic
economic policies. Nixon added that he would ask Connally to undertake some special assignments, and speculation continued that the two men would remain close
together.

One explanation for the resignation was that Connally had originally agreed to take the job for only a
year, a report that had great credibility among his close
associates, who commented, "It is part of Connally's

pattern to do a job and then leave at the crest of a wave."

It also seemed that the Texan was restless for a return to private life, to something less structured and less demanding of his time and interests. One associate noted, "Every time I have talked to him, he has talked about coming home. He likes private life more than any public official I know. He is a universal man, and he feels too restricted when he is expected to spend all his time on the job."

Connally himself spoke about the possibility of buying a home in Spain or Italy to live abroad for a while, though he emphasized he had no intention of "withdrawing from the human race."

There was also speculation, though not confirmed, that Mrs. Connally had used the occasion of the assassination attempt on Gov. George Wallace as leverage on her husband to step out of government.

President Nixon named George Shultz, Director of the Office of Management and Budget, to be the next Secretary of the Treasury. The decision was made in discussion between the President and Connally, so Big John even had a large voice in naming his successor.

There was some surprise over the suddenness of the resignation, especially since there was a Paris meeting coming soon, and everyone knew how Big John loved to do battle in the international monetary arena. Yet there were precedents, as those most critical of Connally's hit-and-run political techniques are quick to point out. At college he would take on a project, build it up and then abandon it. He quit as president of the Curtain Club to run for president of the Student Association. Then he quit as president of the Student Association to concentrate on grades. He quit worrying about grades and school altogether to go to work for a new Congressman named Lyndon B. Johnson in 1938. In later years, he would quit being Secretary of the Navy to run for

Governor. He would quit lawyering to become Secretary of the Treasury. He would quit Secretarying to become a lawyer again. . . .

In any case, the meeting of the Organization for Economic Cooperation and Development, a body significant in forging a new international monetary system, would have to go along without the Texan, whose only comment was, "Charging up that hill to do battle hasn't been as exciting the last nine months as it was the first six."

April 30, 1972. President Nixon spends the night at the Connally Ranch, Floresville, Texas. Here the President talks with a cowboy as the Secretary of the Treasury, Mrs. Nixon and Mrs. Connally look on. *Credit: United Press International Photo.*

[7]

Democrats for Nixon

What were the real origins of "Democrats for Nixon"?

Did the idea first leap into John Connally's mind during the spring and summer of 1968, when his old friend and crony, President Lyndon Johnson, did not encourage or promote him as either a potential President or Vice President?

Did it come from some dark recess of American political history, perhaps a lineal descendant of "Whigs for Franklin Pierce" in 1852, or down through the annals of Texas, like "Alamo Defenders for Santa Anna"?

Was it hatched during Connally's days in Washington in 1971, while he watched President Nixon's well-scrubbed, clean-shaven hordes sweep through the city with all the delicacy of barbarians in Rome and dreamed his own dreams of even more raw and ruthless power than even Johnson had commanded?

Or, in that Washington period, was it conceived in some brief, anticlimactic moment of mental union between the President and his Secretary of the Treasury, perhaps following a warmup period during which things like interest rates or the vice presidency were discussed?

No matter. . . .

Since Connally had always stood with both feet firmly planted in the oil lands and the farm lands of Texas, any discussion that smacked of anti-establishment flavor was to him only a step or two short of treason.

Democrats for Nixon was announced in August 1972, was publicly discussed in the San Antonio *Express-News* in May 1972 and was known to Ben Barnes, the Lieutenant Governor of Texas and Connally's protégé, many months before that.

Bob Bullock, Texas secretary of state, said a month before the 1972 election: "Connally has indicated he is supporting Nixon because he would not support McGovern. Yet Lieutenant Governor Barnes . . . knew of his plans to leave the Democratic party nine months before Senator McGovern received the *nomination*—and at a time when Senator Humphrey appeared to be the front-runner for the nomination."

Connally in fact supported Nixon during the 1968 campaign, though the action was generally sub rosa. Connally snubbed Hubert Humphrey on the Vice President's first campaign swing through Texas, and it was not until later in the race, when Humphrey began to gain strength, that Connally endorsed him. There was strong speculation that Connally was busy raising money for the GOP candidate, largely on the basis that Nixon was interested in keeping the depletion allowance high and the interference in offshore wells low, while Humphrey had refused to stand for a high depletion allowance.

The reward was the invitation to Washington to be Secretary of the Treasury. Being the major Democrat in the Nixon Administration was another point of prestige, perhaps even a reverse feeling of status and class, always important things for Connally.

County and senatorial districts in Texas held conventions on May 13, 1972, and McGovern supporters did well in several areas, including gaining 70 percent of the delegates from Bexar County, which includes San Antonio. On the surface, that was exciting to the McGovern forces, but the San Antonio *Express-News* commented the next day that few conservative Democrats had participated and added, "After all, Secretary Connally announced during the week that he had serious doubts that any of the present Demo candidates were fit for the job and he would have more to say about them later, hinting he may vote Republican. First the party at the Connally Ranch. Then the indifference to the conventions. Can it be that something like 'Democrats for Nixon' is just over the horizon?"

Two weeks later the *Texas Observer* was again speculating on the Nixon-Connally relationship, saying, "John Connally was a hawk as a Democrat, he'll be a hawk when he becomes a Republican and that day may not be far away. Connally said, 'I have no plans to do so, but the possibility certainly exists that I could do so.' In a recent United Press International column from Washington, Helen Thomas quoted three lengthy paragraphs of Connally's praise for Nixon ("scholar . . . as disciplined a man as I have ever known, mentally and physically . . . slender and boyish looking . . . tenacity and perseverance . . ."). Thomas pointed out, 'In all the years that Lyndon B. Johnson occupied the White House, his protégé, Connally, was never heard to utter such encomiums about his Texas friend and mentor.' "

There was obviously further discussion of Connally's forthcoming relationship to Nixon and the Republicans when the men feasted on barbecue at Connally's ranch.

The May party was most notable, perhaps, for a comment from H. R. Haldeman to a reporter who asked if the President would enjoy running against McGovern.

"Wouldn't you?" cracked Haldeman as he reached for a sparerib.

By mid-July Connally had taken a round-the-world trip as Nixon's personal representative, visiting seventeen countries and talking to political leadership in all of them. He also had apparently decided his course of events—or else Nixon had made the decision for him.

The men met at the President's San Clemente villa and Connally then made his campaign plans public at a press conference at the villa itself, far more important than at a nearby hotel, where most of the President's subordinates made their announcements.

Connally not only jumped onto the Nixon bandwagon, but he pushed off with both feet against McGovern, a tactic he was to continue throughout the campaign.

Connally denounced McGovern on almost all fronts, saying that although he still considered himself a Democrat, he could not support the candidate because his ideas are "all too isolationist in character and also too radical in character." Connally also charged that the Senator's pledge to bring American prisoners of war home ninety days after his election "sabotages the efforts of the Administration and of the peace negotiators in Paris to try to bring the war to an end on a negotiated basis." He added that the pledge was "unfair" because "obviously a President of the United States has no capacity, no power to bring home prisoners of war in the hands of the North Vietnamese."

The harangue continued on all fronts, with accuracy not always a hallmark of Connally's comments. He criticized McGovern for what he termed his plan for "giving amnesty to draft dodgers," adding, "To me, this is a glorification of men who refuse to serve their nation." Connally ripped into McGovern's plans for reducing the military budget by saying, "This means cutting the heart out of the defense establishment and a retreat from responsibilities in world leadership."

Connally incorrectly accused McGovern of plans to cut the defense budget by $30 billion a year, when the Senator had talked of that amount of reduction over a three-year period.

Overall, Connally said that he was going to support Nixon for President in 1972 and would spend all his time up to the election urging other Americans to do the same. He explained away his resignation as Secretary of the Treasury on almost the same basis, using some wonderful hindsight to say that he had expected "someing like this" and had "wanted to be free, as a private citizen" to follow the dictates of his conscience. The fact that he apparently had been considering some action of this type for many months, and against any Democratic candidate, was conveniently unsaid.

The statement took some amazing turns, even leading Connally through a discussion of previous presidential campaigns when he said that 1972 offered "for the first time in my life, a clear choice in this country." When asked to explain, Connally noted that 1960 (Nixon versus Kennedy) had not presented such a clear choice because the men differed primarily in means, not ends. He ignored the 1964 campaign between his old crony Lyndon Johnson and Barry Goldwater, who had campaigned on the premise of "a choice, not an echo."

Where Connally's own future was concerned, he was vague. He did not repudiate the vice-presidential candidacy that Nixon had not offered, but he did allow that he "was not closing any doors" on the possibility, which had been bandied about in the press all spring. That type of conversation was apparently as close as it ever got to real fruition.

The *National Review* looked back on the Nixon-Connally meeting and its subsequent statements, and decided: "But with this now public and absolute commitment to his cause by this intelligent and forceful Democrat, who is very influential not only in his own Southwest but in all sectors of the Democratic party except the ideological Left that is unreachable by any means, Mr. Nixon has got the maximum John Connally has to offer—more, in all probability, than he could get from a turncoat Connally on the Republican ticket. This would seem to be the cold, hard political fact, and about politics Mr. Nixon reasons both hard and coldly."

Connally's actions also were noted by James Reston of *The New York Times,* who wrote: "Nobody would mind if John Connally thought the Democrats were wrong and the Republicans right on the war, the economy, taxes and welfare and then switched, like Mayor Lindsay of New York, to the other party. Or even if he stayed as a Democrat in the Republican Administration and stuck with his job and struggled on with the Administration's problems. But Mr. Connally seems to want the best of everything—to use the Democrats who are dominant in Texas to be Governor of the state and to use them again when they have executive power in Washington to be Secretary of the Navy, and then, when they lose their power, to go over to the Republicans as Secretary of the Treasury. One of the troubles with the attractive and dogmatic Connally is that when he gets bored with his jobs either under the Democrats or the Republicans he gets out and goes home to his ranch. Personally it is a good deal but otherwise it seems a little selfish. The pattern is quite clear. He comes and goes as he pleases, and now he is just back from his 'round-

the-world trip in San Clemente and is vilifying the
Democrats for foreign and domestic policies he says he
cannot support and praising a Republican party he will
not join."

The arrival of the former Texas Governor into Nixon's
camp gave the President another major weapon. He now
had two men—Connally and Spiro Agnew—whom he
could use for scalding attacks on his enemies. Both were
experts at political diatribe, and the President could
stand quietly in the background while his executioners
did the dirty work. The Agnew scandal and the Connally
clouds were yet to come.

Connally started rapidly in another direction, too,
leaning heavily on Democratic leadership around the
nation to defect from McGovern and support Nixon.
He spoke with more than just normal political or Texan
persuasiveness, and his power again came directly
from the White House. Connally used what Lawrence
F. O'Brien, McGovern's campaign manager, termed
"strong-arm tactics." O'Brien accused Connally of using
promises of federal aid—either increased or decreased—
as a recruiting lever.

When O'Brien was asked if he was accusing Connally of "political blackmail," the Democrat replied,
"Yes, that's exactly what it is."

Whether or not there had been any last-minute discussion of the vice presidency between Nixon and Connally, the Republicans renominated the Nixon-Agnew
ticket, and speculation on the Texan's role then moved
to the Cabinet level, perhaps as Secretary of State. It
seemed that whenever there was a Republican job opening, or even the hint of one, Connally's name was at the
head of the list. There were few reports of what the
President was thinking, however.

Connally was blandness and party loyalty person-
ified when he discussed the Republican ticket.

"I never assumed that it was going to be me," he said. "I have assumed all along that it would be Mr. Agnew. I think the Vice President has been a man of great courage. I think he's been a very controversial figure. I think he has been loyal. I think he has been faithful to the President in carrying out his assigned duties, but if being controversial precludes a man from being on a major ticket, then I think the Democrats ought to reconvene their convention and reconsider their nominee because I think Mr. McGovern is . . . controversial."

Connally's campaigning never stopped, and he took every opportunity to continue shooting at the Democratic nominee while courting the Democratic party.

On the one hand, he could say about the candidates: "I think their objectives in foreign policy are vastly different. I think President Nixon is an internationalist and I think Senator McGovern is basically an isolationist. . . . They certainly differ in their views on welfare programs . . . on permissiveness . . . in many other areas. . . . They differ primarily because Senator McGovern and his adherents are talking about changing or destroying the system, the establishment. Well, in any free society there has to be an establishment. There is an establishment that runs our road system and our school system and our governmental system. Everybody has to be a part of a system and you can't just tear it asunder . . . without doing violent damage to this country and what it stands for."

And on the other hand, at the same time, he was filled with pious blandishments about the wonderful party that bore the name of Democratic, saying, "I don't concede that Mr. McGovern is the Democratic party. I think he and his supporters, frankly, are not really concerned about the Democratic party at any level. I think they are promoting an ideological course, irrespective of party.

. . . Just because I can't support Mr. McGovern is no sign I am going to, in effect, give him the Democratic party."

The fact that a presidential candidate has long been regarded as the leader of his party seemed not to worry Connally in the slightest.

As always, however, he kept all options open. He was lined up with the Republicans for 1972, but when 1976 was discussed, he responded with a cliché-ridden loyalty pledge that could have come from a precinct captain on his first campaign.

"I hope I am at the [1976] Democratic Convention laboring in the vineyards as I have all of my adult life," he crooned. "I do want to indeed try to lead a revival of broad support within the Democratic party to recapture the machinery. That is all we have lost. We haven't lost the party—we have merely lost the machinery."

Whether Connally was serious, or whistling in the dark or thinking only of Texas Democrats is hard to comprehend. The party establishment had lost more than machinery. It had gained a new base of support, new people, new ideas and policies. The establishment group, on many levels, would never again control the party or make it a mere errand boy for special interests.

Although Connally himself had been actively campaigning for the reelection of the President, it was assumed that a formal Democrats for Nixon organization was in the works, probably with the former Texas Governor at its head, but with major names on the roster so as to give it respectability, an aura of real power to gather support, enough diversity so as to attract as broad a base of political and social thinking as possible and, most important, a solid list of many-figured bank accounts.

When the organization was announced on August 9, it met a number of those qualifications. Connally was

named chairman and the vice chairmen included Frank
Fitzsimmons, president of the Teamsters Union; Leonard
Marks, former director of the U.S. Information Agency;
Farris Bryant, former Governor of Florida and close
associate of Lyndon Johnson; John F. Collins, former
mayor of Boston; Mayors David Kennedy of Miami and
Beverly Briley of Nashville, Tenn.; and James Roosevelt,
son of the President and former Democratic Congressman.

At the same time Connally announced the formation of an auxiliary group to attract independent voters
rather than just Democrats. This section was led by Jeno
Palucci, a Minnesota frozen-food magnate who had been
a major contributor to Hubert Humphrey in the 1968
election and in the 1972 primaries. Palucci had leaped
into the national spotlight with a series of offbeat television commercials, guided by Stan Freberg, which had
made his products famous and himself a very rich man.

Connally, of course, never lost a moment to continue firing at McGovern and attempting to divide him
from the Democratic party.

While he was announcing the formation of his new-
est little establishment empire, Connally said he hoped
to raise between $2 million and $3 million for Nixon,
and then attacked McGovern for harming the party.

"According to a national poll just completed," he
intoned gravely, "twenty million Democrats have already
decided that their choice this year will be President
Nixon over Senator McGovern. We open our doors to
all those millions of Democrats who realize that in this
presidential election President Nixon is simply the better
choice. Far from becoming a more open party, the Democratic party under Senator McGovern's leadership is
becoming an ideological machine closed to millions of
Americans who have been the party's most loyal and
steadfast supporters."

Connally, in attempting to attract all those poor, huddled masses yearning to be free, was lifting a golden lamp beside the door, but in his case, it was probably diamond-studded.

Ever since Connally had joined the Nixon entourage, there had been speculation involving Lyndon Johnson and his own position in the race. Johnson and McGovern differed in numerous areas, especially foreign policy as it related to Vietnam. There were those who wondered if Connally was serving two masters—Nixon and Johnson—and if the former President was going to take an active part in the campaign.

On August 15 Johnson spoke strongly in favor of McGovern and, in effect, in criticism of Connally. The date was six days before the Republicans were to renominate Nixon, a day on which Johnson and McGovern would meet at the LBJ Ranch.

"I believe the Democratic party best serves the needs of the people," said the former President. "Therefore I intend to support the 1972 Democratic ticket. I shall vote for George McGovern and Sargent Shriver for President and Vice President of the United States.

"It is no secret that Senator McGovern and I have widely differing opinions on many matters, especially foreign policy. Senator McGovern has not refrained from criticizing policies of mine with which he disagrees. Neither shall I refrain from stating my disagreements with any position of his when I believe that the public interest demands such action. The differences between us need not be minimized. The Democratic party can accommodate disagreement."

No politician can avoid the self-serving statement when the opportunity shows up on the horizon, and the former President could hardly avoid adding, "I have welcomed and supported—in retirement as I always did in public service—the growing participation in the affairs

of the Democratic party by the young, by women, by
blacks, by Mexican-Americans and others who have far
too long been outside the political system. Such participation represents a fulfillment of goals for which I
worked throughout my public career."

The Nixon campaign to woo Democrats was carefully planned, carefully worded to make it seem as if
any repudiation was primarily of McGovern and not of
the lesser party lights. The President did not want to be
accused of trying to destroy the other party, but the
politicians' dream of constant overkill was always there.

For example, the Republican platform, at the express orders of Nixon, with John Ehrlichman the aide at
the site, had no reference to any endorsement of so-
called right-to-work laws.

At the convention, three registered Democrats, who
said they would vote a straight Democratic ticket with
the exception of the top line, were picked to make
seconding speeches for the Nixon nomination. John
Volpe, Secretary of Transportation, offered a resolution
to welcome "all disenfranchised Democrats to a permanent or temporary home in the Grand Old Party," which
he then renamed "the party of the open door." Palucci,
the former Humphrey supporter and contributor, par-
roted the new party line when he said, "Senator Mc-
Govern does not represent the Democratic party. His
movement is a McGovernite movement, a temporary
fixture of American politics until the Democratic party
once again receives leadership consistent with the thinking of the rank and file."

The Republicans did show a wisdom and subtlety
not usually associated with politics and politicians when
they kept the prize Democrat, John Connally, away
from the Miami convention. He had been scheduled to
appear, and a fancy hotel suite had been arranged for
him. However, at the last minute, cooler and apparently

wiser heads prevailed. Convention strategists realized
that the best Democrat to display was one who was not
a regular visitor to Republican functions, and not one
who had been a Cabinet officer and a constant crony of
top Republican officials. The exposure could have opened
the party to serious criticism on one level, and certainly
to ridicule and wisecracks on another.

Therefore Palucci was the Democrat in the spotlight instead of John Connally.

The move did not escape all notice around the
country. The *Texas Observer,* now a virulent adversary
of the new Democrats for Nixon organization, analyzed
Connally's absence perfectly, especially in terms of Texas
politics:

"Republicans, at least the kind who come to the
convention, distrust Connally. It's not that they dislike
him. It's just that it is Us and Them and they're not
about to forget that Connally was one of Them. The same
problem has ever plagued Texas Republicans: if your Republican loyalties don't go at least back to Taft, you are
not considered a Republican."

The *Observer* didn't explain, but the Taft was obviously William Howard rather than Robert.

With normal political reasoning, the GOP felt that
if one former Democrat should make a statement, many
former Democrats should make statements so that everyone would hear at least one statement by one former
Democrat.

While the convention was forming, James Roosevelt, then American representative to the United Nations
Economic and Social Council, took his turn as the statement maker, with comments that echoed much of what
had been said before.

The sixty-four-year-old Roosevelt pointed out that
it was the first time he had endorsed a Republican candidate and added, "I don't think this is a time when our

government can afford such a radical change of leadership as is being proposed. I have made this decision after weighing most carefully the best interests of our country, particularly remembering there are times in a nation's history, no matter how reluctantly, that it is imperative to put one's views of the interests of the country first."

Since it always raises political capital to refer to the names of people who cannot respond, and to sprinkle some high-sounding and patriotic memories around, Roosevelt added, "Prior to World War II, Secretary [of War] Henry Stimson and Secretary [of the Navy] Frank Knox, both Republicans, not only supported a Democratic candidate but went on to serve in his administration. I believe that history has proven our country was the gainer."

August turned to September and summer began to wane. The campaign went in the other direction. McGovern repeatedly challenged Nixon to "come out of hiding" and join the fray, but the President was happy to have his hirelings do the campaigning. Nixon, with the big bloc of Texas votes at stake, even made a rather dangerous decision and announced he would kick off his personal campaign with a dinner at Connally's ranch.

McGovern forces moved to the attack, with the candidate and his supporters talking often of "John Connally and his oil billionaire friends" lining up behind the President and his "special-interest Administration."

The strategy had its effect in some areas of the electorate, but the special-interest groups, knowing they had a big-money representative of both parties active in the Nixon Administration, kept those cards and letters and checks flowing in.

The *Texas Observer* kept firing at both Connally and Nixon. The publication described the Democrats for Nixon as "John Connally's groupies" and named more Texan establishment personalities, many of them onetime officials under Connally's own state administrations. A September list included Jim Lindsey, former Texas House speaker; W. Hunter McLean and George Cowden, both former chairmen of the Texas Insurance Board; Dr. Leonidas Cigarroa of the state Board of Mental Health-Mental Retardation; Jenkins Garrett, University of Texas regent; Tom Sealy, former chairman of the regents; and J. Doug Toole of the Texas Water Quality Board.

Not everyone in Texas was following the former Governor, however. Godfrey Connally, a brother of John and an economics professor at San Antonio Junior College, spoke out strongly in praise of McGovern's economic proposals.

The peculiarly American type of political campaign tries to leave no stone unturned, no special interest or minority group ignored. There is no issue too small to receive comment, though there often are those which are too large.

For example, Nixon held a major strategy meeting at Camp David over a September weekend. The names of those in attendance were potential headline makers in themselves, and, in months to come, their faces and stories would become familiar to the nation. However, on that September weekend, with a slight nip in the Catoctin Mountains air, the group was still known only as Nixon's first team. It included Connally; Clark MacGregor, director of the Committee to Re-Elect the President; John Mitchell, his predecessor; and H. R. Haldeman.

Meanwhile, back at the White House, press secretary Ron Ziegler was making several announcements, none of them of any real significance but all of them appealing to possible voters. There was the announcement that the President was going to meet with Democratic Mayor Frank Rizzo of Philadelphia to receive a

group of high school students. The students were to
present a petition, signed with 400,000 names, pledging
their "support for the respect of parents, teachers, law
and order, property and the rights of others." Then there
was the announcement that the President had proclaimed
October 11 as Casimir Pulaski Day, in honor of the
Polish officer who had fought with George Washington
in the American Revolution and who still was a hero in
the Polish-American community. And then there was the
announcement that the President had written a memorandum to all federal departments and agencies, stressing
the importance of "older Americans" as potential federal
employees.

Something for everyone. . . .

While Mrs. Connally was busy cleaning house,
trimming the lawn and making preparations for the gala
party scheduled for September 22, the former Governor
of Texas, former Secretary of the Navy and Secretary of
the Treasury was receiving a plum of his own from the
President.

John Connally received the privilege of making the
first Republican television commercial.

The Democrats, with Charles Guggenheim as film
adviser to McGovern, were moving heavily into use of
the medium and had budgeted $3.5 million for airtime
purchase. The advertising approach was similar to the
pre-primary tack by McGovern, that of answering un-
rehearsed questions but not being critical of the opposition.

The Republicans, with Connally as their spokesman,
moved in a different direction. The first commercial was
a frontal attack on McGovern and his policies. The
emphasis was on what the Republicans termed inconsistencies and contradictory positions taken by McGovern
and they planned to use the candidate's voice, if not his
face.

Connally's appearance on network television was an effectual denial of the previous line by Connally and his Democrats for Nixon. They had claimed they would run an independent campaign, raising their own funds and running their own television commercials, but the first spot made it obvious that the White House and the Committee to Re-Elect the President were working hand-in-hand with Connally and his forces.

During the past ten years or so, Connally's land holdings have trebled in Wilson County, Texas. The countryside is beginning to flatten out on its way to the Gulf of Mexico, and it is not as wooded as the hill country, some seventy-five miles to the north, where the LBJ Ranch is located. Still, it has trees and flowers and is not as barren as the western part of the state. Picosa, the site of Connally's ranch house, covers some 3,600 acres. Another 1,200-acre ranch nearby is named for his children, and there are about a thousand more acres that also comprise part of the homestead. Some years ago, Connally also bought about 1,500 acres of prime Texas ranch land from Delhi Properties for over $250,000.

The Connally mansion at Picosa was finished for him just as he completed his first term as Governor. The two-story house is a mixture of French provincial and LBJ Texas. It's high on a hill, where Connally can survey his holdings and be a distinguished version of the Marlboro Man. There are only eight bathrooms, but each is well decorated with antiques Connally has collected during his world travels. He enjoys bragging about the two handcarved teakwood doors that weigh some 800 pounds between them.

When Cabinet member Connally once again became lawyer John, he also bought a modern house in the very exclusive River Oaks section of Houston. And, of course, there is the plantation in Jamaica. Big John's plush hacienda on the sea was built on property allegedly donated by Pollard Simons, one of President Nixon's big campaign contributors.

John Connally never hesitates to mix business with pleasure. Instead of just enjoying the lush scenery of his Jamaican hut, he is taking an active interest in a local-based multimillion-dollar beef and dairy cattle operation with his benefactor Simons.

When the press started describing Connally's hideaway in Montego Bay, Big John got upset at stories claiming he had spent $250,000 to build it. He said the figure was high and pointed out that only *his* bedroom was air conditioned. Either way, it's still a long way from the Wilson County peanut fields where John Bowden Connally, Sr., and his wife Lela nurtured their family of five children.

The weekend was going to be a big one, with gala events scheduled for Friday, September 22, at the ranch and on Saturday at Denton, just north of Dallas. Couturiers around the state—and the country—had been busy for weeks, and the design problems were just slightly intricate. After all, how formal can things be at a party on a ranch followed by a party in a horse barn?

President Nixon got things started with a trip to Texas that had several aspects of bipartisanship, along with an excuse to charge at least part of the journey to the American taxpayer. He invited several members of the Texas congressional delegation—Senator Lloyd Bentsen and Congressmen Abraham Kazen, Jr., and Eligio de la Garza, all Democrats, by the way—to accompany him on Air Force One. That part was financed by everyone, with the party journeying from Washington to Rio Grande City, an ironic location. The town, deep in the Rio Grande Valley, is the county seat of Starr County, where organizing attempts by farm workers of the Mexican-American community had given birth to the deep hatred of Connally by members of that minority group.

Nixon picked up Republican support in Laredo, where he was joined by Senator John G. Tower, the senior Senator from Texas.

Party invitations were for sundown, and some three hundred guests were on hand, all Democrats who had decided they'd rather switch than fight. The swimming pool was filled with chrysanthemums, and the oak trees housed spotlights so that everyone could see and, more important, be seen. The barbecue motif included plenty to drink, along with Mexican hors d'oeuvres followed by roast beef.

Guests mingled madly. James Roosevelt had come from California, and his brother, Elliott, from Portugal. Teamsters' boss Frank Fitzsimmons was on hand, and so were investment banker Leo Cherne of New York, former Virginia governor Mills E. Goodwin, Jr., and George L. Killion, a former film executive from Beverly Hills. Others invited included Perle Mesta, formerly the nation's number one Washington hostess and onetime Ambassador to Luxembourg; Angier Biddle Duke, former chief of protocol; and even Robert E. Lee (Sam) Huff, who had made his name as a football player for the New York Giants and who had made an unsuccessful attempt at running for Congress from his home state of West Virginia. Huff also was an employee of Marriott Hotels, whose founder, Willard Marriott, was a close Nixon confidant.

The price of drinks and dinner, as at all functions of this type, was to listen to a speech by the guest of honor. The President spoke for close to thirty minutes, a reasonable enough dinner tab, and reiterated his earlier statements of the need for strength in international relations and the need for the preservation of freedom of opportunity at home.

He also took note of the step across party lines taken by the guests, saying that the organization's title, Democrats for Nixon, was really not proper, and that they should be termed "Americans for Nixon."

"I know the risk that you have taken," he said. "I know the heat you are taking, but I can only assure you that if we prevail in this election, I am going to do everything I possibly can to make your votes and your support look good for America."

The Saturday night party was even more Texan, more ostentatious and more successful in terms of raising lots of money for the Republican campaign.

It was billed as "A Gathering of Eagles" and was hosted by Rex Cauble at his Ranch and Show Arena. Cauble is an oilman, banker, investor and owner of thousands of acres of Texas land. His arena, larger than a football field, houses offices, private eating and drinking facilities, plenty of room for horses to exercise and stable facilities for Cutter Bill, world champion cutting horse, now retired to stud, and numerous of his offspring. The arena, by the way, is not limited to political fund-raising events or quarter-horse demonstrations. It has been the site of many parties, including one a couple of years ago for a prestigious and obviously influential group of men whose Sunday afternoon function is designing and supervising halftime shows at National Football League games. The bandsmen and others were impressed by Cutter Bill, his record, his diet, his enormous stud fee and the brief cutting demonstration he put on, though several more recalcitrant people were loudly rooting for the cow to win. They also were envious of the huge, rain-protected, dirt-floor arena, feeling that it was a splendid place for halftime entertainment, if not for football.

The Eagles of September 23 were Connally, movie star John Wayne and Herb W. Klein, Dallas big-game hunter and gas, oil and real estate magnate. They were honored for their "love of country, love of outdoors and love of sportsmanship," and each received a special rifle designed by Homer Koon, described as "the foremost rifle designer in the world."

The program included a private party for the top contributors, whose dinner enjoyment was only slightly challenged by odors of disinfectant and horse manure, along wtih a chorus which sang "The Green Leaves of Summer" and "God Bless America," among other popular hits.

During pre-meal activities, which centered around the bar, Klein was generally lost in the shuffle as Wayne and Connally received all the attention. After all, Wayne was the legendary "Duke" of the Western movie, and Connally had shaken hands with the President only the night before.

Connally received his rifle and heard the audience reminded that he had "felt the sting of the assassin's bullet," but he made a generally nonpolitical speech, emphasizing the anti-gun legislation stand that "a hunter is not a killer, a hunter is a conservationist."

Wayne, however, was anything but nonpolitical. He fondled a $50,000 rifle, inlaid with rubies and gold, as he said, "Recently I had the privilege of talking to the President and Mr. Kissinger, and if Mr. Connally had heard the nice things they said about him, he'd know why we all want him in '76. I'm willing to help start it, anytime."

The cheers were deafening, and as they began to lessen, a voice arose from the crowd, "John Connally, '76!" It, too, was echoed loudly.

The public finally was admitted to the arena in time to see the Eagles' departure.

It was a glorious weekend. Money had been raised,

parties had been attended, expensive dresses and fancy suits had been worn, and the catering and liquor interests had seen a brief economic boom.

Six weeks remained until Election Day.

John Connally produced another string to his bow in September. He had been a fund raiser, television commercial announcer, speech maker and foreign emissary for Richard Nixon. Now he was an author, too, with an article in *Reader's Digest,* a publication never known for its liberal approach. It was called "A Time for Toughness in America," and subtitled, "We can no longer afford the limitless largess of the past."

Whether the article was written as a trial balloon for Nixon economic and trade policies, or as a Connally application to show what a superb Secretary of State he would be cannot be determined, but the article took a hard line regarding foreign trade and seemed aimed at Japan and Canada, the only two countries discussed in any depth.

Connally wrote with reverence and awe of the Marshall Plan, without, of course, any mention of the President under whose aegis it had been begun. But the glories of the Marshall Plan soon were subverted by the ardent capitalism of other nations, who manufactured lots of things and sold them cheaply to Americans.

There was, of course, some preelection philosophy that appeared here and there throughout.

"The winds of change have also swept over our own country," the writer pontificated. "A regrettable but necessary war has aggravated deep cleavages in our society, weakened our will and sapped our resources. Turning inward, we perhaps did not fully apprehend [sic] what was happening around the world as a result of what we had started through our generous post–World War II international economic policy."

Connally also had to bring up his own recent trip abroad. "As an envoy for President Nixon last summer I told the heads of seventeen nations of the developing areas of the world that the time of our limitless largess is at an end. It is not a question of lack of concern or compassion, or of a wish to withdraw; it simply is our inability to afford it any longer."

There was thunder in his typewriter as Connally said that the American people could no longer be regarded as the guarantors of the security and integrity of the free world without receiving equal economic treatment.

His economic platform included demands that foreign investors be given more opportunity to buy American securities, and that American companies should be able to secure more local financing. He concluded by reminding Americans that toughness had been eroded by affluence, and restated the Protestant ethic of industry, frugality, sobriety with a four-point program: "We must not become slothful in our work. We must not allow expanded leisure time to lull us into becoming smug and complacent. We must not lie back and expect our Government to cure all the nation's ills. Above all, we must not stand still while the rest of the world grows."

The article may have been written by Connally himself, but the tone was as Nixonian as could be imagined. The implied criticisms of social help, welfare and internationalism were clear and strong and anti-McGovern.

Connally, of course, was ever the politician, too shrewd to mention a political candidate by name, regardless of affiliation. The magazine helped when it described the author very briefly and added that he had been "appointed a special presidential envoy to Latin America and Asia." Based on his background as Secretary of the Treasury, Connally could be expected to have knowledge of economic issues, and there were continuous overtones of social and political comment that would easily be accepted by a commuter who skimmed the article with his eyes still blurred from the night before.

Although Connally was still seriously regarded in most circles as a clever and tough, if devious, politician, with the same survival instincts as his better-known Texas friend, Lyndon Johnson, there were occasional signs that Democrats for Nixon was an organization that could hurt Connally.

William Shannon, in a *New York Times* analysis that also described Nixon as "a keen mind ruined by a lifetime of servitude to a salesman's instincts," ripped into Connally: "If this tall, handsome, dynamic Texan is the more natural, self-confident politician, his alliance with Mr. Nixon in this campaign does nothing for his image. Once regarded as a serious figure, Mr. Connally now heads a paper organization called 'Democrats for Nixon.' It is composed of former Mayor Vincent 'Impy' Impellitteri of New York, Mr. Elliott Roosevelt, a clutch of dim Southern ex-Governors, and Mr. Frank Sinatra. Presumably only his probation officer kept Mr. James Hoffa out of this incongruous assembly."

The campaign was getting bitter as the October days shortened. McGovern tore into Connally on October 4 with the rhetorical question, "How much did John Connally and his oil company friends invest to protect their stake in the oil depletion allowance or the oil import quotas that cost every American family from $100 to $150 a year?"

Some of the McGovern approach was aimed at persuading some of the defectors to re-defect. He continued comments like, "The Republicans are welcome to him, as long as we have the people on our side." The comment usually drew cheers but did not seem to have much effect on campaign funds or on public opinion polls that showed anywhere from 35 to 43 percent of the nation's Democrats endorsing Nixon.

Connally continued to show strength, and Nixon continued to show more strength, and Senator Ralph Yarborough, Connally's old enemy, probably was whistling in the dark when he said, "His defection has caused resentment among some old-line Democrats, a resentment that will spur them to go out and work for the ticket."

Another Texas Democrat, more realistic, mourned, "Nobody can raise money like John Connally, and he's hurt us by cutting off some money we might have gotten."

By now there was no pretense of independence in the Democrats for Nixon camp. The group borrowed $180,000 from CREEP for newspaper advertising, used their campaign's talent to write television commercials. Connally met regularly with MacGregor and Mitchell, and the continual theme was to convince the usually Democratic voter that he would find himself in good company by voting for Nixon. Connally and his group, as nominal Democrats, also could lead the way in vicious attacks at McGovern and then claim it was being done for the good of the entire party and not aimed at all Democrats, just the man who was leading the ticket.

Connally concentrated on swing states like Michigan, New York and Illinois and stayed out of California except for the Los Angeles area. Texas and Florida, with good-sized electoral votes, also were worked over, with both money and votes as the targets.

The gadfly tactics of the *Texas Observer* continued even in its letters to the editor. One writer said: "If Connally can't carry Texas, there's always the possibility that in the bargain we'll get ourselves a less arrogant President. But if we should have to suffer four more years, at least we shouldn't endanger the world. If Connally can't carry Texas, maybe Nixon won't want to reward him with a big job (like Secretary of State)."

Connally's most virulent attack, however, was delayed until later in the campaign, when it was felt it could do the most good. A lot of money was spent for television time, and Connally was delegated to make sure it was spent wisely.

It was a bitter and personal attack, termed by the *Texas Observer* "the central act of Connally's life and career. It was so low, there is no way to discuss Connally hereafter without conscious or unconscious reference to it. The essence of the job was Joe McCarthyism —and all in the name of the Democratic Party."

Connally unleashed all the spectres and demons of godless communism and handed the empty leash to McGovern. He charged that the South Dakota Senator would "wrench American foreign policy out of the great traditions" of the last six Presidents, four of them, of course, Democrats. He accused McGovern of policy cowardice and of the kind of thinking that would leave the nation defenseless against the Mongol hordes. He invoked the name of Harry Truman on a half-dozen occasions, and made numerous references to Franklin D. Roosevelt, John F. Kennedy and Lyndon Johnson, each time with a picture of the man showing on the television screen.

Several of the more massive critical assaults were either shaded or were basically untrue. For example, Connally said that McGovern "rallied to the cause of Henry Wallace in 1948." McGovern said several times that while he had initially supported the Iowan, he did not even vote for him. More important, Connally cited McGovern as having favorably compared Ho Chi Minh to George Washington. A spokesman for the Connally group said the sources of the allegation were a *Playboy* magazine interview in September 1971 and a McGovern biography by Robert S. Anson. None of the three indexed references to Ho Chi Minh in the Anson book have any reference to McGovern, and the *Playboy* magazine interview carried no such remark.

Still, Connally went on. He introduced himself to his television audience as "a Democrat who, along with many of my fellow Democrats, has become convinced that it is in the best interests of the country to reelect President Nixon." He roused the ghost of John Kennedy to say that in "the fundamental question of confidence," many Democrats "agree with John Kennedy that 'sometimes party loyalty asks too much.' "

Another interesting visual display to the huge television audience was a passport, reportedly that of President Nixon. It showed a typed legend, "The bearer of this passport is the President of the United States," and the audience saw page after page stamped with visas of the various countries he had visited. According to the Protocol and Passport Office of the State Department, however, the President does not carry a passport. Heads of state don't need them, though television audiences might.

Connally also charged that McGovern "wants to cut the muscle out of our national defense," and said that if those proposals were carried through, "the total United States armed forces level would be cut to a point lower than at the time of Pearl Harbor."

A politician can only chop an opponent so far, and even John Connally got into the position of damning with faint praise when he allowed that he did not question McGovern's sincerity, "or even his good intentions, but sincerity and good intentions are not enough."

It was not even enough for Connally to invoke the

ghosts of Democratic presidents. He even brought up a defeated candidate, Adlai Stevenson, and quoted him as saying, "If the voters ever stop looking at the record and character of the candidates and look only at a party label, it will be a sad day for democracy." Connally did not believe this would happen because "the people of this country will reject George McGovern's call for retreat and reaffirm America's leadership by reelecting Mr. Nixon."

This TV-radio ad campaign was a savage example of political minds at work. Polls were showing a solid lead for Nixon in all areas, and the election was practically assured. If the election had been a sporting event, bookmakers would have taken it off the boards weeks before. Still, the necessity for overkill was felt strongly in the Nixon camp. The results of the necessity belong to history.

McGovern battled back valiantly, but it was a case of much too little, much too late, and he didn't have enough renegades on his side. A parting shot was, "If Americans vote for Richard Nixon next week, they will be voting for Watergate corruption, Nixon recession, Connally oil and Republican reaction."

So in the end, Nixon won and Connally, smiling broadly, took a deep bow.

It remained for feisty Bob Bullock, Texas Secretary of State, to add a postscript to the matter. Bullock decided to start an anti-Connally crusade in the last days of the election, saying, with grim but whimsical humor: "Now, you might think that me bein' just a minor state official and him a member of Richard Nixon's Cabinet that it is kinda like the case of the flea that crawled up a elephant's leg with rape in mind. But I got some ideas on Mr. Connally. He ain't never done nothin' but get shot in Dallas. He got the silver bullet. He needs to come back here and get hisself shot once every six months. I attack

Connally on his vanity. He's terrible bad vain, y'know. Hell, if George McGovern got hisself a $600 Cardin suit and dyed his hair blue like Connally does, maybe he could do him some good. Connally gets his face lifted, too. That's one I'm spreadin' around."

John Connally abandoned the Washington, D.C., bullring and returned to Texas to breed the four-legged variety. Here he admires one of his entries in the 1973 Texas State Fair. *Credit:*

[8]
Epilogue: 1976

As the 1976 presidential election is being seeded, the nation is in a strange mood. Early symptoms of Nixonian paranoia have eased somewhat. Extremists of every variety have enjoyed a calm holiday as the country watches the press and the press watches the Government.

America seems to have finally realized that there are two Chiefs of State. One is the man (for the time being a continuing sexist reality) and the other is the presidency itself. The man in the office will always be hampered by human shortcomings and he will be exposed and irritated in varying degrees dependent upon the political climate. But the health of the presidency must remain inviolate. The spirit of the chief executiveship itself must be "grin and bear it," no matter what the reaction of any single White House resident.

Nevertheless, as the campaign professionals seek out retainers and expense accounts for the next two years, the public remains more curious about what happened than about what will happen. It has been primarily the European press that has taken the initiative in urging bicentennial Constitutional reform designed to reestablish privacy in America and minimize the amazing autonomy the White House has acquired during the recent administration.

Richard Nixon looks as if he is reflecting upon the words of Louis XVI, who pondered, "What have I done that they should hate me so?" The man who, with or without justification, will be remembered solely as the Watergate President must forego the luxury of anointing a successor. It will take more than his all to stay afloat until the country inaugurates a new president.

When Henry Kissinger was still in his pre-Nixon phase and a staunch supporter of Governor Nelson Rockefeller for the 1968 GOP nomination, he expressed the view of many in public life about being the nation's chief executive. "If you've seen one President, you've seen them all," he replied to my question as to his feelings about Nixon. Perhaps he was right. Certainly the Haldeman-Ehrlichman-Mitchell-Dean revelations clearly document the power of the staff and the influence of outside forces on even a so-called strong White House incumbent.

The simple truth is that merely calling ourselves a democracy and holding free elections are not convincing evidence of inviolable national excellence. Yet we must vote in 1976—if for no other reason than to lend dignity to the claim that American voters are either more or less apathetic than last time. Suddenly we are running out of desirable candidates. Many are well known, but most of the leading contenders and not-so-dark horses have in common clay feet or mouths. Our need is to renourish the presidency and lend a fresh but stable new look to our sagging democratic pride. It just doesn't seem important what labels are given to our choices as long as they are credible and perhaps a little valiant.

New York's perennial Governor Rockefeller is rich and reasonably competent. Unfortunately, at the insistence of his consensus-conscious advisers, Rocky's philosophy has drifted right, left, and now right again, with such self-righteousness that he has lost his base of support among moderate Republicans.

Ronald Reagan was a fair actor and is a surprisingly agile Governor of California. Despite continued attacks on his reactionary approach to any number of state problems, he has remained nationally popular and enjoys wide conservative support. But urban Republicans who must inevitably compromise in finding a GOP nominee could never endorse the Californian who banners his conservatism as further right than Barry Goldwater.

Senator Charles Percy of Illinois, the only other often mentioned would-be GOP starter, is strictly a second choice despite the fact that he tries harder.

And then there is the incarnate Lyndon Johnson. The peripatetic John Connally is weaving in and out of GOP finance meetings, congressional offices, and Republican State Committee headquarters with the devoted enthusiasm that only ambitious new converts can sustain. He is being well received.

At the moment of truth, many more seasoned Republicans have fallen short of ideas and available finances to back their campaign. Nearly half of the major corporate supporters of the Grand Old Party rejected the President's pleas for substantial donations (channeled through individuals) to assist key Republicans in their difficult congressional reelection campaigns. It is no surprise, then, that John Connally is looking fresher than ever as he delivers oil and gas and banking monies to the near-drained GOP coffers. No one ignores the import of each such bundle of campaign fuel—support for Connally at the 1976 Republican Convention.

The lawyer from Texas who became sufficient of an economist to survive as Secretary of the Treasury quickly takes credit for the phases that worked. He is equally quick to disassociate himself from the less popular price controls that alienated too many constituents of too many incumbent candidates in the U.S. Senate and the House of Representatives. With newfound modesty, economic experts like Arthur Burns are acknowledging that "the rules of economics are not working quite the way they used to." Yet the political rule of bowing or disappearing depending upon the mood of the crowd, still works well. John Connally knows when to explain and when not to meddle with pocketbook decision making.

In fact, he has not yet subscribed to fixed positions on many issues or public figures. Even his totally expected party switch was low key. Lately there has not been any fervor or pizzazz in his comments on anything. Perhaps that is wise, since no one seems able to assess the nation's mood on any given issue for more than a day at a time. The Connally tactic seems to be based wholly on saturating the country with an awareness of his personal competence. He is, indeed, the three-time Democratic Governor of Texas; the wounded companion of an assassinated President; twice a cabinet officer; and a somewhat self-made rancher, banker, lawyer, and a corporate officer of millionaire tastes and near-millionaire means.

Some time ago I interviewed Congressman Paul McCloskey, the rebel Republican from California. It was McCloskey who first made the Vietnam war a campaign issue and who challenged Nixon in the New Hampshire primary elections. Again it was McCloskey who first brought to the floor of the House a discussion of what dozens of other Congressmen have whispered about for weeks—the possibility of impeachment. The ex-marine hero is candid, precise and considered in his views. Whether or not you accept his obvious anti-Nixon prejudices, you are impressed with the sincerity of his observations about the presidency. I wanted his instant reaction to certain names—a kind of human Rorschach test. When I said "President Nixon," he replied quietly, "Sad that he didn't measure up." I've thought about that since. No President since Thomas Jefferson has enjoyed greater credentials for the presidency than Richard Nixon when he took the oath of office in 1968. I thought too about Emmet John Hughes, who while Nixon was Vice President wrote *America the Vincible*. There Hughes warned that self-rightousness, self-delusion, lack of humor and inflexibility were leading the United States to disaster.

In anger and despair during the Nixon Administration Americans have asked and now demand reform of presidential power. This could mean a new kind of presidential candidate. John Connally's greatest tool in Texas politics may be his Achilles heel nationally. Big John is so much the product of LBJ's tutelage that one cannot always separate the late teacher's words from the pupil's. More recently he has seasoned that image with his political identification with Richard Nixon. The product may be too rich for 1976 consumption.

We have long since passed the day when a mother fondly wishes that her newborn son might someday be president. Loving parents would not curse their offspring with that hope, for the presidency has become a well-tailored suit of pierceable armor that doesn't fit anybody. Yet Connally continues to tread the path to Pennsylvania Avenue. Can a poor boy from Texas find happiness in Washington, D.C.? Will the former Secretary of the Treasury become bedeviled by those who suffered his economic impositions, or is Big John just a phase we're going through?

There was an incident involving Connally during his brief sojourn at the White House as a post-Watergate presidential adviser. The encounter was brief and unimportant, at a time filled with vital presidential news, but it gave witnesses a rare peek at Big John under sudden pressure. Connally emerged from the White House by the front entrance after holding a scheduled impromptu news conference. As expected, he expressed his faith in the President and avoided elaboration on the story that he was leaving the White House counseling staff because no one ever asked for counsel. Connally was then approached by a group of the regular White House pickets who rotate their placards as if they were assigned by Abbey Rents for whatever campaign is in vogue. One suddenly jumped in front of the former Texas Governor and extended his hand. "Governor, I'm from Houston, how are you?" he shouted, while still holding an anti-Nixon sign. Connally coolly said hello, but didn't extend his hand until the young man urged him on. "My folks voted for you. Aren't you going to shake my hand?" Big John reluctantly extended his hand to the young man and a cheer came from the crowd of fifteen protesters. For a moment it looked like another Connally conquest right outside the House he hoped to live in.

But then came the young man's next remark: "I read you might become a Republican, but my father says you once said in Texas you'd never trust a man who switched parties." Connally turned red in the face, pivoted and marched off with his entourage close behind. Only a few near him heard his comment: "That dirty little son of a bitch." But the damage was done.

It took only a few hours for an alert Washington columnist to learn the story. It took another few hours to have Connally's Texas speeches checked and to prove that Connally's taunter was correct. In the heated race for the governorship in his home state in 1962, Big John had attacked his Republican opponent because he had some years before switched parties. The scene was set. When Connally made his move and formally joined the ranks of Republicans, he would be vulnerable to the charge of hypocrite, and a lot of loyal party members would know it.

At any other time Connally's untenable position would have been the subject of widespread ridicule. Watergate drowned out any other sensationalism.

After hearing Congressman Paul McCloskey's cryptic comment about President Nixon, I asked him his views of John Connally. Before he could stop the word from rushing out he had mouthed "fraud." He then qualified his instant reaction by adding that he hoped he was wrong and perhaps it was just Big John's blatant ambition that gave him that look. Three days later I talked with former Congressman John Schmitz, who had received over a million votes for the presidency as the American Party's stand-in candidate in 1972 after George Wallace was shot. Schmitz's reaction to Nixon was softer than that of McCloskey, and the conservative also called Connally "a great Texan." He later confided that either Big John or Governor Ronald Reagan would be acceptable GOP nominees for the presidency in 1976. Most of the dissident liberals still active in the GOP do not resent Connally's conversion to their party's ranks, but are suspicious of his motives.

Big John's support for Hubert Humphrey's campaign in 1968 was last-minute and light. His willingness to serve in the Nixon Cabinet repelled loyal Democrats when it became apparent he was only parroting the Nixon economic philosophy and establishing groundwork for a 1972 endorsement of the President. The crowning blow was his defection to become chief spokesman for the Democrats for Nixon reelection drive.

After that John Connally was finished as a candidate for public office on any level so long as he wore a

Democratic label. The significance of Connally's switch then became limited to an awareness of his personal desperation. Every politician who has tasted victory by votes wants more. Connally is a classic non-exception.

But for all the obvious gain and the welcome from the President, there was still a powerful irony in the fact that he was deserting the party of LBJ and John F. Kennedy—the party that had thrice made him Governor and nurtured his needs since his fledgling days as a law student learning politics in Texas.

Historically, party-switchers enjoy instant limelight if they win, and cynical good-byes when they fail. Only a Connally-sized ego, which surpasses all in Government save that of his rival Henry Kissinger, would try to overcome such a precedent.

John Connally's good looks and charm were enhanced by the charmlessness of the rest of the Nixon Administration. Jim Kilpatrick seemed enamored with the Supertexan when he wrote this about Big John's arrival in the nation's capital:

". . . John B. Connally seems to have something special.

"Part of his appeal doubtless arises from the contrast he brings to his drab surroundings. The Nixon administration has its merits, but pizzazz it has not . . .

"Now comes Connally, a six-feet-two, silver man, with a handsome phiz and a he-man tan. He stands straight as the shaft of a six-iron. In private conversation —even in a press conference—he looks you straight in the eye, but it is not like it was with Lyndon. Mr. Johnson had the flinty gaze of a faro dealer. Connally has the friendly gaze of a good coach or a parish priest. Want to buy a used car? This guy could sell an old Toyota to Henry Ford.

". . . Here in Credibility Gulch, he possesses one

attribute more precious than nuggets of gold—the appearance of absolute candor. . . . Connally has the look of eagles; and he is flying high to somewhere."

And yet . . .

For a time it seemed that the milkman of the 70's was destined to be Mark Spitz, who, his many medals much in evidence, praised the dairy industry's virtues nightly on all channels. But it now appears that Spitz has been outdistanced by Big Bad John as Dairyland's most noteworthy personality.

In a copyrighted story released by the North American Newspaper Alliance on November 10, 1973, I wrote that a San Antonio dairy executive named Bob Lilly would be the key witness as the Senate Watergate Committee and the Special Prosecutor focused in on John Connally.

Under investigation was an alleged multimillion-dollar contribution promise by dairy conglomerates to the Nixon campaign in exchange for preferential treatment on milk price controls.

And then questions arose about Connally's role as the middleman and about monies he allegedly received for opening the White House door for the swag-toting milkmen. In an unprecedented moment of candor, Connally was asked by a newsman whether the dairy investigations would hurt his presidential aspirations. "They won't help," Big John quipped.

There were a few, of course, who believed Connally's claim that the cash that passed had no influence on quickly changing federal controls on milk prices. "It's only a coincidence," Connally boldly asserted.

Those few believers will also accept the tooth fairy these days.

Index

Advisory Council on Executive Organization, 176–179
Aerospace Medical Health Center, 36
AFL-CIO, 115, 133–134, 140, 142, 145, 155, 158, 239–240
Agnew, Spiro T., 9–10, 186, 226, 251
Air Force, U.S., space program of, 94
"Airstrip set," 78
Air Transport Command, 97
Alamo, battle of the, 8, 51, 167
Alger, Bruce, 22
Algeria, fee paid by, 188
Allee, Capt. A. Y., 114
Allford, Don, 145
Alpha Psi Omega fraternity, 53
America the Vincible (Hughes), 291
American Bankers Association, 217
American Broadcasting Co., 118–119
American Fact-Finding Committee, 35
American General Insurance Co., 7
American Motors Corp., 211
American Society of Newspaper Editors, 248

"American Sportsman" program, 119
American Telephone & Telegraph Co., 176
Americans for Democratic Action, 20, 86
Anderson, Adm. George K., Jr., 180
Anderson, Jack, 170
Anderson, Robert, 71, 83
Andrade, Erasmo, 172
Andrews, George, 197
Anson, Robert S., 283
Arnold, Thurman, 66
Ash, Roy L., 176
Ash Council, 176–178, 187
Atlantic magazine, 82, 226
Atlas Corp., 3
Azores Conference, 237

"Back-room bosses," 1
Bailey, John, 35
Baker, George P., 176
Balance-of-payments deficit, 229, 249
Barnes, Ben, 127, 146, 163, 165, 224, 226, 258
Bass, Bill, 106
Bass, Perry, 191–192, 226
Bator, Francis M., 233
Bayh, Birch, 213

Beckworth, Lindley, 23
Belli, Melvin, vii–viii
Bentsen, Lloyd, 170–171, 192, 226, 274
Bernal, Joe, 115, 118
Black sailors incident, 92
Black voters, 28, 30
Blimps, U.S. Navy, 93
Boeing Aircraft Co., 212
Briley, Beverly, 266
Brill, Idanell, *see* Connally, Mrs. John
Briscoe, Dolph, 122
Brown, Hank, 134, 145, 155, 158
Brown, Pat, 21
Brown & Root Construction Co., 58, 169–170
Brown Bros., Harriman & Co., 185
Bryant, Farris, 112–113, 266
Budget deficit, 245
Bullock, Bob, 284
Burke, Adm. Arleigh A., 90, 190, 212–213, 222–223, 290
Burns, John, 129
Bush, George, 171

Cabell, Earle, 34
Cambodia, bombing of, 178
Carpenter, Liz, 8
Carr, Mrs. Billie, 146
Carr, Waggoner, 122, 133
Case, Francis, 82
Cauble, Rex, 276
Chamber of Commerce, U.S., 245
Chapman, William, 187
Chase Manhattan Bank, 184
Cherne, Leo, 275
Cheshire, Maxine, 197
Chicago Tribune, 99
Chicanos, 172
Childs, Marquis W., 188
Chile, expropriation by, 219
Christian, George, 6, 137
Cigarroa, Leonidas, 271
"Citizens for Johnson" movement, 2
Civil rights legislation, 24
Clark, Ed, 63
Clark, Ramsey, 135
Clifford, Clark, 152, 165
Collins, John F., 266
Committee for Natural Energy, 187
Committee to Re-Elect the President (CREEP), 250, 281
Common Market, 233, 253
Connally, Carmen (sister), 51
Connally, Godfrey (brother), 271

Connally, John Bowden (father), 50
Connally, John Bowden, Jr.: abstemiousness of, 199; Achilles heel of, 291; Algerian retainer to, 188; on "American Sportsman" program, 119; anti-Kennedy attack by, 2–4, 75; as arm-twister, 197–198; assassination aftermath and, 44–46; "awe" of Nixon toward, 196; birth and early years, 50–52; booing of by Mexican-Americans, 116–117; "candidacy" of, 98–100; clothing styles of, 103–104; compared with LBJ, 67–69, 197; conflicting loyalties of, 9; "court" of, 7–8; dapper appearance of, 62; directorships held by, 6–7, 169–170, 244; and economic crisis of 1973, 217–218; economic ties of, 85–87; endorses Eisenhower, 70; endorses Humphrey, 167; on energy crisis, 238; establishment and, 216; fascination for politics, 54; as favorite son (1968), 139, 145–146, 154; as fiscal conservative, 227; "fiscal responsibility" of, 185; on Foreign Intelligence Advisory Board, 179–180; as "fraud," 293; on fuel shortage, 238; fund-raising efforts of, 164, 289–290; gold price and, 234–235; as Governor of Texas, 4–5, 21–23, 99–173; and gross national product, 207; vs. Haldeman and Ehrlichman, 195–196; as hard worker in Treasury Department, 198; in Humphrey campaign, 6, 159–160, 167; "international policy" of, 231–233; Jamaica home of, 6, 274; Johnson and, 8, 17–18, 54–58, 65–70, 76–78, 197, 291; Kennedy Administration and, 29–30; and Kennedy assassination, 37–44; land holdings of, 273; Latin American loans and, 219–220; legal career of, 54; liquor laws and, 110–111; as lobbyist, 82–84; and Lockheed loan, 204–206, 213, 243, 248; and McGovern candidacy, 260–261, 281–284; as "manicured man," 50, 101; on Martin Luther King, 143; Meany and, 241–242; as "martyr," 15;

Navy commission for, 61; and New Frontier, 88–89; and 1976 presidential nomination, 11–12; Nixon and, 167, 196, 201, 215–216, 259; in Nixon Cabinet, 8–9, 177–178, 187, 201, 215–216; as Nixon spokesman on wage-price board, 214; as Nixon's "economic guru," 175–255; oil depletion allowance and, 280–281; oil reserves and, 84–85; as opportunist, 9–10; as orator, 102–103; Oswald and, 42–43; "overreaching" of as Treasury Secretary, 250; on pay raises in Texas, 111–112; personal appearance of, 62, 103–104, 227–228; Picosa mansion of, 273; political activities of, 206; political plight of (1963), 32–33; poll tax and, 31–32; on pollution, 171; as post-Watergate Presidential adviser, 292; as potential President, 16, 277–278, 294–295; as power merchant, 1–3; private aid to Nixon by, 167; as private citizen after 1968 convention, 172; public attitude toward, 8; and radio station KVET, 63–64; *Reader's Digest* article by, 278–279; as "Republican hypocrite," 292–293; Republican party membership of, 4, 10, 294; Republican TV commercial by, 272–273; resigns from Navy post, 98; resigns as Treasury Secretary, 253–254; responsibilities as Treasury Secretary, 186–187; on revenue sharing, 208–210; Richardson Foundation payments to, 191; rift with Kennedy Administration, 29–30; as Secretary of the Navy, 3, 18, 79–82, 85, 88–97; as Secretary of the Treasury, 6, 8–9, 180–183, 186–188, 196–197; snubs Humphrey in 1968 campaign, 164–165; source of strength in Nixon cabinet, 184–185; visits South Vietnam, 230–231; and SST aircraft, 201–206; support for as "Mr. Texas," 46–47; supports Eisenhower, 70; supports Humphrey, 168; on taxation, 111; telegram intercept by Reagan, 124–125; and Texas Rangers "strikebreakers," 114–

115; tourism and, 103; as true conservative, 102; and two-term limit, 120–124; unit rule and, 154–155; at University of Texas, 52–53; as vice-presidential candidate, 159–161, 225, 251–252; on Vietnam War, 149–150; on wage and price controls, 189–190, 222–223; Wayne and, 277; withdraws from fourth-term campaign, 126–127; as "worst governor," 24; Yarborough and, 121–122

Connally, Mrs. John, Jr. (Idanell Brill), 37–39, 54, 81, 199, 227, 254

Connally, John B. III (son), 70

Connally, Kathleen (daughter), 70

Connally, Mark (son), 70

Connally, Merrill I. (brother), 131

Connally, Sharon (daughter), 70

Connally, Wayne W. (brother), 172

Cooper, John Sherman, 85

Cost of Living Council, 241, 247

Council of Economic Advisers, 190, 198, 221

Cowden, George, 271

Cox, Jack M., 5, 20, 22–23

Cranston, Alan, 212

Credentials Committee (1968), 151–158

Cronkite, Walter, 53

Curtain Club, 53

Cutter, Bill, 276

Czechoslovakia, Soviet invasion of, 148–149

Dairy investigations, 295

Daley, Richard, 160, 162

Dallas, Texas: as "hate capital," 34; Kennedy visit to, 26–28, 37–44

Dallas Memorial Auditorium Theater, 34

Dallas Morning News, 25–26, 34–35

Dallas Times-Herald, 34, 225

Daniel, Price, 17, 30, 82, 99, 105, 119, 124, 151–152

Davis, Will, 138, 157

Dean, John, 178, 288

Deason, Willard, 63

Defense Department, U.S., 96, 201

Deficit spending, 194

300 *Index*

de la Garza, Eligio, 274
Democratic National Committee, 146; fund raising by, 163–167
Democratic National Convention: of 1940, 54–55; of 1960, 73; of 1964, 25; of 1968, 133, 139–140, 147–164; Credentials Committee of, 151–158; and Vietnam War plank, 151, 155; street fighting at, 162–163; of 1976, 265
Democratic party: fund raising by, 163–164; split in, 16–17, 23, 27–28, 120; unifying of in Dallas, 44–46
"Democrats for Nixon," 8–10, 186, 257–285
Depletion allowances, 163–164, 251, 280
Devaluation, Nixon and, 237
Dickerson, Nancy, 225
Dirksen, Everett, 86
Dobbs, Jim, 28
Dockery, Richard, 135
Dollar, devaluation of, 237
Dow Jones Industrial Averages, 244–247, 253
Dugger, Ronnie, 80, 82, 226

Eagleton, Tom, 8
Economic crisis (1973), 217
Economic system, Phase II of, 241
Economist, The, 134
Edwards, India, 74
Eggers, Paul, 144
Ehrlichman, John, 178, 195, 268, 288
Einzig, Paul, 235
Eisenhower, Dwight D., 4, 16, 62, 70, 83, 87, 97
Elkins, J. A., 7
Ellington, Buford, 160–161
Emergency Loan Guarantee Board, 243, 248
Energy crisis, 238
Enterprise, U.S.S., 92–93
Environmental Protection Agency, 244
Erwin, Frank, 138–139, 154, 156, 161
Estaing, Valery Giscard d', 236
Europe, troop reduction in, 217
Expropriation, by Latin American countries, 219

Federal Communications Commission, 63

Federal Reserve Board, 190, 212, 222
Federal revenue-sharing plan, 208, 217–218
Finch, Robert, 182
First City National Bank, Houston, 7
Fitzsimmons, Frank, 200, 266, 275
Floresville, Texas, birthplace, 50
Foreign Intelligence Advisory Board, 188
Foreman, Ed, 22
Forrestal, James V., 62
Forrestal, U.S.S., 90–91
Fortas, Abe, 66
Fortune, 95
Fort Worth Club, 81
Franke, William B., 89
Fuel shortage: Connally on, 238; oil tax and, 207
Fulbright, William, 217–218
Fullingim, Archer, 132

Galbraith, John Kenneth, 212
Garner, John Nance, 55
Garrett, Jenkins, 271
Garrison, Col. Homer, 116
Garrison investigation, 43
General Accounting Office, 248
General Gas Committee, 87
Germany, E. B., 60
Gibraltar Savings Association, 169
Gold, price of, 233–235
Goldwater, Barry, 25, 204, 261, 289
Gonzalez, Henry B., 30, 35, 147, 167
Good Neighbor Policy, 220
Goodwin, Mills E., Jr., 275
Goodwin, Richard, 156–157
Graves, Curtis, 155
Great Depression, 52
Greer, William, 37
Griffin, Robert, 193
Griffiths, Martha, 208
Gross national product, 207
Guggenheim, Charles, 272

Haldeman, H. R., 178, 195, 260, 271, 288
Halliburton Corp., 169
Hamilton, Alexander, 235–236
Harris, Fred, 162, 188
Hartke, Vance, 190
Harvard Business School, 176
Harvard University, 233
Haughton, Daniel J., 205

HemisFair '68, 104–105, 109, 127, 142–143, 147
Henry, Patrick, 53
Herring, Bill, 111
Herring, Charles, 105
Hill, John, 133
Ho Chi Minh, 129, 282
Hodgson, James, 241
Hoffa, James, 2–3, 200, 280
Hoffenbert, Louis, 81
Hoover, J. Edgar, 252
House Banking and Currency Committee, 190, 213
House Committee on Interior and Insular Affairs, 237
House Ways and Means Committee, 200, 208–209, 224, 243, 246
Houston, Sam, 55
Houston Chronicle, 25
Houston Petroleum Club, 163
Houston Post, 60, 103
Huff, Robert E. Lee (Sam), 275
Hughes, Emmet John, 291
Hughes, Howard, 21
Hughes, Richard, 162
Humphrey, Hubert H., 5–6, 76, 86, 139–148, 158–159, 180–181, 187, 266, 293; fund raising for, 163–169; snubbed by Connally in 1968 campaign, 164–165; support for in Texas, 168; on Vietnam War, 166–167

Impellitteri, Vincent, 280
Inflation, unemployment and, 194, 214–215, 249
Institute of Texas Culture, 109
Institute on Oil and Gas Law and Taxation, 171
Insurance Securities, Inc., 243
Interest rate ceiling, 199–200
Internal Revenue Service, 58, 71
International Monetary Conference, 217
International monetary crisis, 217, 223–224
International Monetary Fund, 22, 230, 234, 236
International monetary policies (1971), 228–229
International Telephone & Telegraph Co., 119

Japan, trade advantages of, 232
Jawboning, 194, 222
Jefferson, Thomas, 291
Jenkins, Walter, 63

Johnson, Lady Bird, 8, 63, 68–69, 167
Johnson, Lyndon B., 2–4, 8, 20, 22, 25–26, 28–30, 34, 36–37, 54, 63–64, 73, 81–82, 88, 92, 95–96, 106, 109, 116, 121, 128, 135, 147–148, 150, 156, 179, 182, 186, 194, 197, 216, 254, 259, 261, 266–267, 280, 282, 289; "Addison's disease" smear and, 74–75; campaign funds of, 58–59; as "campaign manager" for Connally in 1972, 170; Connally and, 65–70, 76–78, 197, 291; and Democratic National Convention of 1968, 156–157; distrust of, 17–18; Locke and, 130–132; McGovern and, 267; physical weariness of (1967), 137–138; as President, 44–45; renounces second term, 138–139; Senate campaign of, 54–60, 65–67; supports Humphrey (1968), 160–161, 168; and Vietnam War, 124–125, 128–130, 136, 164, 171
Joint Economic Committee, 206, 216
Jones, Bill, 22

Kappell, Frederick R., 176
Kazen, Abraham, Jr., 274
Keating, Kenneth, 86
Kellam, J. C., 63
Kellerman, Roy, 37–38
Kennedy, David, 181, 196, 266
Kennedy, Edward M. (Ted), 146, 160, 162, 165, 204, 227
Kennedy, Jacqueline (Mrs. John F. Kennedy), 38
Kennedy, John F., 2, 4, 17, 23, 73, 88, 96, 99, 140–141, 150, 172, 282–283; "Addison's disease" charge against, 2, 74; assassination of, 5, 15, 24–25, 37–44; Texas visit, 26–27; "wanted" posters of, 35
Kennedy, Joseph P., 75
Kennedy, Robert F., 74–75, 128–130, 139, 144–145, 168
Killion, George L., 275
King, Martin Luther, Jr., 142–143, 159
Kissinger, Henry A., vii, 10, 178–181, 201, 234, 237, 252, 277, 288
Klein, Herb W., 276–277
Knox, Frank, 270

Koon, Homer, 277
Korth, Fred, 42, 96–98
KTBC radio station, 63–64
KVET radio station, 63–64

Latin American countries, expropriation by, 219
League of United Latin American Citizens, 114, 116
Lilley, Bob, 295
Lincoln, Abraham, 49
Lincoln, Evelyn, 77–78
Lindsay, John V., 162, 271
Lindsey, Jim, 271
Linkenhoger, Edgar M., 95
Litton Industries, Inc., 176
L-1011 Tri-Star plane, 201–206
Locke, Eugene, 130–133, 141, 144
Lockheed Aircraft Corp., 201–207, 211–213, 220, 243, 248
Long, Russell, 188–192
Long, Stuart, 64
Long Beach, U.S.S., 92
Los Angeles Times, 21
Louis XVI, 288

MacArthur, John, 206
McCarthy, Eugene, 128, 139, 141–142, 144, 147, 149–150, 158, 161, 167–168
McCarthyism, 150, 282
McCloskey, Paul, 290, 293
McClure, Sarah, 35
McCracken, Paul, 190, 198
McDonnell-Douglas Corp., 212
McGovern, George, 8, 10, 149–150, 156, 165, 258, 260–261, 263–264, 282, 285
MacGregor, Clark, 271, 281
McLean, W. Hunter, 271
McNamara, Robert S., 3, 77, 93, 127, 137, 152, 161
Mansfield, Mike, 203
Maria Immacula Orphanage, Naples, 90–91
Marks, Leonard, 266
Marriott, Willard, 275
Marshall Plan, 229, 278
Maverick, Maury, 35, 154
Meany, George, 133, 239, 242
Mecom, John, 71
Medrano, Pancho, 117
Mesta, Perle, 275
Mexican-Americans, problems of, 30–31, 112–118, 120–121, 147, 155, 157, 159, 172, 268, 274–275
Milk prices, controls and, 295

Mills, Wilbur, 199, 208–209, 217, 224
Minimum wage laws, 112
Mitchell, John N., 196, 271, 281, 288
Mitchell, William, 247
Mobley, John, 171
Mondale, Walter, 159–160
Monroney, Mike, 87
Montoya, Joseph, 204
Moorhead, William S., 205
Morse, Wayne, 85
Muskie, Edmund, 162, 165, 168, 239

National Arbitration Association, 115
National Association for the Advancement of Colored People, 91–92, 135, 143
National Football League, 276
National Governors' Conference, 124
National Review, 262
National Security Affairs, 178
National Security Council, 148–149
National Tax Association, 210
Natural gas bill, 82–84
Navy, U.S.: defense budget and, 89; as large source of employment, 89; oil purchases of, 85; space program of, 93–94
New Braunfels, march on, 117
New York Central Railroad, 4
New York Stock Exchange, 181
New York Times, The, 16, 34, 45–46, 96, 184, 191–193, 232–234, 245, 262
Newsweek, 12, 227
Nixon, Donald, 21
Nixon, Richard M., 2–3, 7–8, 71, 162, 165, 167, 171; Connally and, 179–183, 195–196, 201, 215–216; Democrats for, 257–285; economic views of, 193–194; Four Point plan of, 222; and International Monetary Fund, 228–229; "last press conference" of, 21–22; as one-party thinker, 175; "salesman's instincts" of, 280; and Vietnam War, 184; on wage-price controls, 223; as "Watergate President," 288
North American Newspaper Alliance, 295
North Dallas Democratic Women's Club, 114

Nuclear-powered ships, 92–93

O'Brien, Lawrence F., 263
O'Daniel, W. Lee ("Pappy"), 55–60
O'Donnell, Ken, 33
Office of Management and Budget, 190, 254
Offshore oil, 106–107
Oil and gas tax, 206–207
Oil depletion allowance, 163–164, 251, 280
Oil industry: as political power, 107; pollution and, 108, 171; tax loopholes for, 163–164
Oil Policy Committee, 187
Ordaz, Gustavo Diaz, 117
Organization for Economic Cooperation and Development, 230, 255
Organization of Spanish-speaking People, 31
Orr, Roy, 154
Oswald, Lee Harvey, 26, 41–43

Pacific Missile Range, 95
Packard, David, 212
Paget, Richard M., 176
Palucci, Jeno, 266, 269
Parkland Memorial Hospital, Dallas, 39
Partini, Ed, 200
Patman, William N., 106
Patman, Wright, 190, 221
Pay Board, 241–242
Pearson, Drew, 83, 170
Pena, Albert, 31
Percy, Charles, 204, 289
Phase II, of new economic system, 241
Phillips, Rev. Channing, 161
Phinney, Bob, 63
Pickle, J. J., 28–29, 63
Picosa Mansion, Texas, 273
Pierce, Franklin, 257
Playboy, 283
Poll tax, 24, 31–32
Pollution Control Board, 108
Pompidou, Georges, 234
Pool, Joe, 34
Porter, Paul, 66
Powell, Wirtz and Rauhut, law firm, 70
Power, influence of, 1
Presidential campaign (1968), 128–130; of 1976, 287–295
Price Commission, 241–242
Price controls, *see* Wage and price controls

Protestant ethic, 49
Proxmire, William, 3, 73, 85–88, 203, 211, 248

Railroad Commission, 46
Rayburn, Sam, 77, 88
Raymond, Morris, Knudson, Brown, Root and Jones firm, 150
Reader's Digest, 278
Reagan, Ronald, 124–125, 289, 293
Rebozo, Bebe, 21
Republican National Convention (1972), 265–266; prospects for 1976, 287–295
Republican party: Connally's switch to, 4, 10, 292–294; in Texas, 16–17; after Watergate, 289–290
Reston, James, 262
Revenue sharing, 208–210, 217–218
Ribicoff, Abraham, 150, 165, 167
Richardson, Sid W., 3–4, 70–71, 81, 83–88, 95, 191
Richardson and Bass firm, 3
Richardson Foundation, payments from, 191–193
Rickover, Adm. Hyman, 237–238
Rio Grande Valley, problems of, 112–118, 120–121, 274
Ritter, Jack, 28
Rizzo, Frank, 271
Rockefeller, David, 184
Rockefeller, Nelson, 288–289
Rogers, William P., 178, 220
Rolls-Royce, Ltd., 201–206
Roosa, Robert V., 185
Roosevelt, Elliott, 275, 280
Roosevelt, Franklin D., 55–56, 58–60, 282
Roosevelt, Franklin D., Jr., 77
Roosevelt, James, 266, 269–270, 275
Roosevelt, Theodore, 77
Russell, Richard B., 84, 86
Rutherford, J. T., 23
Rutherford, Pat, 78

Safeway Stores, Inc., 247
Salinger, Pierre, 34, 150
San Antonio Express-News, 258–259
Sargent, Francis, 186
Sato, Eisako, 245
Schlesinger, Arthur, Jr., 77
Schmitz, John, 293
Scott, Hugh, 185

Sealy, Tom, 271
Senate Appropriations Committee, 202, 204
Senate Armed Services Committee, 3, 83, 192
Senate Banking and Currency Committee, 210, 248
Senate Finance Committee, 188, 191
Senate Foreign Relations Committee, 218
Senate Labor Committee, 134
Senate Watergate hearings, 10–12, 58, 178, 204, 295
Shannon, William, 280
Sheppard, Morris, 55
Sheraton-Park Hotel, 199
Sherrill, Robert, 99
Shires, Tom, 40–41
Shivers, Allan, 16, 71
Short, Bob, 164
Shriver, Sargent, 267
Shultz, George, 190–191, 242, 254
Simons, Pollard, 274
Sinatra, Frank, 280
Sirica, Judge John J., 12
Sixth Fleet, U.S., 90
Smith, Preston, 122, 133, 135, 144, 164, 169
Solis, Lalo, 20
Solow, Herbert, 95
South Vietnam, Connally visit to, 231; *see also* Vietnam War
Southwest Legal Center, Dallas, 171
Soviet Union, invasion of Czechoslovakia by, 148–149
Space program, U.S. Navy and, 93
Spears, Franklin, 107
Spitz, Mark, 295
SST aircraft, 201–206
Staats, Elmer B., 248
Starr County, Texas Rangers in, 115–116
Stassen, Harold, 228
State Department, 178, 219, 250
States' Rights, 106
Steger, Bill, 23
Stevenson, Adlai, 16, 34, 65–66, 70, 284
Stevenson, Coke, 64
Stimson, Henry, 270
Stinson, William, 39
"Stop Roosevelt" bloc, 55
Sulzberger, C. L., 234
Surtax debate, 234
Syers, W. E., 63

Taft, William Howard, 269
Talmadge, Herman, 195
Tax laws, large families and, 237
Tax reform, 208–212, 249
Tax relief program, 224
Taxation, in Texas, 111
Teamsters Union, 266
Teapot Dome Scandal, 84
Texas: Congressional districts of, 33; liquor laws in, 110–111; one-party system in, 101; as test case for South, 32; two-year governor's term in, 120–124; University of, 53, 271
Texas Bar Association, 218
Texas Council of Churches, 114
Texas Democratic Executive Committee, 139
Texas Democrats for an Open Convention (TDOC), 153–160
Texas Department of Correction, 135
Texas Instruments, Inc., 7, 169, 244
Texas Insurance Board, 271
Texas Observer, 80, 110, 150, 160, 190, 193, 226, 269–270, 282
Texas oilmen, fund raising from, 163–164
Texas Rangers, Mexican-Americans and, 113–116
Texas School Book Depository, Dallas, 33, 38, 41
Texas Water Quality Board, 108, 271
Thayer, Walter N., 177
Thieu, Nguyen van, 230–231
Thomas, Albert, 35–36
Thomas, Helen, 259
Time, 95
Times (London), 9
Toole, J. Doug, 271
Tourism, promotion of, 103
Tower, John G., 17–18, 98–99, 123, 185, 226, 275
Transport Co. of Texas, 94–95
Treasury Department, U.S., 201–206, 218–219, 253–254
Truman, Harry S., 97, 136, 229, 282
Tulia Herald, 119–120
Twain, Mark, 109
Two-term debate, 120–124

Udall, Stuart, 106
Unemployment, inflation and, 194, 214–215, 221

United Auto Workers, 117
United Farm Workers, 115
United States Trust Co., 170
Unit rule: death of, 161; power through, 154–155
Unruh, Jesse, 157, 165
U.S. Information Agency, 266

Vanderhooven, William, 156–157
Vanik, Charles A., 209
Vantage Point, The (Johnson), 137
Vietnam War, 124–125, 128–129, 136, 138, 147–152, 155, 162, 178–179, 184, 229–231
Vinson, Elkins, Searls and Connally law firm, 6, 169
Volpe, John, 268

Wage and price controls, 189–190, 214, 223, 239–240
Wall Street Journal, 63, 177
Wallace, George C., 144, 146, 166, 254, 293
Wallace, Henry, 282
Wallach, Eli, 53
Warren Commission and Report, 5, 38, 41–43
Washington, D.C., in World War II, 61–62
Washington, George, 272, 282

Washington Post, 187, 197
Water Quality Board, 108, 271
Watergate hearings, 10–12, 58, 178, 204, 295
Watson, W. Marvin, 124
Wayne, John, 276–277
Whitney Communications Corp., 177
Wilkins, Roy, 92
Willkie, Wendell, 227
Wilson, Will, 98
Wirtz, Alvin, 56, 59–60, 64, 66, 69
World Bank, 127
World War II, 61–62, 75–76, 229, 233
Wright, Jim, 163
Wright, Lela (Mrs. John Bowden Connally, mother), 50

Yarborough, Donald, 19–20, 28, 133, 144
Yarborough, Ralph, 17, 19, 24–25, 27, 29, 36, 114, 116–117, 120, 122–124, 133, 140, 142, 147, 158, 167–168, 170–171, 192, 281

Ziegler, Ron, 240, 271